The Jazz Man Record Shop, 3323 Pico Blvd., Santa Monica, California, October 1975.
(Blow-up frame from film Without a Song *by Cary Ginell)*

Hot Jazz for Sale

Hollywood's

Jazz Man
Record Shop

Cary Ginell

Cover design by Holly Fraser

For Dar

Blessed be the names of record collectors,
For their perseverance and insight
Are the torches needed
By those who stumble by firefly-light.

Truly, they have preserved the evidence
And their reissues shall live after them.
Their steps to Salvation will resound
On tapes all the days of our lives.

Go and do likewise.
— Myra Menville, 1977

Myra Menville co-founded the New Orleans Jazz Club and was the former editor of *The Second Line* magazine. Used by permission of her daughter, Myra Loker Menville.

Contents

Where Everybody Knows Your Name

In an article in *The New York Times*, a consortium of record stores and trade groups declared Saturday, April 19, 2008 to be "National Record Store Day," a day celebrating the culture of buying and selling phonograph records. Promotions, sales, and free concerts were presented at record stores across the country, at traditional hole-in-the-wall mom-and-pop outlets as well as national chains. As of that weekend, there were still a reported 2,400 independent record stores still in existence, but their numbers had been rapidly diminishing. In its article, the *Times* reported that over 3,000 record stores had closed since 2003, half of them independents. With the rise of iTunes, Amazon.com, Internet piracy, and escalating real estate prices, the neighborhood record shop appears to be headed for extinction.

In the movie *Inherit the Wind,* Spencer Tracy, in his portrayal of the Clarence Darrow-inspired defense attorney Henry Drummond, lamented the side effects of advancing technology:

Gentlemen, progress has never been a bargain. You've got to pay for it. Sometimes I think there's a man behind a counter who says, "All right, you can have a telephone; but you'll have to give up privacy and the charm of distance. Madam, you may vote; but at a price; you lose the right to retreat behind a powder-puff or a petticoat. Mister, you may conquer the air; but the birds will lose their wonder, and the clouds will smell of gasoline."

The neighborhood record shop is dying because sophisticated technology has made it more convenient for us to buy our music from the comfort of our own homes. No longer is it necessary to expend time and energy going down to the local record store. Now, you can audition and purchase just about any kind of music you want online, without having to worry about whether it is in stock or whether your favorite store even carries that genre, much less the record you desire. But what have we lost in the process?

The love of music does not live in a vacuum, nor is it a solitary endeavor. At our neighborhood record stores, we were introduced to music that we might not have found otherwise, met people who were more knowledgeable than we were, and learned from their experience. These were places where the people who ran them knew more about the music than their customers.

I will never forget the first time I heard the music of Django Reinhardt. I was 17 years old and shopping for country LPs in a small San Francisco record store called the Magic Flute, located in a shabby neighborhood near Golden Gate Park, across the street from old Kezar Stadium. Somebody was playing an LP reissue of Reinhardt and Stephane Grappelli's recording of "Minor Swing," and the infectious rhythm and exciting solos they played with the Quintet of the Hot Club of France froze me in my tracks. I was sold. The record-buying experience was made all the more vibrant and memorable when the music was given a physical context, such as that provided by the atmospheric, dusty, creaky stores of the past and the characters who inhabited them. This book is about one of those places, a shop that not only became a community meeting ground for collectors, but had a revolutionary influence on the popularizing of a musical genre: the traditional jazz revival of the 1940s.

The Jazz Man Record Shop survived for more than four decades in Los Angeles. It died, ironically, just as the LP was being phased out by the introduction of the compact disc in the early 1980s.

I discovered the Jazz Man in 1971, when I was a 15-year-old high school student. My brother, who is two years older than me, had visited the Jazz Man earlier in the year after reading an article on record collecting in *Los Angeles Times Magazine*. The shop was then located at 3323 Pico Blvd. in Santa Monica, just off the Santa Monica Freeway (Interstate 10), so one day, he and I headed down there so I could check the place out myself. The two of us had been collecting records since the late 1960s, regularly prowling record stores like Melody Records in Sherman Oaks, the Beat in Encino, and Wallichs' Music City in Canoga Park, looking for 45s that we had heard on KHJ, Los Angeles' Top 40 radio station. Record stores that sold 78s were virtually non-existent in the San Fernando Valley at the time, so we spent nearly every Saturday scouring neighborhood garage sales.

Santa Monica, on the other hand, had a number of haunts for old records, and after I started my freshman year at UCLA, I joined my brother (who also went to school there) in after-school record junkets. Favorite places we found included the Salvation Army thrift store near Olympic Blvd. and 11th Street (where LPs were 40 cents and everything else was a dime) and Jane Hill's House of Records on Main Street, where we mostly bought used 45s for 50 cents apiece.

It was on a Saturday when I first walked into the Jazz Man. The shop was deeper than it was wide and divided into two areas: a large front room and a smaller back room, about a third its size. The shop was almost entirely stocked with 78s, with a few boxes of 45s stashed in the back and LPs stacked in bins in the front. Most of the 78s were displayed on ancient wooden shelves, with each disc categorized and filed in green or brown protective sleeves. Prices starting at 75 cents were scrawled in grease pencil on the run-off grooves. For us, the highlight of the front of the store was the "dime table," piles of sleeveless 78s stacked up like dishware on top of two waist-high cabinets. In the afternoon, the sun would stream through the front windows onto the unprotected records, giving the expression "hot wax" a more literal connotation. Most seasoned customers habitually walked past the dime table to get to the better records in the main part of the shop, but we would always sift through the mountainous stacks up front, occasionally finding a hidden gem buried among the junk.

The Jazz Man was owned and run by a bearded curmudgeon named Don Brown. Although he was only in his early 50s, Brown looked considerably older, with wispy graying hair and bushy eyebrows. If Central Casting had put out a call for a merchant who sold old records, Brown would have been perfect for the part. Even though the Jazz Man had been at this address for only a few years, the records and dingy shelving made the store look older than it was. It was obvious that Brown had given up trying to keep the place clean years ago. The shelves were dusty, and when you pulled a long-ignored 78 out for examination, the occasional silverfish would slither out of its sleeve.

Brown's roost was a stool behind a counter into which a Rek-o-Kut turntable had been installed. Anyone wishing to audition a 78 before buying it could do so, as long as they returned the record to its place in the stacks if they decided not to buy it. I told him that I was looking for records by Spike Jones and His City Slickers, the wildly popular 1940s orchestra that made musical parodies of contemporary hits, such as "You Always Hurt the One You Love" and "Cocktails for Two," utilizing a barrage of novelty sound effects (klaxon horns, slide whistles, and gun shots among them), plus assorted burps, coughs, and sneezes.

Puffing on a cigar, he steered me to the back room, where I encountered a group of older men who were standing around, drinking from bottles of beer and smoking cigars while noisily laughing, telling stories, and insulting each other. I needed to navigate past them in order to get to the shelves that housed the Jones records. I wondered why these men were there, ignoring all this great music surrounding them, talking instead of listening.

Seeing me, they grudgingly but politely cleared a path, and continued their chatting and laughing. I sensed that I was invading their lair. To a 15-year-old kid, the atmosphere in the back room was somewhat forbidding, with the pungent smoke and loud laughter mixing with the musty air and dim light. I selected four Jones 78s and also a few by the Jack Teter Trio, ranging in price from 90 cents to $1.50 each.

Thus began a ritual for me as I started learning about the world of 78 rpm records. While rummaging through the back room, I heard enticing sounds coming from the front area and its constantly spinning turntable. By the late 1970s, I had expanded my horizons, beginning with a newly found passion for western swing 78s from the 1930s.

In 1976, I landed my own radio show at KCSN, the campus radio station at Califonia State University Northridge, where I regularly played my recent acquisitions on the air. At the Jazz Man, the rowdy collectors in the back room had slowly begun to accept me. All of them had different tastes and specialties in their own collecting and I learned something from each one of them. I became acquainted with intoxicating new sounds: pre-war Cajun music by Joseph Falcon, hot stride piano by Fats Waller, big band jazz by the Casa Loma Orchestra, and hotel dance numbers by Leo Reisman. For me, the Jazz Man was a veritable university extension course in the history of popular music of the first half of the 20th century.

Through fellow hillbilly record collectors Eugene Earle, Harvey Newland, and Donald Lee Nelson, I became a big fan of western swing bands like Milton Brown and His Musical Brownies and Jimmie Revard's Oklahoma Playboys. In addition to other collectors, I also met owners of small independent record companies, who came to find copies of discs to reissue on LP. One of these was Bill Givens, a boorish, blustering, bear-like bohemian who swilled beer and pontificated about anything and everything, whether it related to jazz, politics, or the current baseball season. It didn't matter whether anyone was listening; Bill still prattled on, like a demented, lisping Walter Winchell, although there was an element of perverse logic in every opinion he had. Givens was a jazz and blues fan who owned the Origin Jazz Library record label. At the time I met him, he had developed an interest in 1930s western swing as well, and asked me to annotate two LPs of music by band leaders Ocie Stockard and Roy Newman. After we got to know each other, he convinced me to return to UCLA to get my master's degree in folklore, where I learned to conduct oral histories from the esteemed folk music scholar D. K. Wilgus.

In my chats with the members of what Don Brown called "The Saturday Crowd," I learned a little about the history of the shop. Its previous location (reverently referred to by all as "The Old Shop") had been in a run-down neighborhood on West Pico Blvd. a few miles from downtown. I also found out that the Jazz Man's roots went back to the 1930s, and that it once spawned its own eponymous record label. I never thought much about the shop's history until the spring of 1983, when Brown solemnly announced that the Jazz Man was shutting down. The restaurant next door wanted to expand into the shop's space and its owner offered to pay the landlord more rent than what Brown could afford, so Brown was given 60 days to vacate the premises. On two successive Saturdays in May, I conducted interviews with Brown and many of the Saturday Crowd regulars about their memories of the shop and the friendships they had developed by coming in week after week. When Brown finally went out of business, the shop resurfaced for a brief period in Burbank, but it was just a last gasp of stagnant air before expiring. It closed for good in early 1984.

As time went on, I discovered that there was still a great deal to learn about the Jazz Man. When it opened its doors on Hollywood's Sunset Strip in 1939, it was the first shop on the West Coast to specialize in selling used jazz 78s to record collectors. Through its eponymous record label, it released the first recordings by Lu Watters' Yerba Buena Jazz Band, a San Francisco group that spearheaded the traditional jazz revival of the early

1940s. For 44 years, researchers, musicologists, and writers all paid regular visits to the shop. Musicians playing gigs in town would often stop by and say hello, including such luminaries as Louis Armstrong, Mel Tormé, and Rex Stewart. One of the shop's biggest fans was RKO's *enfant terrible*, actor/director Orson Welles. The social network that developed because of the Jazz Man became almost as important as the shop itself.

A lot has been written about jazz since Frederic Ramsey and Charles Edward Smith's landmark book *Jazzmen* was published in 1939. But up until now, few books have focused on the places where jazz records were sold. Increasing interest in early jazz 78s started in the 1930s, when records on such desirable labels as Gennett, Paramount, and OKeh became harder to find. A few collectors shops sprang up, most notably, the Commodore Music Shop in New York. In 1939, the Jazz Man became the first collectors' shop on the West Coast, and with Dave Stuart at the helm, it quickly developed into one of the most respected purveyors of jazz records in the country. Although the Commodore went out of business in 1958, the Jazz Man lasted for another quarter century, influencing an additional generation of jazz fans.

What makes the story of the Jazz Man Record Shop particularly provocative is that it is not just about a record store. It concerns the lives of a handful of entrepreneurs who ran the store during its nearly half-century of existence. Each of them had other ambitions; some were realized, others were not.

Dave Stuart, the shop's founder, saw the Jazz Man as a stepping stone to stardom. During his brief and tumultuous two-and-a-half year tenure, the opinionated, egocentric Stuart had visions of becoming a concert promoter, an author, and jazz-consultant-to-the-stars. But each of these endeavors failed, and it wasn't until he decided to start his own record label that he actually succeeded in making history, although his fortune, ultimately, was earned in the art world.

Marili Morden, who married two of the shop's owners (Dave Stuart and Nesuhi Ertegun), had lesser ambitions than either of her two husbands. Still, while in her early twenties, she became an expert on traditional jazz as well as a friend of Los Angeles musicians, such as Kid Ory, and manager of blues guitarist T-Bone Walker.

The Turkish aristocrat Nesuhi Ertegun was the one owner of the shop who parlayed his stewardship into a prestigious career. He took up where Dave Stuart left off, and with the help of his wife Marili, spearheaded a series of groundbreaking recording sessions in the 1940s that helped spread the New Orleans jazz revival. After leaving the Jazz Man, he joined his brother Ahmet's burgeoning Atlantic record label and became a jazz music legend.

Albert Van Court, Jr., a Harvard-trained attorney and jazz fan, didn't know what he was getting into when he bought the Jazz Man. He was the only one of its owners who did not manage the shop; basically becoming an absentee owner. When he finally got rid of the shop six years after he bought it, he sold it for peanuts.

Midwestern transplant Don Brown arrived in Hollywood from Dixon, Illinois in the 1950s, determined to become a television writer. After getting nowhere, he resigned himself to running the shop for the remainder of his days. In the process, he became a local legend, although always teetering on financial insolvency.

Jonathan Pearl was an idealistic young man trying to save an institution from extinction, but he gave up more quickly than any of his predecessors, and was the shop's sixth and final owner.

There were other minor characters in the Jazz Man's life story, but Stuart, Morden, Ertegun, Van Court, Brown, and Pearl were its major players. Although they had completely different personalities, all six shared one thing in common: a passion for jazz records. The story of the Jazz Man resembles the plot of a 1964 film called *The Yellow Rolls-Royce,* which tells the stories of three very different owners of a Rolls-Royce Phantom II automobile. The lives of the six individuals who ran the Jazz Man are as integral to the shop as were the tens of thousands of discs that migrated in and out of its portals.

A quarter century after the Jazz Man Record Shop closed, evidence of its existence still turns up occasionally. At garage sales and flea markets, you can still find copies of records that were once part of the Jazz Man's stock, evidenced by the identifying shop ink stamp on the protective sleeve or an old grease-penciled price scrawled on its run-off groove. Records on the Jazz Man label are still relatively common on the West Coast. The discs, featuring performances by Lu Watters, Bunk Johnson, and Kid Ory, among others, were all influential in the traditional jazz revival of the 1940s.

The Jazz Man, however, was much more than just a record store; it was a place where friendships were established, deals were struck, and even where husbands and wives met each other. Athough many of the shop's regular habitués moved on to other cities, memories of the Jazz Man left indelible memories with them.

During my time as a Saturday regular, the television program *Cheers* was a ratings powerhouse. Its premise: a Boston bar frequented by a regular group of beer-swilling eccentrics, struck a chord with me as I made my regular weekly appearances. As the *Cheers* theme song states,

> *Sometimes you want to go where everybody knows your name,*
> *And they're always glad you came.*

The Jazz Man was that kind of a place.

Chapter One
Outside Start: Hot Jazz for Sale

This book tells the story of the Jazz Man Record Shop, one of the most important record stores in the history of jazz and record collecting. Although it is not our intention to ignore the contributions of other pioneering record stores, we will leave their histories for others to tell. Before presenting the Jazz Man's story, however, it is important to briefly discuss two earlier stores, one on the East Coast and one on the West, both of which set important precedents for the establishment of the Jazz Man and its eponymous record label.

In the early years of the 20th century, a European Jewish immigrant named Julius Gabler opened a hardware store in midtown Manhattan. In the early 1920s, a newfangled invention called radio became the nation's hottest new technology, so Gabler opened another shop around the corner that sold exclusively radios, speaker supplies, and other electronic equipment. The second shop was located at 144 E. 42nd Street, between Lexington and Third Avenues, across the street from Grand Central Station. Gabler named his establishment the Commodore Music Shop after the neighboring Commodore Hotel (named for "Commodore" Cornelius Vanderbilt, who once commanded the largest schooner on the Hudson River). In 1924, Gabler's 13-year-old son Milt (1911–2001) started working at the store, putting in hours while attending Stuyvesant High School in Manhattan. Milt was a fan of hot jazz, having spent weekends and summers in Throgs

1

Left to right: Milt Gabler, Herbie Hill, Lou Blum, and Jack Crystal, at the Commodore Music Shop, New York, N.Y., ca. Aug. 1947. (The William P. Gottlieb Collection)

Neck in the Bronx, listening to black jazz bands play at an open-air dance pavilion.

It was young Milt who suggested that they could attract more customers to the store by playing music that could be heard from the sidewalk by passersby. So the enterprising teenager mounted a loudspeaker over the store's door and started broadcasting New York radio station programming featuring hot jazz by artists such as Bix Beiderbecke and Louis Armstrong. As time went on, customers began asking for the records that they heard while walking past the store. In 1926, Julius Gabler agreed to allow to stock the store with phonograph records. He contacted the major record companies and had them send him the latest jazz 78 releases by artists such as Ted Lewis and Fletcher Henderson. By 1934, the record business had taken over the store.

Nineteen-thirty-five saw the explosion of the Swing Era, following Benny Goodman's monumentally influential engagement at Los Angeles' Palomar Ballroom. In time, hot jazz began to be less and less in demand, resulting in the major record companies putting many of their hot recordings from the 1920s out of print. With its devotion to hot jazz, the Commodore was now attracting collectors of hot jazz records, who would discuss, trade, and barter 78s from their collections with each other. With swing starting

to monopolize radio station air waves, Gabler and a student from Yale named Marshall Stearns (later, the founder of the Institute of Jazz Studies) formed the United Hot Clubs of America (UHCA), whose goal was to preserve and document classic jazz records from the 1920s. Another former Yale student, John Hammond, who happened to be the great-grandson of Commodore Vanderbilt, was named club president. In 1936, Gabler and Stearns struck a deal with the American Record Corporation (ARC) to reissue out-of-print jazz records from the 1920s under the auspices of the UHCA, which would be sold and distributed through the Commodore Music Shop.

The American Record Corporation owned masters released on the OKeh, Brunswick, Columbia, and Vocalion labels, and included early works by Louis Armstrong, Bix Beiderbecke, Bessie Smith, Sidney Bechet, and King Oliver, the five giants of the first decade of jazz on record. A legend above the song title on the labels indicated that the records were issued "for members of the UHCA," with the Commodore Music Shop's name and street address imprinted at the bottom of the label. UHCA records were the first to list full personnel detail on its labels, showing its members' devotion to the contributions of sidemen as well as bandleaders.

In 1938, Milt Gabler decided to record and market new recordings of music performed in the traditional style by artists such as Bud Freeman, Eddie Condon, and Pee Wee Russell, and started the Commodore record label (UHCA reissues of out-of-print masters continued until 1941). He opened his own store a few blocks away, at 46 West 52nd Street, the center of Manhattan's jazz club scene, and hired his brother-in-law, Jack Crystal (father of comedian Billy Crystal), to be the store's manager. The Commodore record label flourished into the 1950s, issuing landmark recordings by Billie Holiday, Hot Lips Page, Wild Bill Davison, and Coleman Hawkins, becoming the most successful independent jazz label to be marketed by a record store.

Five years before Julius Gabler started the Commodore Music Shop, another music store opened up in Los Angeles. It was run by two brothers, Benjamin "Reb" Spikes (1888–1982) and his brother Johnny (1881–1955), who got their start by running an open-air playhouse called the Pastime Theater in Muskogee, Oklahoma that featured traveling jazz and blues singers. One of the performers who passed through Muskogee in 1911 was a young Jelly Roll Morton, then doing a comedy act in blackface.

In 1919, the brothers moved to Los Angeles where they opened the Spikes Brothers Music House, located at 1203 Central Avenue, at 12th Street, where they initially sold sheet music and musical instruments. Within a few years, the store became the place to buy records by "colored" performers as well. In an interview with Floyd Levin years later, Reb Spikes recalled that, at that time, there was no place in town where one could buy recordings by black artists:

Wealthy Hollywood people would drive up in long limousines and send their chauffeurs in to ask for "dirty records." When the local Columbia distributor received a shipment of Bessie Smith records, we'd take the entire lot . . . a few hours later they'd be gone!

In 1979, nearing the age of 90, Spikes told *Westways* magazine:

A lot of motion picture actors would come too. They'd hear about these different records from word-of-mouth, but when they went to the uptown stores, they couldn't find the records. A lot of the people heard about our store because there were so many Negroes working in private families in those days, and they would talk about us.

Its peak came when the Spike Brothers' shop sold one hundred copies a day of Alberta Hunter's Black Swan recording of "Someday Sweetheart," a song that Reb and Johnny wrote.

In addition to running their shop, the Spikes Brothers wrote their own songs and arrangements, performed in groups (both played multiple instruments), and booked acts for local clubs. Since there was no local union for black musicians, anyone who wanted a band knew to go to the Spikes Brothers, because musicians would often congregate at the music store. Johnny Spikes wrote arrangements for many of the bands that were formed there, and also taught piano, trumpet, and saxophone at the shop. The Spikes Brothers also operated a handful of cafés in Los Angeles, including the Dreamland, Reb's Club, and the Wayside Park Café, and opened the Watts Amusement Park, sending for Jelly Roll Morton to be its musical director and star performer.

Sunshine record label, June 1921.

In June 1921, Reb and Johnny Spikes decided to go into the record business, and arranged for a recording session that summer with Edward "Kid" Ory, a 35-year-old jazz trombonist who had been playing at the Wayside with his group, the Creole Jazz Band. Ory was an early jazz musician from New Orleans who had only recently arrived in Los Angeles and was still trying to establish himself.

Only one recording facility existed at that time on the West Coast, which was started by Arne Andrae Nordskog, the son of a Norwegian

immigrant. The Nordskog studios were located on Ocean Park Blvd. in Santa Monica, a few blocks from the Pacific Ocean. Although Nordskog was mainly interested in classical music and opera, he agreed to record Ory's band for the Spikes Brothers in June. Nordskog cut the masters using equipment designed by his father-in-law, Frank Lockwood. Seven songs survive from that historic session, the earliest recordings of New Orleans jazz played by black artists. Ory's band included Dink Johnson on clarinet, Mutt Carey on trumpet, Ed Garland on bass, Freddy Washington on piano, Ben Borders on drums, and Roberta Dudley and Ruth Lee, vocals.

Since there were no pressing plants on the West Coast at that time, the masters had to be sent by truck to Orange, New Jersey, where the records were made. Several of the masters melted in the hot Mojave Desert heat, including "Froggie Moore," a Jelly Roll Morton composition, and an unnamed blues written by Ed Garland. Although the records were supposed to be issued on the Spikes Brothers' black-and-orange Sunshine label, when the brothers received the shipment, what they saw on the records was Nordskog's own label, with Ory's group renamed the Seven Pods of Pepper. Outraged, the Spikes Brothers pasted their own orange and black Sunshine labels over the Nordskog labels. Most of the pressings were sold at their shop, except a few that were shipped to stores in San Francisco and

Oakland. At the Spikes Brothers' store, the records sold like hotcakes at 75 cents each. Five thousand copies were pressed in that initial run, although few survive today. Reb and Johnny Spikes never manufactured records after the Ory session, but the significance of those sides cannot be overestimated. Few African Americans were producing records in 1921; only George W. Broome's Broome Special and Harry Pace's Black Swan labels preceded the Spikes Brothers' Sunshine label.

A few years later, Kid Ory would participate in the most celebrated of all jazz recording sessions, when he became an integral member of the original lineup of Louis Armstrong and His Hot Five, a group that revolutionized jazz through its recordings for OKeh in 1925 and 1926. Along with other members from the band that recorded for the Spikes Brothers, Ory would later play a significant role in the history of the Jazz Man record label.

As different as they may appear, Milt Gabler in New York and the Spikes Brothers in California shared many characteristics, each indirectly leading to the opening of the Jazz Man Record Shop and the start of the Jazz Man record label. The Commodore Music Shop and the Spikes Brothers Music House were both devoted to traditional jazz; both became local gathering points for musicians and collectors; and both defied conventional wisdom and prevailing trends in the music industry in their respective eras and locations. Gabler's foresight led to the first examples of reissues of classic jazz on record while the Spikes Brothers introduced the earliest recordings of jazz made by African Americans. The entrepreneurship displayed by these men set a precedent that would inspire the beginnings of the Jazz Man Record Shop.

TU. 1842   .   ME. 5611
Spikes Bros. & Elsworth
MUSIC HOUSE
We Sell and Repair All Kinds
of Musical Instruments
1203 Central Ave., L. A., Cal.

Label sticker, Spikes Brothers, c. 1920s.

Chapter Two
Music in the Hot Idiom

The idea for opening a shop for jazz record collectors came to Dave Stuart late in 1939, when he was hosting a Los Angeles radio program featuring rare records from his private collection. David Ashford Stuart was born on November 24, 1910 in Scotland, South Dakota and probably moved to Los Angeles in the 1920s, ostensibly to become an actor. When he arrived, he settled in Glendale, about 20 miles from Hollywood, where he attended art school and acted in silent movies.

In November or December 1939, Dave Hylton, a stringer for *Down Beat* magazine, got word of a new record store opening on Hollywood's Sunset Strip. Since he didn't have a car, Hylton got his friend Charles Campbell to drive him to Hollywood where they soon found the shop. There they found two men installing record shelves and racks. One was former silent screen actor Richard Barthelmess (1895–1963), who had recently made a successful comeback in the film *Only Angels Have Wings*; the other was Dave Stuart, the store's new owner. Stuart had been calling himself "The Jazz Man" on his radio program and so his new establishment was christened the Jazz Man Record Shop.

According to Charles Campbell, the Jazz Man was the only record store in the city that stocked only jazz 78s. Stuart was what was later known as a "moldy fig," an idealistic fan who believed that the only music worth listening to was the original New Orleans jazz played by such artists as

King Oliver, Louis Armstrong, and Jelly Roll Morton. Stuart had amassed an impressive personal collection of jazz 78s and thought that the shop could attract other collectors and help preserve the music, which had been rendered dormant since the late 1920s. Stuart was not only ambivalent towards swing, the currently popular musical trend, he was vehemently offended by it. While he ran the Jazz Man, Stuart refused, on principle, to stock records by Glenn Miller, Artie Shaw, Benny Goodman, and their ilk, which probably cost him thousands of dollars in added income.

The original location of the Jazz Man was at 8960 Sunset Blvd., on the western end of the Sunset Strip, between Hilldale Avenue and Hammond Street, strategically located mid-way between the mansions of Beverly Hills and the movie studios of Hollywood. In a short while, the shop became known to Los Angeles' creative community, attracting musicians, actors, writers, and filmmakers, who made connections, listened to jazz on the in-store turntable, and traded or sold records. Among the most distinguished of the early visitors to the shop was composer Igor Stravinsky. "Stravinsky would come in and listen to jazz, especially King Oliver," Stuart told the *Santa Monica Evening Outlook* in 1981. "He loved King Oliver and would just come in, sit down, and listen to the music. He never bought anything."

The heightened interest in early hot jazz recordings in the mid-to-late 1930s was due to several factors. One reason was a backlash against the arrival of the Swing Era, which was triggered by the highly publicized engagement by the Benny Goodman Orchestra on the night of August 21, 1935 at the Palomar Ballroom in Los Angeles.

Although swing bands had been slowly developing from earlier groups since the late 1920s, they exploded on the scene after Goodman's landmark stay at the Palomar. By 1930, traditional New Orleans jazz had basically disappeared from the scene. Its patron saint, trumpeter Joe "King" Oliver, had not recorded since 1931, and had fallen on hard times, working as a janitor in a Georgia poolroom. Jelly Roll Morton also had found his music becoming increasingly in disfavor. His most recent recordings had been made in 1930 and he was spending his time playing piano in a dive bar in Washington, D.C. Of the classic progenitors of hot jazz, only Louis Armstrong was still a successful draw. But Armstrong had been rendered musically inert, as he adapted to the big band trend by softening his hot jazz and fronting a swing orchestra of his own, often utilizing inferior musicians.

The Depression also had a marked effect on the development of jazz during the 1930s. With many musicians out of work, some resorted to working as studio musicians at radio stations, where they would play stock arrangements suited for the general public. Hot jazz always had limited mass appeal during the 1920s, and record companies found that the smoother sounds of dance orchestras made for better business and increased sales. As time went on, the major record companies put their older releases out of print and collectors began to correspond with each other to share information on their favorite recordings.

African Americans who played New Orleans jazz were especially hit hard by the Depression, and many of the best black musicians of the 1920s gave up trying to find music gigs and went back to their homes to do manual labor or find other menial work.

Dave Stuart felt that he was the champion of these displaced musicians, whose records he cherished and played over and over on his radio program. Through his record store, he got to know some of the musicians who had been transplanted to California, and sought to help them out financially whenever he could.

Another element that resulted in the early success of the Jazz Man Record Shop was the formalization of the study of "hot" jazz records in what became known as "discographies," spearheaded by the initial publication on the subject by a French record collector named Charles Delaunay.

The term *discography* was first used by Delaunay in 1936, when he published his *Hot Discography* in Paris. The book presented a formalized listing of so-called "hot" jazz records, which included details such as song titles, record labels, catalog and master numbers, and personnel. In time, other session details would be added, such as session locations, recording dates, and unissued titles, but initially, only the bare-bones information concerning released recordings was listed. The book's layout was clumsy and difficult to follow, as Delaunay organized the book stylistically, rather than in any objective order. Categories of records were divided into sections such as "Originators of Hot Style," "The Great Soloists," "Prominent Orchestras," and "Chicago Style," with only major performers listed.

The first edition of *Hot Discography* sold several thousand copies around the world, which prompted a second edition, reprinted in the United States by the Commodore Music Shop. This edition included updates, additions, and corrections submitted by jazz collectors from around the world. By this time, collectors of hot jazz had begun scouring junk shops and thrift stores for out-of-print 78s by their favorite artists, using Delaunay's work as their Bible, dutifully checking off discs in the margins as they filled in blanks in their collections.

Another major publication to come out in this period was *Jazzmen,* a book written by two of the early scholars of hot jazz, Frederic Ramsey, Jr. and Charles Edward Smith. With the cumbersome subtitle: *The Story of Hot Jazz Told in the Lives of the Men Who Created It,* the book, published in 1939, contained oral histories of pioneering jazz musicians, including the first account of the career of King Oliver.

Discussions of details found in *Hot Discography* and *Jazzmen* resulted in the founding of several small-format periodicals. One of the first of these was *Jazz Information,* a thin publication that was initially edited by Ralph de Toledano and Eugene Williams. Founded in 1939, *Jazz Information* published articles, and included profiles of early jazz musicians, discographical data, letters from collectors, and announcements of new releases of 78s. After a year, de Toledano dropped out, leaving the editor's duties to Williams, who was later joined by Ralph Gleason and Jean Rayburn.

These books and periodicals had a pronounced impact on the burgeoning ranks of hot jazz collectors, and the Jazz Man Record Shop became a magnet for these impassioned collectors. Records on such valued labels as Gennett and Paramount were still relatively plentiful in the late 1930s, and Dave Stuart developed a knack for tracking down collections to acquire for his new store's stock, often going door-to-door, and asking residents if they had any old records lying around that they would like to sell. In addition, he made sure to stock reissues of classic hot jazz released by the United Hot Clubs of America (UHCA) and the Hot Record Society (HRS).

Jazz Information was the first publication to announce the Jazz Man's opening, in its issue of December 15, 1939, as an aside to a note in its "Collector's Items" column.

Dave Stuart, who just opened the Jazz Man Record Shop in Hollywood, gives us three blues records which have piano accompaniment by Lemuel Fowler: Helen McDonald, on Gennett 5193, "Squakin' (?) The Blues — "You've Got Everything a Sweet Mama Needs," masters 8431 and 8432, respectively, and Clara Smith's "How'm I doin'" (142250)— "Whip It to a Jelly" (142251), Columbia 14150, and "Percolatin' Blues" (143140)— "Ease It" (143141), Columbia 14202.

A few weeks later, in its January 12, 1940 issue, another, more formal, notice appeared:

Los Angeles has an exclusive hot record shop at last. It is run by Dave Stuart, who calls himself "The Jazz Man" and is located out on the Sunset Boulevard Strip. Heretofore, it has been necessary for collectors to order the race items and many of the reissues without first hearing them. Dave has been running a daily broadcast playing the good old ones. His is also the first shop in this vicinity to sell and trade rare records.

Earliest mention of the Jazz Man - in Jazz Information, *December 15, 1939.*

Postcard showing Vine Street, Hollywood, looking north, 1940 (from the author's collection).

On February 2, *Jazz Information* announced that Dave Stuart had moved his shop to 1221 N. Vine Street, a few blocks north of Santa Monica Blvd. It was the first of 12 moves the Jazz Man made during its lifetime. Anyone who owns 78s knows how difficult moving the brittle discs can be. Along with the store's bulky shelves, the Jazz Man's stock had to be painstakingly packed in boxes and carefully loaded onto sturdy trucks, and then laboriously unloaded at the new location.

In June 1940, Stuart began running record auctions, which were sent out by mail to customers. The auctions included duplicates of better records that he had scrounged in the Los Angeles area. Minimum bids were set at $1.00. Winning bids utilized the now-accepted policy of reducing the high bids to 25 cents over the second high bid. As Stuart explained in his October 1940 auction, which was printed in *Jazz Information*: "If you bid $7.50 and the next high bid is $5.25, you get the record for $5.50." The listings included items that would make today's collectors drool, such as copies of recordings by King Oliver's Creole Jazz Band, the Wolverine Orchestra (featuring Bix Beiderbecke), and the Bucktown Five on Gennett; Louis Armstrong & His Hot Five on OKeh; and Jelly Roll Morton piano solos on Vocalion, all in new condition.

In July, Stuart started a series of regular correspondences with New

AUCTION!

THE JAZZ MAN RECORD SHOP'S

Fifth Monthly Auction of Rare Records

RULES: Auction ends October 24, 1940. All records will be sent at once C.O.D. The highest bidder will get the item at a 25¢ advance over the second high bid. For instance -- if you bid $7.50 and the next high bid is $5.25, you get the record for $5.50.

				LOW BID
LOUIS ARMSTRONG & HOT FIVE				
Irish Black Bottom - You Made Me Love You	OK 8447	FINE USED		$1.00
ARMSTRONG ACCOMPANIMENT (CLARA SMITH)				
Nobody Knows The Way I Feel Dis Morning	Co 14058	FINE USED		$1.00
BUCKTOWN FIVE				
Hot Mittens	Gen 5518	NEW		$1.00
KING OLIVER'S CREOLE JAZZ BAND				
Snake Rag	Gen 5184	NEW		$2.50
FRIAR'S SOCIETY ORCHESTRA				
Eccentric	Gen 5009	NEW		$1.00
NEW ORLEANS RHYTHM KINGS				
Milenberg Joys - Marguerite	Gen 5217	NEW		$2.00
Mr. Jelly Lord - Clarinet Marmalade	Gen 5220	NEW		$2.50
London Blues - Mad	Gen 5221	NEW		$2.00
SIOUX CITY SIX				
Flock O'Blues - I'm Glad	Gen 5569	LIKE NEW		$2.00
WOLVERINE ORCHESTRA				
Fidgety Feet - Jazz Me Blues	Gen 5408	EXCELLENT USED		$2.00
Copenhagen - Oh Baby!	Gen 5453	EXCELLENT USED		$1.50
Big Boy - Tia Juana	Gen 5565	EXCELLENT USED		$2.00

PIANO SOLOS

JOLLY JIVERS				
Piano Stomp - Hungry Man's Scuffle	Vo 25015	NEW		$1.00
Jookit Jookit - Watcha Gonna Do	Vo 02532	NEW		$1.00
CRIPPLE CLARENCE LOFTON				
Brown Skin Girls - Tore Your Playhouse Down	Me 61166	NEW		$1.00
JELLY ROLL MORTON				
The Pearls - King Porter Stomp	Vo 1020	NEW		$1.00
CASSINO SIMPSON ACCOMPANIMENT (LAURA RUCKER)				
St. Louis Blues - Little Joe	Para 13075	NEW		$1.00
PINE TOP SMITH				
Nobody Knows When You're Down - Big Boy They Can't Do That	Vo 1256	NEW		$1.00
THOMAS WALLER				
Muscle Shoals Blues - Birmingham Blues	OK 4757	NEW		$1.50

IF YOU LIKE THIS TYPE OF AUCTION - MORE LATER.

The Jazz Man
RECORD SHOP
1053 North Vine Street   Hollywood, California

Orleans jazz historian William Russell (1905–1992) that would continue sporadically for the next 30 years. Russell, whose research specialized on the careers of Jelly Roll Morton, Bunk Johnson, and Manuel "Fess" Manetta, was a voracious and meticulous collector of anything that had to do with New Orleans music, accumulating an archive of musical instruments, records, piano rolls, sheet music, photographs, books, and periodicals. Along with Frederic Ramsey and other collectors, Russell was instrumental in reviving the career of Bunk Johnson, who would record for Stuart's Jazz Man record label in 1942.

THE JAZZ MAN RECORD SHOP

8960 SUNSET BLVD.   "ON THE STRIP"   HOLLYWOOD, CALIF.   CR. 19087

Original Jazz Man Record Shop letterhead, early 1940 (The Historic New Orleans Collection).

Stuart's letters were usually written or typed on Jazz Man stationery. On an early example, the letterhead featured the words "The Jazz Man Record Shop" across the top, underscored by the phrase "On the Strip." A list of jazz personages who had frequented the shop was listed under the heading "patrons" along the left margin, and included the names of Duke Ellington, Freddie Green, Jay Higginbotham, Mezz Mezzrow, Zutty Singleton, Muggsy Spanier, and Jack Teagarden. Along the bottom of the letterhead was the phrase "New, Old, Rare Out-Of-Print, Race and Reissues of Music in the Hot Idiom."

The letters Stuart wrote to Russell shed a great deal of light on Stuart's personality and thought processes. They reveal him to be a man who was passionate about the music he loved, but arrogantly opposed to and intolerant of other forms of jazz. He also displays a mercurial temper in his letters, and was resentful of competing stores. It wasn't long before Stuart became impatient with the day-to-day existence of running his record shop. He yearned for the prestige he thought he was entitled to, and during his two-and-a-half year tenure as owner of the Jazz Man, desperately clung to each opportunity afforded to him to escape its clutches.

In his initial letters, however, Stuart focused on the business of finding and selling records. In July 1940, he reported to Russell that he had just returned from New Orleans, where he had observed the current jazz scene, including some sour comments about Texas pianist Peck Kelley:

Heard Peck Kelley and I think he's lousy! To me, he sounds like Duchin, Tatum, Wilson in one — with a very little bit of Sullivan. Sounds like he knew music quite well, but didn't really have any ideas of his own. Once every hour a little phrase comes out that gives you hope, but that's the end.

It wasn't enough for Stuart to complain about Kelley to Russell; he also sent a letter to *Down Beat* about hearing Kelley, which was published in its issue of September 1, 1940. The letter prompted an angry rebuttal from Irving Veret, a musician in Phil Harris's orchestra, under the headline "Who the Hell's Dave Stuart?"

Of the musicians Stuart mentioned, one who he was impressed with was Monk Hazel, who he called "the best in all the South." Hazel, who was known primarily as a drummer, was playing cornet and mellophone when Stuart saw him; Stuart marveled at Hazel's use of the plunger mute in a style that reminded him of fellow horn man Muggsy Spanier.

Stuart also bragged to Russell about "purloining" a street number sign (235 Basin Street) that used to hang outside the infamous Mahogany Hall. The sign was apparently all that was left from the notorious Storyville brothel run by New Orleans madam Lulu White. Stuart bragged to Russell that he planned to put the sign in a "red plush frame" and shine a red light on it to memorialize Storyville, New Orleans' infamous red light district that was shut down in 1917. The hall was immortalized in Louis Armstrong's 1929 recording of "Mahogany Hall Stomp" with his Savoy Ballroom Five.

Some time in late July, Dave Stuart moved the shop several blocks south to 1053 N. Vine Street, on the other side of Santa Monica Blvd., next to a large movie house. By August, Stuart was crossing out the Sunset address and typing in the new Vine Street address on his letterhead.

But after only a little more than six months in the business, Dave Stuart was already getting restless. Perhaps he had underestimated the work necessary to maintain a record store. With no employees to help him, Stuart was bound to the shop and had very little time to travel, hunt for records, or look for other work. His growing desperation manifested itself in three ambitious projects he attempted in the next year; each of which he trumpeted with high hopes and visions of fame and fortune. Each was doomed to failure.

DAVE STUART

JAZZ MAN RECORD SHOP
NEW, OUT-OF-PRINT, COLLECTOR'S ITEMS
HOME RECORDERS

1053 N. VINE   HI. 1588

Chapter Three

From Spirituals to Swing

On August 15, 1940, Dave Stuart breathlessly wrote to William Russell that he had been put in charge of booking talent for a West Coast version of the landmark *From Spirituals to Swing* concerts. Conceived and produced by impresario John Hammond, *From Spirituals to Swing* was promoted as "An Evening of American Negro Music." Two concerts were presented at Carnegie Hall: the first, on December 23, 1938, and the second, a year later, on December 24, 1939.

The 1938 concert was sponsored by *New Masses*, a monthly leftist journal known for its Marxist views that featured articles and editorials contributed by such literary icons as Upton Sinclair, Ernest Hemingway, Dorothy Parker, and Langston Hughes. In 1937, *New Masses* printed a poem by a Jewish high school teacher named Abel Meeropol entitled "Strange Fruit," a searing work describing a lynching in the South. Under the pseudonym Lewis Allan, Meeropol later wrote an accompanying melody for the song, which was recorded in 1939 by Billie Holiday for Milt Gabler's Commodore label. The 1939 concert was sponsored by the Theater Arts Committee of New York, another left-wing organization formed in 1937 that published a journal and also sponsored a political satirical revue called "Cabaret TAC."

In his liner notes to the 1959 LP release of the 1938 concert, Hammond explained that his ambition was "to present a concert that would feature talented Negro artists from all over the country who had been denied entry to the white world of popular music." The first concert was a tremendous success, with an overflow crowd demanding tickets, resulting in three hundred patrons being seated on the Carnegie Hall stage. The performers were brought to New York from all over the U.S. Mitchell's Christian Singers, a black male gospel group, came from North Carolina. From Kansas City and Chicago came boogie woogie pianists Albert Ammons, Meade Lux Lewis, and Pete Johnson. Blues singer Robert Johnson was scheduled to be brought in from Mississippi, but in August 1938, he died mysteriously from an apparent poisoning and was replaced in the show by Arkansas singer Big Bill Broonzy. The jazz world contributed the integrated Benny Goodman Sextet, which included guitar sensation Charlie Christian, vibraphonist Lionel Hampton, and pianist/arranger Fletcher Henderson. Others who appeared at the first concert included Sidney Bechet, Hot Lips Page, Count Basie, Sonny Terry, Lester Young, James P. Johnson, Ida Cox, Sister Rosetta Tharpe, and Big Joe Turner.

The 1939 concert was also a success, hosted by Howard University professor and blues authority Sterling Brown. Although not as electrifying as the first concert, the 1939 sequel was equally representative of the best in African American blues and jazz talent and again included Basie, Goodman, and Terry, plus the Golden Gate Quartet gospel group.

According to Stuart, the third *From Spirituals to Swing* concert was scheduled for October 1940 at Los Angeles' Philharmonic Auditorium. Stuart's letter shows that *New Masses* was returning to sponsor the concert, and promised Stuart "the best publicity men in town" and $1,000 to pay the performers. Stuart said that *New Masses* wanted white performers on the program as well as black ("good for the movement and all!," he wrote).

Stuart's initial proposal for the program was more ambitious than either of the two previous concerts, tracing black music history by including African tribal music, spirituals, string bands, blues, and New Orleans Dixieland. Without being promised a salary or any funds other than the $1,000 stipend for talent, Stuart was prepared to leap into the breech with both feet, and already had an outline planned as to how the program would be ordered.

To save money, Stuart considered hiring locally-based artists, which would have given the concert a decidedly West Coast flavor. For the segment on African tribal music, Stuart asked William Russell whether he should include live or recorded performances. For the former, he suggested an L.A.-based African drummer named Prince Modupi, who led a small troupe of percussionists. For the latter, he mentioned a friend of his from Beverly Hills who had a large collection of African 78s.

Following this would be a segment on spirituals, or "holy rollers," in Stuart's words, for which he recommended "some fine small groups around town in churches," but did not name any specific performers. Stuart was equally vague on the next segment, labeled as "string band," describing it as an "old time religious 'swing' string band of five pieces."

To represent blues, Stuart recommended either guitarist T-Bone Walker (who was then playing with the Les Hite orchestra) or Amos Easton, a.k.a. "Bumble Bee Slim," who Stuart believed was playing "around town." He also said he was going to investigate unnamed Victor and Decca blues artists who also might be in the Los Angeles area.

The centerpiece of Stuart's plans was, without a doubt, the reuniting of Kid Ory's "Original Dixieland Orchestra," which had not performed in more than ten years. In its segment on New Orleans jazz, the 1938 *From Spirituals to Swing* concert featured Sidney Bechet's New Orleans Feetwarmers, featuring stride pianist James P. Johnson and trumpeter Tommy Ladnier. Stuart was busy writing an article on Ory, which was to be published in *Jazz Information*, and had traced all six members of the group that had recorded for the Spikes Brothers in 1921, including cornetist "Papa" Mutt Carey, drummer Ben Borders, pianist Fred Washington, clarinetist Dink Johnson, and bassist Ed Garland. Stuart noted that "they are all here" and that he had located Johnson playing clarinet in nearby Santa Barbara, an hour's drive from Hollywood. Stuart had talked to Ory, who had told him that the group would be able to play "with a week's practice." He also suggested that the legendary Bunk Johnson could even be brought out from New Orleans to play cornet.

Stuart was intent on bringing boogie woogie pianist Jimmy Yancey in from Chicago, even if he had to pay Yancey's train fare himself. For this segment, he proposed teaming Yancey with Meade Lux Lewis, whose appearance at the 1938 concert had made the rotund pianist a sensation.

In keeping with *New Masses'* request to include white musicians, Stuart proposed including Wingy Manone and His Orchestra. ("Manone says he'll stay on the coast to do this, just as soon as I can assure him it goes.") Obligated to anchoring the show with a popular swing band, Stuart was unsure who to hire. Grasping for straws, he wrote:

The only thing I can do is hope some band happens to be in town at the time. Perhaps with the two new ballrooms there will be someone. At the present, Lunceford is the only one here. I don't like him too much but with a little talk perhaps he could see the light and play some good things.

Stuart saw three groups used for the segment on swing, proposing hiring a 14-man swing band that could be broken up into smaller units of five and seven pieces. Chafing at the meager money he was promised by *New Masses,* Stuart wondered if he was going to run into resistance from the local musician's union. ("Can this be done as Charity? It really is – I'm not getting a red cent. All goes to the *New Masses.*")

Desperate to get out of Hollywood, Dave Stuart was going to do all he could to bring the West Coast version of *From Spirituals to Swing* to fruition, believing that it was his ticket to becoming a nationally-known authority on jazz like John Hammond. He pressed Russell for his recommendations on his ideas about the concert, but in a fit of purist's fervor, gave one final caveat about its traditional content:

I'll be damned if I get one commercial number on the program! It is a good chance for me to really unload some oldtime stuff on the city. Anyway, if this Philharmonic thing bangs, I'll have a fair name and that won't hurt!

In a follow-up letter sent a few weeks later, Stuart complained to Russell that he hadn't heard from him yet, but indicated that the concert had now been pushed back to November. He told Russell that he was personally going to finance bringing Jimmy Yancey out for the concert and that he had also lined up pianist Earl Hines. Muggsy Spanier, one of the few leaders of a traditional New Orleans band playing at the time, was going to bring his five-piece unit to Los Angeles and play for free. Stuart was also trying to convince Sidney Bechet, who had played in the 1938 concert, to come as well and indicated that Kid Ory had agreed to play several numbers.

There was no further mention of the concert in any of Dave Stuart's remaining letters for the rest of the year. The plans had apparently fallen apart, although there is no indication as to why. It is possible that when *New Masses* called Stuart in August, they were merely floating the possibility of staging a concert in Los Angeles. Stuart impetuously started making phone calls and began working on a program without ever getting a contract, a written proposal, or any monetary advance from *New Masses*. The nation was big band crazy in 1940, and it's possible that the concept of presenting material that was no longer commercial 3,000 miles away from New York, the jazz capital, was as ill-conceived as it was ill-timed. So the project was still-born, and it is likely that the "suggestion" that Dave Stuart received over the phone was just that: a mere suggestion.

By the summer of 1940, Dave Stuart had quickly established a national reputation with his Jazz Man Record Shop. It was because of this reputation that *New Masses* contacted him in the first place. Although the Jazz Man was never more than a local hole-in-the-wall record store, Dave Stuart's name was becoming known through articles he was writing for *Jazz Information* as well as the auction lists of rare jazz 78s he was posting in the magazine.

In the letters that he wrote to William Russell, Stuart was openly resentful of those more successful than he, such as Columbia Records' impresario/talent scout John Hammond and the Commodore Music Shop's Milt Gabler. He was particularly jealous of Gabler, whose series of reissues of 1920s Columbia masters on his UHCA label was doing well.

In the fall of 1940, Columbia Records started reissuing material on its own, including versions of masters already released on UHCA. In September, *Jazz Information* excitedly announced the label's plans to inaugurate its new series by releasing four albums of recordings by Louis Armstrong, Bix Beiderbecke, Bessie Smith, and Fletcher Henderson, in addition to 15 single release 78s. Subsequent monthly releases would be featured on Columbia's new red label 78, which were priced at 50 cents. Following UHCA's lead, the labels would feature full session details, including the original recording date and full personnel listings.

Dave Stuart crowed that Gabler and his New York rival, Steve Smith, owner of the Hot Record Society (HRS) label and record shop, which also reissued Columbia masters, were "scared stiff" of the Columbia reissue series and that it would invariably put their respective reissue imprints out of business. But Gabler had already started the Commodore label, featuring new recordings of traditional jazz to combat the ever-increasing surge in the popularity of swing. The Commodore label made Gabler famous, and Stuart, chafing at this, felt isolated on the West Coast, 3,000 miles away from New York, the hotbed of jazz. Charles Rossi, who had at one time worked for Stuart at the Jazz Man, had left Los Angeles for New York, and it was plain that Stuart wanted out of Los Angeles also, but he wasn't ready to give up his record store just yet, as he told William Russell:

Chuck Rossi —remember the fellow in the shop? Well, he now lives in N.Y. and wants me to come back there and open the shop. Says that both Steve and Milt are doing nothing about their cut-outs, that they have no interest in the collector but in the money only. The records are back there — the musicians are back there — the business is back there, so how about me doing it? The main thing is that I live on very little money, as you can damn well guess with my business! So [even] if it would just ease by, it would be fine with me.

November came and went, and by the end of the year, the concert Stuart had put so much hope into had been forgotten. It was a bitter disappointment for him, and most likely an embarrassment as well, since he had led so many musicians to believe that the concert was definitely going to happen. Late that fall, Stuart moved the Jazz Man to 1731 N. Vine Street, in the same building as the old Hollywood Playhouse, across the street from the site where the Capitol Records tower now stands. In 1935, the Playhouse was renamed the WPA Federal Theatre, which was used for government-sponsored programs. In 1939, it changed again to the El Capitan. (The building would later become the home of the ABC television program, *The Hollywood Palace*.) Now that he was in the heart of Hollywood, Stuart could monitor the goings-on around town and begin attracting specialty clients in the movie industry.

It was at this location, probably in early December 1940, where Stuart greeted a very special visitor who had just arrived in town after completing a harrowing cross-country drive from New York. He was a bedraggled man of about 50 who looked much older; Once upon a time, he was a major star in the jazz world but was now down on his luck and looking to jump start his flagging career. Ill and broke, the man just wanted to talk to somebody about the good old days, when hot jazz could be heard everywhere instead of the swing music Stuart destested. In Stuart, the man discovered a kindred spirit, and it wasn't long before the two became friends, playing records in the shop and talking endlessly about the early days of jazz. The man's name was Jelly Roll Morton.

The Hollywood Playhouse, 1735 N. Vine St., shown in 1937. The Jazz Man moved into 1731 in 1940, which would have been the storefront to the left of the theater marquee (From the author's collection).

1735 N. Vine St. in 2009, now the home of the Avalon Theater. The storefront where Jelly Roll Morton and Marili Morden first met Dave Stuart in 1940 no longer exists, but the building lives on (Photo by Cary Ginell).

Chapter Four

Jelly's Last Jam

As Dave Stuart was coming to grips with the fact that the *From Spirituals to Swing* concert was not going to happen, Jelly Roll Morton left Manhattan to move to Los Angeles. Morton, who had turned 50 on October 20, was a desperate man. The one-time leader of Jelly Roll Morton's Red Hot Peppers, a popular recording band for Victor Records, Morton had fallen on hard times due to the Depression (which had decimated record and sheet music sales), the changing of America's musical tastes (Morton's music was long since out of favor), and his on-going battles with publisher Walter Melrose. As Morton's publisher, Melrose had made a fortune by adding lyrics to Morton's songs without his permission, thus enabling him to label himself as "co-creator," and eligible to receive half of all Morton's royalties. This practice, which Melrose used to bilk hundreds of thousands of dollars from Morton as well as other black songwriters, made Melrose a rich man. Denied entry to ASCAP, the performing rights society that paid royalties to songwriters, Morton earned nothing from his compositions.

By 1940, Melrose had sold the songs he had swindled from Morton to Edwin H. Morris Co., which inherited his catalog, but not any of Melrose's liabilities. Too late, Morton complained to *Down Beat* that he had been robbed of three million dollars in royalties, and filed a lawsuit with the Justice Department against ASCAP, which had been paying royalties only

Jelly Roll Morton in Washington, D.C., c. 1940 (Courtesy the Frank Driggs Collection).

to Melrose. Unable to prove the frequency or usage of his music, Morton was handed a token payment of $185 to cover his losses, a ludicrously small amount, considering the body of work he had created, for which he received next to nothing.

Refusing to declare defeat, Morton started writing music again. He created a series of big band arrangements that he thought would surely bring him back to the forefront of the music industry. Realizing that he could not afford the cost of a rehearsal hall in New York, Morton called an old friend from his New Orleans days, bassist Ed Garland, who was then working in Los Angeles in a band led by trombonist Kid Ory. When Morton told Garland about his new arrangements, Garland promised to round up some New Orleans musicians he knew in the L.A. area so that Morton could start his new band. In October, with forty dollars in his pocket, Morton set out for the West Coast, driving a new Lincoln sedan, which he hitched to a 1938 Cadillac loaded with his few possessions. Morton's health had been declining for some time (he blamed his condition on a voodoo curse), which was only exacerbated after he was knifed in a bar fight in 1939. Despite this, he embarked on what was, in 1940, a dangerous cross-country trip, at a time when interstate highways had not yet been built.

Morton hoped to make some money by playing in towns along the way, but he was rejected everywhere he went, including places where he had been famous decades before. In those days, Morton was a dandy man-about-town, wearing custom-made suits and silk underwear, flashing thick wads of cash, carrying a pearl-handled pistol, and sporting a half-carat diamond embedded in his front tooth. But now, his friends had long since left town and his name meant nothing to anyone he met on his westward journey.

As it turned out, Morton's trip took on Odyssean proportions; instead of taking a direct route in a southwesterly direction, Morton chose to take a northern route, through Pennsylvania, Ohio, Indiana, Illinois, Missouri, Kansas, Wyoming, Idaho, and Oregon, before turning south. When he reached Pennsylvania, a series of tremendous storms followed him all the way across the country. In Wyoming, a sleet storm forced his two-car caravan off the road. When he arrived in Montpelier, Idaho, the road conditions were so treacherous, he had to abandon his Cadillac and continue with only the Lincoln. Near the town of John Day, Oregon, the Lincoln got stuck on the slippery, icy road and Morton had to have a police car tow him to safe ground.

On November 9, he wrote to his wife from Eureka, California about his weather-related escapades. Four days later, he arrived in Los Angeles, worn-out, tired, and sick, but still determined to revitalize his career. He had sent his scores ahead of him in two trunks, which arrived a week later, however, he was nearly broke, and couldn't afford the $42.29 he needed to claim them. After a few days of rest, he contacted Garland and began rehearsals with his new band at the Elks Hall on South Central Avenue. He rented a room at 4052 Central Avenue, a few blocks away from the Elks Hall, and began contacting movie studios as well as Reb Spikes, with whom he hoped to start a new publishing partnership.

To populate Morton's big band, Ed Garland had scrounged up

several stellar New Orleans musicians, including the venerable trombonist Kid Ory, trumpeter Mutt Carey, drummer Minor "Ram" Hall, and guitarist Bud Scott. Eventually, Morton assembled a powerhouse lineup consisting of three trumpets, two trombones, three saxophones, violin, guitar, bass, and piano. Morton himself wanted to be free to conduct the band, so he brought in Buster Wilson to play piano in his place.

When they began rehearsing, the musicians realized that Morton's arrangements showed amazing advancements to the big band style, an avant-garde sound that took swing to another level. In tunes such as "Ganjam," Morton introduced unusual key changes, exotic rhythms, and a structure unheard of in jazz at that time.

Unfortunately for Morton, his new band did not last long. Los Angeles Musician's Union Local 767 found out that Morton was using non-union musicians in his group and shut down the band for good. His band had only been together a short while, but after this major setback, Morton saw his plans for a comeback go up in smoke. Resigned to the fact that he would probably never record again, Morton began looking for a way to cement his place in history. It was around this time that someone told him about a record shop in Hollywood that sold only records made by traditional jazz artists. He was directed to the Jazz Man at 1731 N. Vine Street.

It is not known when Morton became aware of the Jazz Man Record Shop, but Charles Campbell estimates it to have been around December 1940:

Dave told me that Jelly Roll Morton had been brought into the Jazz Man shop and they had a good talk. Dave and I talked about meeting up with him and planning to do a "life story" of his. I was very good at shorthand (about 150 words per minute) so Dave figured out how to get in touch with Jelly. He was in the Central Avenue district, living with his brother-in-law, Dink Johnson. We got together and arranged to meet Jelly and take him to lunch in the Central Avenue district and talk with him about the early days in his life. I did not have to be in my office job on Saturdays, so this worked out OK.

Jelly was very proper and friendly, not in any way of being the so-called "boasting guy." My problem was that I could hardly eat since any questioning we would ask him, he took about 10 or 15 minutes to answer in a most fascinating way. Anyway, I took it down, typed it up, and we sent it all to Bill Russell. I was living with a girl who was born in New Orleans; a very attractive girl named Frances. We heard that Morton was in a rest home on West Adams, so we went to talk with him. He was quite taken with Frances and they talked and he perked up immediately.

Dave Stuart's letters to Russell do not mention Morton until June 10, 1941. Since Morton was bedridden for much of the time leading up to his death in July, it's mystifying why Stuart did not mention Morton to Russell in his previous letters. It is most likely that he conducted his interviews with him shortly after Morton came to Los Angeles in November 1940. In his letter, Stuart told Russell that Morton came to Los Angeles on the orders of his doctors.

When he first landed in town he stood around the corner of 42nd and Central and blew his top about what a great figure he was and is. Then he got a group of fellows together for a band but it went the wrong way. He had some idea of a 14 to 18-piece band. This is silly as the town can't support a seven-piece outfit.

He played with Papa Mutt [Carey], Bud Scott, and a couple of other guys at the Silver Dollar at 8th and Main for a few nights, then took really sick and it looked like the end. Well—he's up now, drinking vegetable juices and looks a lot better, but his wind comes slowly. I've been seeing the guy about twice a week and oftimes spending the entire of a Sunday with him riding around in one of his fine cars.

So—now he wants me to write a book about him—what he did for New Orleans music—how he created jazz and finally set it to the right tempo—how he is the greatest in everything to do with music, etc. Chas. Campbell has been with me on several occasions and we have a book full of notes taken down in short hand and typed.

A frustrated Stuart then went on to ask Russell about the veracity of the many stories Morton told him. Stuart revealed that he already had made the acquaintance of legendary trumpet player Bunk Johnson, who Russell and *Jazzmen* author Frederic Ramsey had re-discovered in 1938. Stuart, who only had *Jazzmen* with which to verify facts about Morton's life, noted that many of the dates Morton told him were incorrect, which led him to question other stories Morton related.

Stuart also said that Morton was obsessed with W.C. Handy, with whom he had had a running feud ever since Handy was introduced on the *Ripley's Believe It or Not* radio program of April 26, 1938 as "the originator of jazz, stomps and blues." On the front of *Down Beat's* August 1938 edition, a headline blared, "W.C. Handy Is a Liar! Says Jelly Roll." Two years later, Morton was still fuming about Handy, as Stuart related:

He can't stop yelling about Handy a minute. This is no good as it never gets anyplace. Who cares if Handy stole or copied everything he has under his own name, it can't bother Ferd's early life in N.O.—but he believes it did.

Despite the inconsistencies with *Jazzmen,* Stuart appeared to show some sympathy for Morton. He told Russell that Ramsey and co-author Charles Smith had given Morton short shrift in their book.

I honestly believe that the Jazzmen fluffed him off pretty poorly. If Nichols rated a chapter, Ferd should have a book.

But Stuart was plainly flummoxed about what to believe and what not to believe of the stories Morton told him. Having given up on the *From Spirituals to Swing* concert, Stuart thought that by writing Morton's biography, he would attract some modicum of respect and find a way to move out of Los Angeles. Although Morton had been interviewed at length by Alan Lomax at the Library of Congress in 1938, the interviews would not be published for another 12 years, so in 1940, there was still very little known about Morton's life. Dave Stuart believed that when Morton shuffled into the Jazz Man Record Shop, he could set the record straight about Morton's importance and publish a rebuttal to what he thought was a skewed history of jazz as presented by Ramsey and Smith in *Jazzmen*. The two became friendly and Stuart would often play records for Morton at the Jazz Man.

By this time, Stuart had become extremely frustrated with the record business and especially the public's insatiable thirst for swing records. Charles Campbell remembered that Stuart would often refer to Benny Goodman derisively as "Benjamin Badfellow."

I'd like to sell this shop and beat it to N.Y. That's the place for me. I think Hammond would put me on at Columbia and keep me alive. I'm tired of this shop business—too many people want Miller, Shaw, Goodman, and the rest.

After a few weeks, Morton's health kept getting progressively worse, and finally, the interviews with Stuart and Campbell ceased altogether, with Morton confined to a small house at 1008 E. 32nd Street. Stuart soon realized that he would never be able to complete his interviews with Morton, as he reluctantly concluded:

With the material I have it would be quite useless to attempt a book. He was quite sick most of the time and we really got little done. Usually on Sunday afternoons we went for a ride to get him some fresh air. He didn't talk much the last month or so. However, I'd like to get in touch with Lomax and see what he has.

On June 30, Stuart wrote to Russell again:

The sad news is that Jelly is as sick as a dog and it looks like it won't be too long. He is in a little puss-pocket of a joint in L.A.—can't afford any more. That guy has really taken a beating. I saw some receipts where he

Jelly Roll Morton's last home: 1008 E. 32nd Street in Los Angeles. Photo taken in 1958.

1008 E. 32nd Street, as it appeared in 2009 (Photo by Cary Ginell).

got but 85 bucks for all of his songs during the years 1930 to 1938. He says he has received very little for all of his tunes! I've been going down to see him about twice a week and taking the stuff down in short hand— I take someone else with me.

On July 28, 1969, William Russell interviewed Stuart about Morton's final months in Los Angeles. Russell and Stuart later condensed the interview down to a narrative:

When Jelly Roll came to Los Angeles in the fall of 1940, he came to my record shop on Vine Street. I was a fan of his and got the idea of having him write his life story. So we'd take the old Cadillac that he had. Jelly and I sat in the front. I'd ask some questions and Charlie Campbell sat in the back seat and would take it down. Charlie Campbell was a secretary at one time and could write shorthand. So we started to write this thing that we thought would be a good book. We got less than 50 pages (actually only 11 typed pages) since he became ill. I think the first time we ever took him anyplace was to see Mutt Carey, who was playing down at the Silver Dollar at 8th and Main. The band sat up in a sort of slot, high above the floor level. It was a terrible joint. When we walked in there with Jelly, Mutt Carey yelled, "Here comes The Roll!" You know, like he just couldn't believe it. And I remember Jelly got up and played "Finger Breaker." He played that for them. Broke them all up. They couldn't believe he still played that way. Mutt and all the guys, they absolutely worshipped that man.

Probably the funniest thing in driving around was trying to get him together with the trombone player Zue Robertson. Zue lived in a converted chicken coop at his sister's, out in Watts. Morton had told us funny stories about how he had to keep a pistol on Zue when he played with Jelly. He'd get up and leave the band ever so often and Jelly claimed he had a revolver on his piano so he could pick it up and hold it on him. So Zue was living down in this hen house and we kept telling Jelly we were going to take him down to visit an "old friend." And he kept trying to find out who this old friend would be. We got him almost down there and he said, "It has to be Zue. He's the only man that could be out here." He said, "I won't go see him, he'll kill me." He just wouldn't go see him, never did. So he turned around in the car and drove right back.

Most of the stuff that we took down was while driving around town with Jelly. And we'd stop every hour or so at one of those health food stands where you drunk up a mess of potassium broth or vegetable juice. That's all he was drinking was health foods. Finally, I got him one of those presses where you can take carrots and press the juice out of them. He was absolutely delighted. We'd go out and get a bunch of carrots so he could have carrot juice.

When Jelly stayed with Dink Johnson and his wife Stella, I heard him play quite often on Dink's piano. In fact, he played anyplace there was a piano; he loved to play.

I never got to know Anita very well. After Jelly died, I got his scrapbooks and a few photos. There was a trunk full of music which I tried to get but never did. I wound up with only the photographs because I made the great mistake of loaning the scrapbooks to Mabel Morton. She said she'd return them. Naturally, she never did. It's a shame because the scrapbooks were wonderful, full of newspaper clippings and things like that.

I remember one time when Jelly Roll was standing on the corner of Central Avenue and talking to the one-legged tap dancer Peg Leg Bates. Jelly was telling the most outrageous stories you've ever heard, but they probably were all true, except that you could hardly believe them. And with Bates standing there, Jelly said things like, "You know, I can tap dance better than anyone in the world." Peg Leg said, "You can't tap dance as well as I can. I'm much better even with one leg." Jelly said something like "I could cut my feet off at the ankles, man, and whip you."

They would argue at the corner with this big group of people always standing around whenever Morton was talking, just, listening to these horrendous stories. They'd shake you up. And if you check them out, they were all right. One day, we were sitting, talking, and he said, "I used to write a tune every night when I was traveling with Benbow's show in the South." He'd sit down in a hotel room and write a new tune, then go down and play it in the show every night. This was the show that had one fellow who Jelly thought was the funniest man alive. He wore black underwear so he wouldn't have to wash it.

You'd think it was impossible for him to write a new tune every night, and he claimed he'd written, I can't remember how many, hundreds of tunes. But then you find out he had a couple hundred copyrighted, so it probably was true. A fantastic man.

When he came out here in 1940, the diamond in his tooth was gone. He had no diamonds left when I knew him, only the Cadillac. He was really broke. When they first put him in the hospital, they put him back in a kind of a broom closet. It was a hell of a mess to get him into an actual hospital room. He was pretty thin, and with the beard that he grew, he looked like a black Jesus. Yes, he let his beard and mustache grow. So he had this big black full beard on and he looked absolutely fantastic. He actually looked like a black Christ. A magnificent looking man.

I didn't expect him to last long because he was pretty miserable and unhappy, and I don't think he really gave a damn whether he lived or died. He was really far out at the end. I don't think it was possible that he could have written a will the last few days – No way. He never talked. I really don't think he was capable of talking. He'd not answer you if you asked him a question. I'd sit by the bed and he'd just hold my hand. I always thought he recognized me, but wasn't sure. He would smile at me. I was last there a day or two before he died.

Jelly Roll Morton died on July 10, 1941 at the age of 50.

On July 16, Morton's funeral was held at St. Patrick's Church, a gothic structure that had been severely damaged during the great Long Beach earthquake of 1933. *Down Beat* reported that only about 150 people came to mourn the man who had done so much to bring jazz to the world. Reb Spikes wanted to attend his friend's burial, but not having a car, he had no way to get to the cemetery from the church, so Dave Stuart offered him a ride and they arrived together. Stuart was the only white person to attend the service.

Jelly Roll Morton's sad final days were a tragedy in the life of one of jazz's most talented innovators, however, it was doubly tragic for Dave Stuart as, once again, an opportunity to make a name for himself went unrealized. He thought that by publishing Morton's biography, he could finally be recognized as a major authority on jazz's early development, which would enable him to move to New York and escape the day-to-day drudgery of running the Jazz Man. With his book unfinished and Morton dead, Stuart had to look elsewhere again.

Jelly Roll Morton's grave marker (Courtesy Darlene Brown).

Chapter Five

Marili

Around the time Stuart was interviewing Jelly Roll Morton, a strikingly attractive young woman in her early twenties walked into the Jazz Man on Vine Street and introduced herself to Dave Stuart. Her name was Marili Morden.

Marili was born in Hood River County, Oregon on December 11, 1919. Her father, Ranslaer Augustus Morden, married Phyllis Hope Goins in 1918 and, sometime thereafter, moved the family west to Portland, where he worked as a foreman for an outdoor advertising company.

Some time around 1940, Morden relocated to Los Angeles, probably to be closer to the music world. Soon after she arrived, she became involved in the local music scene around Central Avenue. Marili was a record collector, with a particular fondness for blues and early jazz from the 1920s. She befriended many musicians, both black and white, in the Los Angeles area, and it was these musicians who showed Marili around town and introduced her to others, including trombonist Kid Ory, who became a close friend. All the musicians liked her because she was kind, respectful, and best of all, colorblind when it came to race. She treated all people equally and was often enraged when she saw an injustice paid to a black musician.

At some point, she became acquainted with blues guitarist T-Bone Walker, who was then appearing at the Little Harlem club on 125th Street.

Marili Morden with T-Bone Walker, Los Angeles, c. early 1950s
(Courtesy Irving S. Gilmore Music Library, Yale University).

Marili had become well-known around town, especially at the all-black clubs where she would often be the only white person in attendance. In Helen Oakley Dance's biography of Walker, Marili recalled:

I wasn't all that great at it, but I loved to dance. If I was invited onto the floor by a good dancer, we'd have a fine time. My escorts were usually musicians, and since it's hard to get them to dance, it was OK. But after a time one of the Brown sisters [who ran the club] *asked me to stop by her office. "You're very welcome here," she said, "but please–no mixed dancing." I gaped. Growing up in Oregon I was raised to think we lived in a democracy. I really believed it! In Los Angeles my eyes were opened a bit, but I hadn't run into anything like this before. "My God," I thought, "Now I know how it feels."*

Marili thought so much of Walker's ability on the electric guitar, which was still considered a novelty instrument in 1940, that she convinced him to let her try to book him into better establishments than the run-down clubs near downtown. Aiming high, she set her sights on the Trocadero, a fashionable nightclub on the Sunset Strip. She advised Walker to dispense with gimmicky stunts like playing behind his back and dressing like a backwoods bumpkin. Marili dressed Walker in tux and tails, and his shows became smash hits. From there, Walker played Billy Berg's club on Vine Street where, initially, black patrons from Little Harlem were shunted upstairs to the balcony. After becoming aware of this pratice, Marili called a meeting with Berg and told him:

I'm sorry, but this is not it. You knew T-Bone had a following when you hired him. You have a chance now to make a lot of money. The word should go out that you're running your club right–everyone welcome. Something new for the West Side!"

As a result, the crowds became so large that Berg had to move to a larger building. Black performers had broken through the invisible wall and were not only playing white-owned establishments, but they were attracting mixed crowds as well. In an article published in *The Record Changer* in October 1947, Walker reminisced about his early years in Los Angeles:

At that time I was playing at Little Harlem in the south part of Los Angeles, and a girl used to come to hear me every night. Finally she got tired of coming so far to hear me so she arranged for me to get a job with real good pay in Hollywood and then I started to get my name. I played at Billy Berg's Capri Club and the Trocadero and lots of other Hollywood spots after that.

On December 14, 1956, Walker wrote and recorded an instrumental titled "Blues for Marili" in honor of the woman who helped him achieve the status and respect he deserved as a performer. The session, which was produced by Marili's ex-husband Nesuhi Ertegun, was released on Walker's LP *T-Bone Blues* (Atlantic 8020).

It is not certain when Marili Morden became aware of the Jazz Man, but Charles Campbell recalls that he first saw her in the shop at 1731 N. Vine Street, which would have been around the time he and Stuart were squiring Jelly Roll Morton around. She had either read about the shop in jazz collectors magazines or happened upon it while nightclubbing in

Hollywood, but soon, she found herself enjoying talking to the Jazz Man's knowledgeable proprietor. Flattered to find someone so attractive who was interested in early jazz, Stuart spent hours playing rare records from his collection for her. Campbell recalled when he first saw Marili:

One day, I came to the shop after my job and there was a very pretty chick at the counter and Dave was playing some of his favorite records for her: Oliver, Hot 7s, Morton, etc. She was from Portland and her name was Marili Morden.

Marili had a large collection of records by Bessie Smith, "The Empress of the Blues," and was looking for early records by King Oliver and Louis Armstrong. Stuart and Marili became close through their shared love for jazz and blues, and in time, Stuart talked her into helping him run the Jazz Man. Stuart was getting busier and busier with his outside activities, so in a short while, he had Marili running the shop by herself.

At the time, Charles Campbell and Stuart were sharing a large house in Hollywood. Campbell and Stuart each had one room to themselves, and they rented out the other rooms to local record collectors. One day, Marili told Stuart that she and a screenwriter were driving to Las Vegas get married the next day. Stuart not only talked her out of it, but proposed to her on the spot, and the two drove to Reno, Nevada, where they were married on February 20, 1941. When they returned to Hollywood a few days later, Marili moved in with Stuart and Campbell in the large house. On March 17, Marili kicked Stuart out, after only 25 days of living together. Although the two remained legally married for some time afterward, they never lived together again. Campbell and Stuart had to vacate their house when the record collectors who were renting the extra rooms got drafted, so Campbell, Marili, and a friend of theirs named Margot Terry, who worked in the record department at the May Company department store, moved into a smaller three-room house. Terry revealed to Campbell that Marili had told her that she "didn't want to have anything to do with another guy ever again."

Marili Morden, in her 1949 Cadillac Series 62 convertible, Hollywood, early 1950s (Courtesy Irving S. Gilmore Music Library, Yale University).

It's not clear what they saw in each other in the first place. Although Marili was an extraordinarily beautiful woman, other than their love for record collecting and early jazz, the two had nothing in common. Where Stuart was effusive and outgoing, Marili was reserved and introverted. The marriage turned out to be one of convenience for Stuart, since Marili was the answer to his desire to escape the day-to-day grind of running the Jazz Man. Charles Rossi, who had helped Stuart run the shop, was now serving in World War II, so Marili's stewardship gave Stuart the freedom to scavenge for jazz 78s and travel.

For Marili, the marriage may have been a sudden impulse due to her respect for Stuart's knowledge, his position of influence in the community, and possibly her own loneliness and insecurity at not being able to find anyone who measured up to the level of sophistication she had developed at such an early age. For whatever reason, she realized quickly how incompatible they were and ended the romantic part of their relationship.

Despite being separated as husband and wife, Stuart and Marili continued as business partners. According to Marili's third husband, musician Art Levin, Marili despised Stuart, and found him egocentric, argumentative, and always needing to have the last word. On November 10, 1942, Marili finally filed for divorce, citing "grievous bodily and mental suffering" caused by Stuart's deserting and abandoning her. The divorce papers claimed their marriage had made her "sick, nervous, and distressed to the extent that further married life or association with defendant is intolerable and impossible." Stuart, who was in the Ferry Command at the time she filed, did not contest the divorce, and it was ultimately granted by default. In a five-minute hearing on February 20, 1943, the Los Angeles Superior Court ruled in favor of Marili with Stuart duly notified of the verdict. On March 16, Stuart signed a waiver that was sent to him in Washington, D.C. whereby he relinquished rights granted to him by the Soldiers' and Sailors' Civil Relief Act of 1940. The divorce was finalized one year later, on March 22, 1944. By this time, Marili had resumed using her maiden name. In the divorce settlement, Stuart gave Marili the Jazz Man Record Shop, realizing that he no longer wished to be tied to it.

Dave Stuart rarely mentions Marili in his letters to William Russell. With Marili running the shop, Stuart no longer had to worry about keeping it open while he pursued other endeavors, including hunting down record collections, promoting the Jazz Man label, and developing his contacts in the now burgeoning world of the traditional jazz revival. Not only was Marili knowledgeable about records, she was young, attractive, and had her own personal connections to the Los Angeles jazz scene. Soon, she became acquainted with all of Stuart's friends and contacts and the local jazz collectors who regularly frequented the shop. Although she had to give up her work as a promoter for various Los Angeles acts, musicians came to appreciate not just her knowledge, but her kindness, reverence for them as human beings, and her generosity. She became known as the go-to person if anyone needed to hire a jazz or blues musician in town. Her marriage to Dave Stuart may have failed, but Marili Morden most likely saved the Jazz Man Record Shop from shutting its doors for good in 1942.

Chapter Six

It's All True

As Jelly Roll Morton lay dying in Los Angeles County Hospital, Dave Stuart excitedly wrote to William Russell that he was going to be making a motion picture with Hollywood's reigning *wunderkind* filmmaker Orson Welles (1915–1985). The 26-year-old Welles was riding high on the critical success of his debut motion picture, *Citizen Kane,* and was one of the first members of Hollywood's elite to patronize the Jazz Man Record Shop. Charles Campbell recalled walking into the Vine Street shop one day and seeing Welles "romping" to Clarence Williams records. Welles was almost as passionate about New Orleans jazz as Stuart was, and enjoyed playing records and talking with Stuart about jazz on the numerous occasions he dropped into the shop. Although both were fans of traditional New Orleans jazz, Welles's taste also extended to more modern exponents of the music, including Duke Ellington.

Welles's project was to be part of a documentary anthology entitled *Pan-American,* which would showcase aspects of life in North and South America. The idea for doing the film was proposed by the minister of propaganda and popular culture of Brazil to combat Nazi anti-American sentiment in the country. The film was soon retitled *It's All True,* with the jazz segment, tentatively titled *Jam Session,* serving as one of four vignettes. One, *My Friend Bonito,* was to be based on a short story by filmmaker Robert

43

Orson Welles on the set of The Magnificent Ambersons, *1942
(Courtesy RKO Radio Pictures, Inc./Photofest).*

Flaherty (famous for his documentary *Nanook of the North*), a sentimental rendering of a Spanish folktale about a friendship between a young boy and a fighting bull. Two other segments would focus on North America, one of which would explore the development of jazz as seen through the eyes of Louis Armstrong. It is likely that Welles was merely indulging his passion for New Orleans jazz and was shoehorning it into his film. Although his motion picture debut, *Citizen Kane,* was shaping up to be a box office disappointment, critics lauded the film, which gave Welles the power to do just about whatever he pleased in subsequent projects, no matter how esoteric the subject matter.

For the film's soundtrack, Welles hired Duke Ellington to write the score, at the extravagant salary of $1,000 a week. In addition, Ellington was allowed to play a role in the film and would retain publishing rights to the music. The script for *Jam Session,* which was soon renamed *The Story of Jazz,* was to be written by Elliot Paul (1891–1958), a journalist known mainly for writing detective stories who was friends to such literary stalwarts as James Joyce and Gertrude Stein. Welles also put Dave Stuart on retainer to work with Paul in establishing the historical framework of the story. Stuart was ecstatic, and in his letter to Russell, he bubbled with excitement as he aggrandized his status as a mere script consultant to that of Welles's virtual co-creator:

I am going to be making a picture with Orson Welles on jazz! It will really be the thing! He wants to do a job about Louie's life from New Orleans to New York BUT with colored people! Just as little about the Austin guys and with the main idea in mind that the big bands are not fine jazz. I suggested he wind up with the Lu Waters (sic) band as one of the few bands trying to play the stuff as it was. The way it will go and the way he will do it I am SURE that no crap will come out of it. I turned down two jobs, one with Warner's and one with Paramount because the story was a cinch to wind up with the Original Memphis Five. I know this is going to be good. Did you see his other picture? If not, have a

Chicago, August 15, 1941

Orson Welles Jazz Movie Will Star Louis Armstrong

by CHARLIE EMGE

Los Angeles — Louis Armstrong will soon play the leading role in an RKO production to be directed by Orson Welles, who has three productions officially scheduled for him at this lot, but who intends to sandwich in his own treatment of a jazz picture.

Welles, who made mincemeat of Hollywood humdrum in his first picture, *Citizen Kane,* and who is a jazz enthusiast, has in mind a "featurette" in the "March of Time" technique, using, wherever possible, roles in the picture that can be performed by the people represented.

Essentially, Orson's story of jazz will be the life of Armstrong, with Louie playing himself except

where he is shown as "Little Louie" at the Waif's Home in New Orleans. Plenty of footage has been planned for other famous jazz performers including the Austin High gang and other Chicago stylists featured on their instruments. When your correspondent phoned the Welles office to verify this some fifth columnist answered a vague "Uh huh, but we're not ready to announce anything yet."

Moguls attached to other big movie mills, who pretend to appreciate Welles' efforts, commented, "Okay. Swell! But how the hell is he going to sell it?"

Leave that to Orson, who will never forget that to educate Joe public you also have to entertain him.

Down Beat, *August 15, 1941.*

David Stuart

THE JAZZ MAN RECORD SHOP

moves again

NEW LOCATION

6331 Santa Monica Boulevard

one block west of Vine Street

HI 1588

(Courtesy the L.A. Institute of Jazz.)

6331 Santa Monica Blvd. in Hollywood: the Jazz Man's home from July 1941 to December 1944
(Courtesy Selma Ertegun).

look quick. It will give you an idea about how he works. He's the only one that ever lit in this town that can do a good job or would ever be allowed to do one. He wants music all the time, rather like an opera, let's say, with the band as the picture, and quick passing shots of Bunk, Jelly, Ory, Bechet, etc., etc., each telling a little about what they remember of the music. I'm sure we'll go to N.O. and take some quick shots of the houses that used to be, perhaps of the fronts with various kinds of music on the screen and the camera passes the houses. I know damn well I'll get Bunk and a few of the guys in the picture so's they can make a few bucks.

Stuart went on to ask Russell if he had any information on Armstrong that was "not too well known" that he could ask Welles to buy from him. His disdain for the "Austin gang," which included white musicians like Eddie Condon, Bud Freeman, Benny Goodman, and others, was palpable. In Stuart's view, these were merely opportunists who made money by watering down the musical ideas of the "authentic" New Orleans musicians. Even Bix Beiderbecke didn't get a break:

I am not going to let Bix into the picture for more than a small shot, as he sits and listens to Louie play. He is the one that everyone will expect to represent jazz, so he gets a fluff off.

In his letters, Stuart continually aggrandized his position on the film, making it appear that it was he, not Welles and not Paul, who would determine who would get to be in the film and who wouldn't. Stuart had full confidence that his opinions reflected those of Welles.

We just got thru playing five hours of records and he can pick the good and bad in a flash, and that counts. He also hates the Goodman period stuff. In fact, Louie and the Oliver band are for him. Jelly's band also gets him.

Shortly after Jelly Roll Morton's death, Stuart moved the shop to its fourth location, at 6331 Santa Monica Blvd., a few blocks west of Vine Street. The store, which had been previously occupied by a real estate

Close-up snapshot of the entryway to 6331 Santa Monica Blvd.
(Courtesy Selma Ertegun).

office, was larger than the old location in the Hollywood Playhouse building. The shop would remain there through the end of 1944.

The design of the building at 6331 Santa Monica Blvd., which shared a street corner with Lillian Avenue, made it resemble a Mexican hacienda, with a stucco exterior, flat roof, and clay shingles over the entryway, which was flanked by two palm trees. Two narrow windows, fitted with Venetian blinds, were on either side of the entrance, with the street address number painted on the upper panes. Catty-cornered at the intersection of the two streets, the structure's adobe-like façade was thus visible from all angles. To thirsty record collectors, the building's Southwestern appearance must have resembled an oasis. Although he was no longer near the famed corner of Hollywood and Vine, Stuart probably liked the exotic ambience of the newer building better than being squashed in the annex to the El Capitan Theater on Vine Street.

In a letter to Russell after the move, Stuart bragged that Welles had put him on salary with a two-month guarantee, expecting to be on staff for four additional months. Despite the fact that Ellington was put in charge of the score, Stuart thought that he would be able to get jobs for musicians he knew who would play on the soundtrack, deluding himself into thinking that he was actually being given that power. His mind raced as he visualized casting the parts of musicians for his fantasy opus:

If you think of any musicians who can play the musical parts of Dodds, Ory, Oliver, Hardin, Dutrey, Johnson, etc., let me know. What about Lu Watters for Oliver, do you think he can play it? What about the trombone on the Rena records? Can Lil play anymore? And who can sing like Bessie? Anybody?

On July 28, while Stuart was planning a trip to New Orleans to scout local musicians for the film, Welles officially registered his omnibus. Two months later, Stuart reported to Russell that he thought the picture would begin shooting at the beginning of 1942. In August, he began making weekly trips to San Francisco to hear Lu Watters' band play and was beginning to recognize the potential for getting Watters some national attention. But for the time being, his focus was still on the Welles film, as he reported to Russell that Elliot Paul had completed the script.

Orson and myself did a short sketch and Elliot turned it into something that reads like a fine book. It is really a beautiful script. At present, the script stands at six reels.

But Stuart was fearful of Duke Ellington's presence on the film. Ellington had put the members of his own orchestra on the payroll, but had not done any real work on the score as yet. he was busy performing in his revue *Jump for Joy* that summer and had little time to work on Welles's project. He later remembered that he eventually wrote a horn solo, which was promptly lost, but wrote nothing else. Despite Stuart's desire to hire authentic New Orleans musicians to work on the soundtrack, only Ellington and a few others (including Louis Armstrong and keyboardist Hazel Scott) received any money. Ellington himself was paid $12,500 for what would result in that one lost solo.

In Ellington, Dave Stuart saw not a collaborator, but an enemy; one who would infuse the score with his own modernistic ideas, and thus, destroy the integrity of what Stuart saw as his golden opportunity for fame. In a letter to Russell dated October 1, 1941, Stuart jealously gnashed his teeth over Ellington's major role in the film:

To ease your fears that Ellington will do any real music for the picture, HE WON'T – NOT OVER MY DEAD AND BEAT BODY! That guy knows nothing – NOTHING – about jass. He never heard the Oliver band, knew nothing about Oliver except what Bubber [trumpeter James "Bubber" Miley] *told him. I've sat at his apt. day after day playing records: Olivers, Louis', Mortons, etc., trying to show him what jass sounded like in those days. After a month of this, I asked him to write something he thought fit behind a tune Bolden would play and the next day, he comes to the studio, sits down, and whacks out a ditty which is an Africoamerican adaptation of* Afternoon of a Faun! "This," *he says,* "Will get it!" Orson howls, "Duke, if you knew half as much about jazz as I do, you would still know less than Oliver's aunt!" *With that, Duke becomes our figurehead. You see, I was going to use Jelly to put the music together. Now I don't know what to do unless Duke can tie up "Didn't He Ramble" with another tune so it won't sound like the Ellington band, but just a short background bridge. How about you? Can't you write this kinda stuff? Enough to patch the music?*

Obsessed with his own part in the film, Stuart probably had no idea of the trouble Welles had gotten himself into. In October 1941, Welles began shooting principle photography on his next feature, *The Magnificent Ambersons,* while simultaneously working on another film, *Journey Into Fear,* for which a script had been completed in July. Welles was now burning his candle at three ends. Stuart, who was now writing his letters on Welles's Mercury Productions stationery, disappointedly informed Russell of the latest developments:

Orson just started on a picture and it will be the first of the year, if at all, that the jazz opus comes up. Looks just fair at present as another company on the lot is making another one of those stinkers about jazz that may leave a familiar taste in the mouth of the public. I'm still on the pay check business so it may work out. Who can tell about things out there?

The film Stuart so disdainfully made reference to was probably *Birth of the Blues,* a Paramount film that starred Bing Crosby. Brian Donlevy, and Mary Martin. In the film, Crosby plays a fictional New Orleans clarinetist in the 1890s trying to catch on with his jazz band (which includes Jack Teagarden, among others). Unable to contain his enthusiasm for *The Story of Jazz,* and bridling at Hollywood's attempts to steal his thunder, Stuart started leaking information about the film to *Down Beat, Jazz Information,* and *Metronome.*

The blurb that appeared in the November 1941 issue of *Jazz Information* describes the film as a "cinematic variety show planned by Welles, Elliot Paul, and Dave Stuart" that stars Louis Armstrong playing himself. Although Duke Ellington is listed as being set to "write some special music for it," the magazine reported a "rumor" (no doubt perpetrated by Stuart) that "Lu Watters' San Francisco jazz band will get a break."

The *Metronome* article resulted from some off-the-record comments by Stuart that were reported without his knowledge. The magazine's headline screamed, "Louis Film Director Slaps at Duke," with Stuart quoted in an embarrassing sub-heading: "'Ellington Knows Nothing About Jazz,' Technical Adviser Claims, Boasting." The article went on to paint Stuart as a "west coast swing radical, one of whose claims to fame is his much publicized refusal to sell any Glenn Miller records as a matter of principle. Stuart owns a small record store." Dripping with sarcasm, the article went on to deride Stuart's claims against "the great leader and composer," referring to him snidely as "The Amazing Authority." Stuart babbled on, saying that Ellington was only hired because it was "good publicity" for the picture. It was a humiliating turn of events for Stuart, who was made to look like a fool in his claims about Ellington's lack of knowledge about the music that he had been playing for 20 years. Word of the article got to RKO like quicksilver, and from the tone of Stuart's next letter to Russell, it was clear that the outspoken record store owner had been taken on the carpet.

That article brought the wrath of the Welles unit down on me for a day. I believe it is all over now – I hope. It was that snotnosed moppet of an owner. He walked in the shop one day and said, "I like Goodman, Dorsey, etc., etc. Why don't you, you old fashioned jass man?" Then we talked and he said that nothing was for publication. The next thing I hear is someone tells me that there is an article in Met. I sell the thing but never read it.

The Japanese invasion of Pearl Harbor on December 7 only served to further complicate Welles's calendar. Nelson Rockefeller, a major stockholder in RKO, persuaded Welles to shoot his picture in Brazil to cement friendly relations between the two countries. Fearing the Nazi influence on the Brazilian dictatorship, the U.S. State Department appointed Welles special ambassador to Brazil. Welles was subsequently ordered to go to Rio de Janeiro and spend a million dollars documenting the country's Carnival season, simply as a good-will gesture. A few days after Pearl Harbor, Welles flew to Brazil to begin preparations for Carnival, which would begin the following February. This only served to further stall work on *It's All True.* Because of this, Welles had to shoot the final scenes from *The Magnificent Ambersons* and *Journey Into Fear* simultaneously on adjoining sound stages. The shooting of *My Friend Bonito,* the first segment of *It's All True* to be filmed, was suspended. As it turned out, Orson Welles did start work on a documentary about a musical style; but it wasn't Dave Stuart's New Orleans jazz, it was a history of samba, the Brazilian music associated with Carnival, which Welles had fallen in love with. *The Story of Samba* was incorporated into *It's All True,* along with another segment, *Four Men on a Raft,* about peasants from an impoverished Brazilian village who travel 1,600 miles on a small raft to petition the government for welfare.

Surviving clips from *The Story of Samba* feature Welles rhapsodically describing the vibrant music over scenes from Carnival. "Dig that rhythm, you cats!," he gushes, during his narration of his documentary, as if he were talking directly to the impatient Stuart, waiting back in the States for the famed director to return to begin shooting *The Story of Jazz.* But unbeknownst to

Stuart, RKO had decided that *The Story of Jazz* was not commercially viable and the segment was dropped entirely. The remaining three stories from *It's All True* were put on the back burner where they stayed. The project was eventually shelved on May 1, 1942. Charles Campbell recalled that even though the project was going nowhere, Stuart remained on retainer for six months until early 1942. Campbell recalled Stuart making weekly trips to the RKO studios to pick up his payroll check, which was about $50.

It's All True* proved to be a failure not just for David Stuart but a catastrophic event in the career of Orson Welles. Because of the Carnival project, Welles was forced to drop *It's All True* and edit *The Magnificent Ambersons* while still in Brazil. After a California screening of *Ambersons* garnered mixed response, RKO panicked and had editor Robert Wise slash 45 minutes from the movie, which included a softening of the ending.

Welles Jazz Film May Be Shelved

Louie May Never Be Immortalized in Great Movie

Los Angeles — Hints that the much balled up Orson Welles movie treatment of the life of Louis Armstrong may never be made are found in cryptic statements issued from Welles' Mercury Productions studios in Culver City.

Inquiries concerning the Welles jazz opus bring guarded remarks to the effect that no starting date has been set, and — recently — a more significant remark that "no contractual commitments or obligations" on the picture have been made.

Armstrong, currently at the Casa Manana, has received no notice to report to work in the near future.

The Welles jazz treatment, as announced, was to be one subject in a feature containing several subjects and entitled *It's All True.* Welles is still in South America where he has been working on production of another subject for the same feature.

Down Beat, *May 1, 1942.*

Welles believed that had the studio permitted him to edit it down himself, *The Magnificent Ambersons* could have been his greatest film. Instead, it was a commercial failure, and it was years before he was able to get another directing assignment. Welles was relegated thereafter to scramble to make "B" pictures for the rest of his career (some of which, such as *Touch of Evil,* he turned into cult classics). Orson Welles and the Jazz Man never did complete their collaboration, but Welles and the Hollywood record store would join forces again several years later.

Elliot Paul's script for *The Story of Jazz* ended up as the genesis for a 1947 film called *New Orleans,* a Hollywood-ized fictional story that bore little resemblance to what Paul and Stuart had envisioned. (Stuart was not credited in the film's final release.) The movie depicted the closing of New Orleans' notorious Storyville district in 1917 and the migration of jazz to Chicago, just as Paul and Stuart had proposed, but the new plot dealt with a love story between a gambling hall owner and a society matron's daughter, with jazz relegated to the background. Nevertheless, it is a worthy document, if only for its performances by Louis Armstrong, Billie Holiday (in her only feature film appearance), Kid Ory, Papa Mutt Carey, Meade Lux Lewis, and many other jazz musicians.

In an intriguing twist, the lead female character in *New Orleans,* played by Dorothy Patrick, is named Miralee. She is a young opera singer who becomes transformed by the jazz sung by her maid, played by Holiday, and aspires to learn to sing jazz herself. One wonders if Marili Morden saw the film and noticed the resemblance between herself and the naïve, new-girl-in-town, who rhapsodizes over the music of the black musicians. (Jazz historian Sherrie Tucker defines the character as the "Jazz Virgin," one who appreciates the music for itself and not from where it was derived. This is in opposition to Krin Gabbard's "Jazz Nerd," who is usually a white record collector who admires black musicians that are viewed as being "hip.") In Marili's mind, it's possible that she saw in Miralee Dave Stuart's image of her: a musical innocent who he transformed, *Pygmalion*-like, into a hip, savvy jazz aficionado.

For Dave Stuart, the failure of *It's All True* was the third in a series of ambitious projects he hoped would help him achieve the fame and respect he so desperately desired. First came the stillborn West Coast version of *From Spirituals to Swing*, which never went beyond the planning stage. This was followed by his plans for a major Jelly Roll Morton biography, which were dashed when Morton died. With the abandonment of *It's All True,* Stuart had now flopped in three arenas in less than two years: live concerts, publishing, and motion pictures. His next obsession, however, which came on the heels of the foundering Welles film, would prove to be the landmark event he was looking for, an event that would change the history of jazz forever.

Chapter Seven

The Good Herb

The Jazz Man's new home, at 6331 Santa Monica Blvd, was its fourth location in less than two years. The shop's address, however, was the only thing that was moving. By July 1941, Dave Stuart's career had stalled. Jelly Roll Morton was dead, and with him went Stuart's plans to publish Morton's life story. Although Stuart was excited about his collaboration with Orson Welles on *It's All True,* the next few months would prove that this, too, would remain unrealized.

About this time, Stuart became aware of a band that was creating quite a stir up in San Francisco. It was led by a tradition-minded cornet player named Lu Watters. Watters' obsession with the traditional jazz of New Orleans made Stuart and other West Coast record collectors take notice. Curious as to how this band sounded live, Stuart carefully started following its progress on the Bay Area club scene. He eventually made plans to hear the group for himself.

Stuart had been toying with the idea of starting a record company some time during that year, but his plans initially involved reissuing long-out-of-print classics, much like the East Coast-based Commodore and HRS labels were doing. Stuart noticed that these two labels, especially Commodore's, were helping to publicize the record stores both were associated with, and Stuart sought to duplicate that success for the Jazz Man by spinning off his own record label. But what should he release? Since 1938, Commodore had been making new records of traditional jazz, mostly featuring exponents from the so-called "Austin High School Gang," Chicago-based musicians like Eddie Condon, Bud Freeman, and Joe Sullivan. To Stuart, these were merely pretenders; if he had his own label, he'd make sure that he recorded only "real jazz." If only he could find a currently working band that played this music. It was then that he came across the Watters band.

Lucius Carl Watters was born on December 19, 1911 in Santa Cruz, a coastal community less than an hour from San Francisco. Shortly afterward, the Watters family moved to Rio Vista, a small town near the state capital of Sacramento. By the age of 10, Lu was already playing bugle in a drum-and-bugle corps at St. Joseph's Military Academy. In 1925, the family moved to San Francisco, where Watters played trumpet in the school band and orchestra. He earned a music scholarship after graduating and was set to start taking classes at the University of San Francisco. Before doing so, however, he worked as a ship's musician, playing aboard vessels that traveled as far as New York City. It was during one of these trips that Watters began writing arrangements.

But music had a stronger pull on him than academia and Watters joined the musicians union and dropped out of college to become a full-time musician. He made his first recordings in 1929 with Jack Danford and His Ben Franklin Hotel Orchestra, recording two songs: "Alabama Stomp" and "On the Alamo," which were released on the Phonograph Recording Company label of San Francisco, a small, private company located in the Kress Building on Market Street.

In 1930, Watters joined the Lofner-Harris Orchestra, which held forth at the St. Francis Hotel on Union Square. The orchestra was one of the city's most popular dance bands, led by pianist Carol Lofner (born Laughner) and drummer Phil Harris. After graduating from high school, Watters sold Lofner an arrangement he had written of "Alice Blue Gown" for $50.00,

*Lu Watters (far right) in the Carol Lofner horn section, 1931
(Courtesy the Frank Driggs Collection).*

so Lofner was happy to have him join his group in the trumpet section. For the next five years, Watters played cornet and wrote arrangements for the Lofner Orchestra, making records with the group for Victor in October 1931. Watters' career took a positive turn when Bing Crosby, who had just left the Paul Whiteman orchestra to become a solo act, heard the Lofner orchestra and hired Watters to be his first official arranger.

By this time, Watters was tiring of the riff-driven swing arrangements he was playing and wanted to explore music with more substance to it. He began thinking about playing early jazz, the spontaneous ensemble music from New Orleans:

I was beginning to know more tunes. I had bought a lot of Louis Hot Fives, Mortons, Olivers, when I was on the road with Lofner. I was also buying a lot of classical records. In Lofner's band, which was a very commercial band, we all listened to jazz records all the time. I liked Louis especially.

One night, while playing with the Lofner orchestra at the Club Forrest in New Orleans, Watters was invited to sit in on a jam session with a group of black musicians. It was then that he realized in what direction he wanted to go.

After ending his stint with Lofner in 1934, Watters played on the road with a cooperative band led by Chuck Glasspool. He became friends with two members of the band who he found had similar thoughts about playing New Orleans jazz: bass player Squire Girsback and pianist Paul Lingle. Stranded in Reno after the ballroom they were to play in burned down, Watters met trombonist Turk Murphy and clarinetist Bob Helm, two musicians who were also from Northern California. The five became friends and promised to stay in touch with one another once they returned to San Francisco.

Around 1936, Watters organized his first band, a five-piece group that played at the Ambassador Ballroom on Fillmore Street in San Francisco. Work was sparse during the Depression and swing music was on the rise. Dance bands generally consisted of saxophones, a muted trumpet, flyswatter drums, and simple piano arrangements. Traditional jazz instruments such as tuba, trombone, and banjo were rarely used.

In the summer of 1938, Watters formed a big band that was designed to be versatile enough to play hot jazz as well as sweet dance music. As an arranger, Watters liked to have a brass frontline sandwiched in between three clarinets (doubling on saxophones) playing freely above the line and two trombones playing below. The band played at the Sweets Ballroom in Oakland, across the bay from San Francisco. This group played to enthusiastic crowds as large as 3,200 before its life ended suddenly in the fall of 1939. By this time, Watters had grown weary of playing stock arrangements, which sounded exactly the same way at every performance. He vowed that the next band he formed would allow the musicians the freedom to play whatever they wanted. It was a difficult period for a jazz musician, as the

Rehearsal at the Big Bear Tavern in Oakland, c. 1939-40. Bob Helms called it the "experimental laboratory of jazz." L-R: Wally Rose, piano; probably Clancy Hayes, banjo; Turk Murphy, trombone; Lu Watters, trumpet; Bill Dart, drums; Bob Scobey, trumpet; Ellis Horne, clarinet (Courtesy the San Francisco Traditional Jazz Foundation).

old New Orleans style he was fond of was no longer fashionable.

Then he found the Big Bear Tavern.

Located in the hills overlooking the college town of Berkeley, just north of Oakland, the Big Bear Tavern was described by clarinetist Bob Helm as "the experimental laboratory of jazz." Free-thinking jazz musicians went there to woodshed at jam sessions, where they exorcised their frustrations in having to play stock arrangements in dreary hotel orchestras for a living. Although most jam session repertoires relied on standards such as "Oh, Lady, Be Good" and "Honeysuckle Rose," musicians at the Big Bear Tavern brought back traditional New Orleans classics like "High Society," "Panama," and Scott Joplin ragtime numbers such as "Maple Leaf Rag." The attraction for these songs was their multiple melodic strains, which gave musicians the opportunity to stretch out musically, rather than be stuck playing a simple verse-chorus pattern. When they weren't jamming at the Big Bear, Watters and his friends scoured record stores, looking for old 78s by King Oliver, Louis Armstrong's Hot Five and Hot Seven, and Jelly Roll Morton. The musicians who frequented the Big Bear Tavern would turn out to be the nucleus of the rediscovery and subsequent explosion of traditional New Orleans jazz during the 1940s.

In early 1940, Lu Watters felt he was ready to assemble a regular jazz band, and began rehearsals at the Mark Twain Hotel on Fillmore Street, a decidedly unglamorous part of town, mostly inhabited by poor blacks. Of all the records he had been listening to, Watters had an affinity for the twin-cornet sound of King Oliver's Creole Jazz Band, which featured Oliver's young apprentice, Louis Armstrong on second cornet. Joining Watters in this role was a New Mexico-born trumpet player named Bob Scobey.

In August 1940, Watters and his group were invited to play at a meeting of the Hot Music Society of San Francisco, which was held at a former basement speakeasy called the Dawn Club. The club was located in the Monadnock Building at 30 Annie Street, a small alleyway located south of Market Street, a short distance from the St. Francis Hotel, where

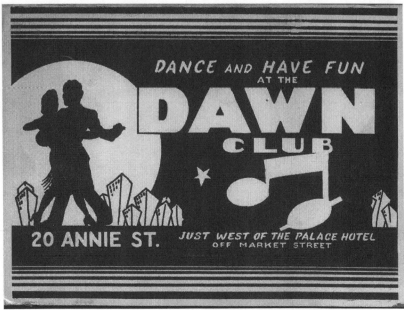

Souvenir photo album given away at the Dawn Club in downtown San Francisco
(From the author's collection).

Watters had played with Carol Lofner. That initial engagement (Watters did not attend) led to a regular Friday night gig at which the band played New Orleans jazz tunes they had learned at their jam sessions at the Big Bear Tavern.

The Dawn Club's patrons were initially repelled by the cacophonous sounds the band produced. Accustomed to the melody-driven songs played by swing orchestras, San Francisco's music fans balked at this unusual group, which played songs whose titles they did not know nor could remember, since few vocals were featured. Although the personnel varied from week to week, the group's stalwart members included Watters and Scobey playing cornet or trumpet, Turk Murphy on trombone, Bob Helm on clarinet, Squire Girsback on tuba and string bass, Russ Bennett and Clancy Hayes on banjos, and Bill Dart on drums. With no regular pianist in the group, Watters invited a classical music teacher named Wally Rose to join, but Rose didn't want to give up his day job just yet so Watters resorted to using a rotating lineup of guest pianists.

During their initial stint at the Dawn Club, the group chose a name: the Yerba Buena Jazz Band. (The name was Bob Helm's suggestion.) Yerba Buena, which means "good herb" or "wild mint," was the name given to a settlement erected by Captain W.A. Richardson in 1835, which was changed to San Francisco in 1847. The wild mint plants that thrived in the San Francisco Bay Area were an appropriate reflection on the equally tangy and fresh music played by Watters' group. (Yerba Buena is also the name of an island located in San Francisco Bay, which today separates the two spans of the San Francisco-Oakland Bay Bridge.)

Throughout his life, Lu Watters was known for his stubborn, combative, and often defensive personality. It was his inability to compromise that led to his decision to play music strictly devoted to the sounds of old New Orleans. This decision rankled the local musicians unions (then racially segregated), who couldn't understand why Watters insisted on playing antiquated "nigger music" to sparse audiences at the Dawn Club, when he could have been raking in the dough playing dance band charts at the ritzier San Francisco hotels.

In addition, what was supposed to be a cooperative band now changed as Watters renamed the band Lu Watters' Yerba Buena Jazz Band. The band's problems with dynamics and fluctuating tempos triggered a row between Watters and Bob Helm, which resulted in Watters inviting clarinetist Ellis Horne to attend a rehearsal early in 1941. Upon seeing Horne, Helm abruptly walked out, with his friend Turk Murphy close behind in an act of loyalty.

When ASCAP, the performing rights organization, and its new competitor, BMI, began battling for revenue from the performance of live and recorded music, the dispute carried over to the clubs, and the steadily declining audience ended the Yerba Buena Jazz Band's initial engagement at the Dawn Club. Refusing to admit defeat, Watters tried again later in the year, assembling a different group that began playing at the Dawn Club on Friday and Saturday nights. A local radio announcer named Hal McIntyre, who had relentlessly plugged the band on his jazz program on station KYA, convinced the station to broadcast the group's Friday night shows. It is not known how Dave Stuart heard about the Watters band, but on Friday, August 29, he and Charles Campbell drove up in Stuart's Packard coupe to hear the group for themselves at the Dawn Club. They spent the next four days in the Bay Area. Stuart introduced himself to Watters and told him that he was interested in starting a record label, with Watters becoming his first artist. Watters was enthusiastic about the idea and the two discussed their plans for the session.

Since Campbell could not get another Friday off, Stuart drove up himself to hear the group and talk with Watters on three successive Fridays in September. By the end of the month, Stuart was convinced that the band was something special, despite being fully aware of the contentiousness of

Watters' Band Brings Dixie Jazz to Frisco

BY FRANK O'MEA

San Francisco—This city by the Golden Gate, which was the scene of the start to fame of Paul Whiteman and Art Hickman, may soon earn itself redemption by becoming the only place in the country which is supporting a genuine jazz band.

With Lu Watters' new Yerba Buena Band now playing once a week at the Maple Leaf Club's Friday night "Jazz Band Ball," many other local musicians are finding themselves interested in New Orleans music.

Frisco's Top Horn Man

Watters' combo, built along the classic line of King Oliver's Creole Jazz Band, debuted at a dance at the Dawn Club shortly before Christmas. The "Jazz Band Ball" series, designed to catch both dancers and listeners, opened Feb. 14. Two previous sessions designed on the same line drew capacity crowds.

Watters, who plays cornet in a manner reminiscent of early Louis Armstrong, is well known as the town's top horn man, and has turned down several offers with "name" bands.

In addition, the group features Turk Murphy, who plays tailgate trombone that would have made him outstanding in New Orleans' balmiest days, and Bob Helm, considered by local critics as the greatest white clarinet man since Leon Rappolo.

Use Banjo, Tuba

Bob Scobey, one of San Francisco's younger musicians, plays second cornet; Walter Rose, piano, and Bill Dart, drums. In addition, banjo and tuba are used.

San Franciscans who never heard of jazz have proved to be some of the band's most ardent supporters, having learned that good dance music can be played by a band of less than 16 pieces.

In addition to such standards as *Kansas City Stomps, Milenburg, Riverside Blues* and *High Society,* the book includes many pops, and even rhumbas and congas. Watters' own tune, *Yerba Buena Strut* is also featured.

Down Beat, March 1, 1941.

Ad for Lu Watters' first Southern California appearance in 1949, sponsored by the Jazz Man Record Shop. (Courtesy the L.A. Institute of Jazz)

the jazz man

presents

the first Southern California

appearance of

LU WATTERS'
YERBA BUENA JAZZ BAND

JAMES P. JOHNSON

ALBERT NICHOLAS   ZUTTY SINGLETON

Wednesday   8:30 p.m.

JUNE 1

PASADENA CIVIC AUDITORIUM

300 E. GREEN STREET — PASADENA

tickets: 2.40—1.80—1.20 inc. Fed. Tax

TICKETS NOW ON SALE
AT JAZZ RECORD STORES

FOR INFORMATION CALL

HIllside 1588

NOON TO 8 P.M.

Market Street, San Francisco, c. 1940. The Dawn Club can be seen at the lower right.

its leader's personality, as he wrote to Bill Russell:

> *I've been up to Frisco the last four weeks to hear the Watter's (sic) band and it is the best no matter how they fight within the outfit.*

By this time, the rejuvenated band still wasn't drawing large crowds and Watters was rumored to be paying the band members out of his own pocket. Patrons coming to the Dawn Club expecting to see a swing orchestra instead saw a band with a tuba and a banjo playing songs that hadn't been heard in a generation. Although Turk Murphy had returned to the fold, prospects for the band's future success were bleak.

And then, on October 7, the *San Francisco Examiner* reported that Watters had been shot in the hand by the father of Patricia Joyce, a 19-year-old University of California co-ed who Watters was dating. Joyce's father told police that he had warned Watters to stay away from his daughter but when he caught them returning to her house one night, he got into a scuffle with Watters and "accidentally" shot him. Watters blamed the incident on an encounter with a robber, but when no evidence turned up, he recanted the obvious fabrication. Watters wasn't seriously injured and the father apologized soon after (Watters and Joyce eventually married), but the sensationalist newspaper story resulted in increased attendance at the Dawn Club. The new customers found the music the Yerba Buena Jazz Band played unusual but fun to dance to, and in a matter of weeks, the band was now playing three nights weekly: Friday, Saturday, and Sunday.

On October 28, with the Orson Welles project starting to fizzle, Stuart informed William Russell that he was negotiating with Watters to make records on a new label he was thinking of starting, taking his cue from other record stores with their own labels, such as Milt Gabler's Commodore and Steve Smith's HRS (Hot Record Society). Stuart's comment was only half-facetious as he made reference for the first time to the shop's eponymous, yet still non-existent label:

I've been trying to make a deal with the Watters bunch to make a set of three records of them to put out on the famous Jazz Man label.

Unable to provide the seed money necessary to book a studio, design a label, and manufacture the initial run of discs, Stuart looked around for someone who could help defray his expenses. The person he found was a 24-year-old screenwriter at the Paramount Pictures film studios named

Lester Koenig.

Born on December 3, 1917, Lester Koenig grew up in New York; a classic jazz fan who hung out with fellow collectors and listened to the sounds of traditional jazz. While still in his teens, Koenig befriended Columbia Records' eminent talent scout and A&R man John Hammond, who invited him to attend Columbia recording sessions during the 1930s. The excitement of seeing history being made in New York's Columbia studios resulted in Koenig dreaming of the day when he would run his own record label. Koenig's son John recalled:

Hammond was several years older than my father and, at least with respect to jazz and records, he had taken my father under his wing, almost as an older brother would.

A child prodigy, Koenig entered Dartmouth College when he was only 15. It was there that he met an aspiring screenwriter named Budd Schulberg. (Schulberg would go on to write scripts for some of the most acclaimed and controversial films of the 1950s, including *On the Waterfront* and *A Face in the Crowd,* in addition to writing the best-selling novels *What Makes Sammy Run* and *The Harder They Fall.*)

While at Dartmouth, Koenig, who was also a film fan, wrote movie and record reviews for the Dartmouth newspaper, which caught the eye of Budd Schulberg's father, B.P., head of production at Paramount Studios. After leaving Dartmouth, Koenig attended law school at Yale University. Soon after he graduated, he got a telegram from B.P. Schulberg, who offered him a position as a writer at Paramount, which Koenig readily accepted. A man of many interests, including Broadway shows, avant-garde classical music, theatre, and dance, Koenig still harbored a love for classic jazz while working at Paramount, and it wasn't long before he found the Jazz Man Record Shop on Santa Monica Blvd., only a half-mile from the studio gates on Melrose Avenue.

Koenig and Stuart not only shared a love for traditional jazz, but also an affinity for ethnic art. They remained friends for the rest of their lives, even after Stuart left the record business to open his art gallery. When Stuart shared his plans with Koenig to record the Watters band, Koenig agreed to bankroll the upcoming session and travel with Stuart to San Francisco to help supervise the recordings.

On December 2, 1941, Dave Stuart wrote to William Russell:

I dug up a fellow to put $500, or thereabouts, on the line to make an album of the Watters band. Lu was down about a week ago and said he come (sic) to town to make them sometime after the 6th. I think that they might bring their money back – hope so – as it is a pretty good band. I go up to Frisco about twice a month to hear them.

The Watters band had been gaining momentum and status in the record collecting world, especially after being profiled in an article by Eugene Williams, which was published in *Jazz Information*'s final issue in November 1941. The article describes the Yerba Buena Jazz Band as "the nearest thing to Oliver you could find in the year 1941." In his piece, Williams stressed that this was not just a band formed by record collectors, but a group of dedicated professional musicians who wanted to play "real jazz," as opposed to the diluted swing music favored by "fickle jitterbugs." Williams went on to describe the band's make-up, which featured instruments that hadn't been heard in a jazz band for more than a decade: a tailgate trombone, two banjos instead of a guitar, and a tuba in place of a string bass. The use of the banjos and tuba provided the band with the percussive punch it needed to help give the Watters sound the march beat that typified traditional New Orleans music.

While still only a regional phenomenon, the Yerba Buena Jazz Band had gotten the attention of traditional jazz's major underground periodical, and although *Jazz Information* ceased publication with its November 1941 issue, other small jazz magazines, led by *The Record Changer*, whose inaugural issue was published the following July, took its place. To the readers of these journals, the Lu Watters band spearheaded the revitalizing of traditional jazz. Thanks to the recent publication of the book *Jazzmen,* which featured interviews with pioneering New Orleans jazz musicians, the seeds were now sown for the revival. The appearance on the scene of a professional jazz band playing the classic material in traditional ensemble style suddenly made New Orleans jazz relevant again. All that was needed was a supply of new recordings of the music, which hadn't been commercially available since the 1920s. After failing in three consecutive endeavors, Dave Stuart knew that his time had finally come. Nothing was going to stop him from making records of the Watters unit.

But Stuart was also aware that the growing war in Europe was, sooner or later, going to involve the United States. Stuart knew that meant that Lu Watters and members of his band could be drafted any day, which would result in yet another bitter disappointment in Stuart's snakebit career. Watters, too, was anxious to get a session down on wax. He told Stuart that the band sounded terrific ever since Turk Murphy rejoined the group, and "the war scare is about to grab a man or two." Stuart warned Russell on December 2:

If the Russians don't do better pretty soon, I'll be forced to go over and give a hand. After the "coming unpleasantness," things will be different – we may have nothing but reissues.

Five days later, the Japanese bombed Pearl Harbor, and Dave Stuart feared his prophecy was coming true, and that, like the USS Arizona, his latest venture might also go down in flames.

Early appearance by the Yerba Buena Jazz Band at the Dawn Club in San Francisco
L-R: Lu Watters, Bob Scobey, Turk Murphy (Courtesy the San Francisco Traditional Jazz Foundation).

Lu Watters (Courtesy the San Francisco Traditional Jazz Foundation).

Chapter Eight

The San Francisco Style

Five events occurred in December 1941 that combined to trigger the traditional jazz revival on the West Coast. First was the increasing success of Lu Watters' Yerba Buena Jazz Band at San Francisco's Dawn Club. Second was the accidental shooting of Watters, which brought new fans unfamiliar with Watters' music into the club from areas all across the country. Another factor was the invasion of Pearl Harbor, which brought servicemen about to disembark for the South Pacific into downtown San Francisco, looking for entertainment. Fourth was Hal McIntyre's popular radio program on KYA, during which McIntyre sang the praises of the Watters band at every opportune moment. The fifth, and possibly most important factor contributing to the revival occurred on December 19 (which happened to be Lu Watters' 30th birthday), when Dave Stuart and Lester Koenig succeeded in getting the Yerba Buena Jazz Band into a San Francisco recording studio.

The first session took place at Picto Sound Studios, located at 130 Bush Street, only a few blocks on the other side of Market Street from the Dawn Club. The owner of the studios was John Sirigo, a distinguished-looking but sullen man in his early forties. Sirigo, the Athenian Greek son of a shipowner, was educated in Cairo, Egypt, and claimed to speak and write seven languages. The recording engineer was Royal Weisman, an intense

71

Lu Watters' Yerba Buena Jazz Band, broadcasting on KYA San Francisco. L-R: Wally Rose, piano; Turk Murphy, trombone; Bob Scobey, cornet; Lu Watters, cornet; Clancy Hayes, banjo; Dick Lammi, tuba (Courtesy the San Francisco Traditional Jazz Foundation).

young man in his late twenties whose burning desire was to play bass and be recognized as a musician. It was Weisman who apparently struck the deal with Lester Koenig, and it was Koenig who won out, recognizing Weisman's ambition and taking advantage of it by negotiating a deal whereby Jazz Man would pay the studio $5.00 for each side recorded and $2.50 for second takes.

The studio was matted, but the walls were hinged so the room could be livened or deadened to any degree wanted. According to Turk Murphy, the band members had to remove their shoes for fear of excess noise from their feet leaking onto the recordings.

The recording equipment, all new, consisted of a Universal recording turntable with an RCA cutting head, both of which Weisman had installed. The session was co-produced by Koenig and Stuart.

The Yerba Buena Jazz Band's initial recordings featured nine musicians. Koenig's session notes show that Lu Watters played cornet but Bob Scobey played trumpet. The remaining musicians included Turk Murphy on trombone, Ellis Horne on clarinet, Wally Rose on piano, Clancy Hayes on banjo, Dick Lammi on tuba, and Bill Dart on drums. To give the band that "busy" sound, Watters added a second banjo player, Russ Bennett. The use of two banjos and a tuba was unusual for the swing-mad 1940s, but Watters wanted the rhythm to have that extra added punch in the grand tradition of old New Orleans, which string instruments like guitars and basses just could not match.

It was Watters's intent to emulate King Oliver's Creole Jazz Band, which first recorded for Gennett in 1923. That band included a young New Orleans musician named Louis Armstrong, who had recently arrived in Chicago from the Crescent City to join his idol on second cornet.

The band arrived at the Picto Studios at 10:30 p.m. In his session notes, Koenig wrote:

The band took the chairs out of the room, turned off the lights, and played. We didn't tell them when we were making a record. They played everything as though it were being cut. Never played the same tune twice in a row. Just rambled through the eight sides. No records were cut until 1:30, after the band went out for a cup of coffee.

The session went into the early morning hours of December 20. Although the members of the band were likely a little nervous, Watters had made records before, and with the help of a bottle of scotch, they loosened up and started to play. All eight songs were older tunes that had not been recorded in years. "Muskrat Ramble" was written by Edward "Kid" Ory, the trombone player who had recorded for the Spikes Brothers in June 1921. It was first recorded by Louis Armstrong's Hot Five for OKeh in 1926. On the original 78 rpm release of Watters' recording, you can hear two foot-taps, presumably from Bill Dart, setting the tempo before the band starts playing.

Both "At a Georgia Camp Meeting" (1897) and "Smoky Mokes" (1899) were turn-of-the-century cakewalks that had been recorded numerous times (Watters misspelled the latter song "Smokey" on the Jazz Man recording). "Original Jelly Roll Blues" was written by Jelly Roll

Morton, who recorded it as a piano solo for Gennett in 1924. "Irish Black Bottom," by Percy Venables, was another product of Armstrong's Hot Five. "Memphis Blues" was a classic tune written by W. C. Handy and published in 1912. Scott Joplin's "Maple Leaf Rag" was the venerable Rosetta Stone of the ragtime movement, published in 1899.

For the final number of the session, Watters had pianist Wally Rose (whose first name was listed on the record label as "Walter") play George Botsford's "Black and White Rag," using only a rhythm section consisting of the two banjos and Bill Dart's drums. Watters had tried a number of rags using the full band, but the horn parts proved to be clumsy and often out of range. So the song ended up being recorded as it was written: as a piano solo, with Watters adding rhythm. Of the eight sides produced that December day, it was Rose's recording of "Black and White Rag" that became the most popular.

Only three numbers had to have second takes cut. "Smokey Mokes" had to be redone because the previous song, "Black and White Rag," was recorded without brass and the brass mike was still turned off when the next song began. The original take of "Memphis Blues" ran for four minutes, so a chorus had to be cut. The initial take of "Original Jelly Roll Blues" simply was not played well enough. The session concluded abruptly at 3:30 a.m., one hour short of the six hours Jazz Man was allotted. Koenig blamed this on the surly Sirigo ("a sinister influence"), who complained of the incessant cigarette smoking in the studio and the band members putting their instruments on his new $2,600 Steinway piano.

Koenig paid Sirigo $50.00 for the session. The nine band members were paid a total of $540.00 (union scale was $60 per man) with Watters getting an additional $240 for being the leader. Two mothers were made from each master (to protect against accidental damage), and along with the cost of test pressings, the total mastering cost came to $88.50. The masters were then sent back to Los Angeles where they were processed by

Allied Phonograph and Record Manufacturing at 1041 N. Las Palmas in Hollywood. Koenig and Stuart ordered 500 sets of the four discs at $.17 per disc. Incidental costs included $1.60 to Sherman Clay for packing the masters and an unspecified amount for the scotch the band drank.

The initial recordings of the Yerba Buena Jazz Band had an infectious, danceable punch that hit listeners like a ton of bricks. The solid rhythm on the first and third beats of each measure from Bill Dart's bass drum and Dick Lammi's tuba drove the band relentlessly forward, while the banjo rhythm filled in the blanks on the off-beats. The front line of Watters' and Scobey's powerful parallel horns and Murphy's tailgate trombone blasted through, with Horne's effervescent clarinet dancing around them. Even when Rose took a solo on piano, the rhythm didn't let up. Occasionally, Dart cracked his cymbal crisply on off-beats, creating a further insistency to some of the solos by Watters and Murphy. Watters had taken a decades-old tradition that had been relegated to the dust bin, exhumed it, and added his own ideas, resulting in a fresh alternative to the increasingly stodgy sounds of the big band era. Even an old warhorse like "Maple Leaf Rag" became invigorating and exciting when given the Watters treatment. It didn't matter how fast a tune went, the rhythm remained insistent and irresistible.

After the session was over, Dave Stuart returned to Hollywood and began planning up a marketing strategy for the eight sides he had recorded. His new record label consisted of the words "Jazz Man" in red print on a light, cream-colored background. He selected an ornate font style called Annabelle Matinee NF, which he found in the 1942 edition of Alfred Bastien's *Lettering Alphabets for Draughtsmen, Advertisement Designers, Architects, & Artists*. The font was only used for the record label and not at the shop or on its stationery. The design would survive for the duration of the label's life, and was included on every record that was released.

Stuart also decided to adopt Commodore Records' concept of printing the names of all the musicians and their instruments on the label,

Jazz Man #1, originally issued as part of a four-pocket 78 rpm album (From the author's collection).

along with the recording date and, most important of all, the Jazz Man's address.

Mastering began at Allied the day after Christmas and test pressings were ready to send out the following Monday.

On January 6, 1942, an anxious Stuart wrote to William Russell, asking him whether four of the songs recorded at the session: "At a Georgia Camp Meeting," "Smokey Mokes," "Irish Black Bottom," and "Black and White Rag," were in the public domain. In their haste to get the session made, Stuart and Watters had not secured releases for the copyrighted works from the Music Publishers' Protective Association (MPPA).

Stuart also asked Russell if he knew where Steve Smith (owner of the Hot Record Society label and Hot Music Society store in New York) got his record albums made and what they cost. Stuart thought that he could sell more of the Watters discs if they were sold in sets of four, so he started exploring the possibility of manufacturing albums that would house the discs, in addition to selling them individually as singles. "I want to sell as many albums as I can to get off the nut" [i.e. to clear expenses], Stuart wrote. "I'm in about $800." Even though the records had not yet been pressed, Stuart was already looking forward to his next recording project.

If I can get away on this, I'd like to make four sides with Lu (cornet), Bob Helm (clarinet), and—this guy is really *wonderful—Turk; Paul Lingle (piano), Lammi (brass bass), and a banjo. I heard some acetates the other day of this six-piece group and they make any recent records sound pretty sick (this goes for all of Steve's, Milt's, and the rest). I think the Watters records will make them sit up. The tests from the masters sound mighty good.*

Stuart then promised to send Russell a set of discs when they were ready. Eager to make more records, Stuart was intent on selling albums first and then singles after the initial buying rush played out. He was very much impressed with the trio of Watters, Murphy, and Helm, but Watters was adamant about not recording with Helm. (The two would not reconcile until 1946.)

Despite Stuart's enthusiasm over the records, he had no idea how influential the Watters sides would become. In his January 1942 letter to Russell, Stuart estimated that he would sell 150-250 albums in the "north" and 50-100 sets over the counter at his shop. Even before the records were officially released, Stuart was getting so much interest from record stores and the general public that on February 10, he decided to order a second pressing of 500.

On February 15, *Down Beat* reporter Hal Holly prepared the magazine's readers for the inevitable verbal battle over the Watters sides. In the article, titled "Yerba Buena Jazz Band Sounds Good on Wax," Holly reported:

Stuart, proprietor of the Jazz Man Record Shop, the West Coast rendezvous of hot jazz devotees, has arrived in town from San Francisco with the first recordings by Lu Watters' Yerba Buena Jazz Band. Jazz Man Album No.1 will probably split the country's jazzophiles into warring camps, for the band that has been tagged by some of jazzdom's heaviest intellectuals as the "greatest thing in the country today" will also be branded as the "corniest thing on wax" by a large portion of swingdom's cognoscenti, especially that portion which started to absorb its jazz lore about the time Benny Goodman "invented" swing.

Holly went on to describe the Yerba Buena Jazz Band's "old-fashioned" instrumentation, noting that there were no saxophones (staples of the big band era), a brass bass, and ("here it is, kids, hold on to your lids!") two banjos. Although Bob Crosby's Bobcats had recorded Dixieland material as early as 1937, the Watters band "made 'Rampart Street Parade' sound like something recorded last week by Glenn Miller for release next year." Without committing to expressing the worthiness of the Watters records, Holly said that the band awakened something in him which may or not have been born of nostalgic memories of his youth. He concluded by predicting success for the discs on the basis that Dave Stuart "knows the market for real jazz music better than anyone in the U.S. He will more than likely turn himself a nice little profit—besides the fun he will get out of it."

The first run of 500 sets of the Watters sides was released the week of February 16. The albums were priced at $4.50, a premium price in those days. On February 20, Stuart informed Russell that he had sold 325 sets in San Francisco in a matter of four days. Four telegrams arrived from dealers for reorders. A store in Berkeley ordered 80 sets and then placed an order for an additional 25 sets three days later. Sherman Clay, the venerable Bay Area-based piano dealer, sold 85 sets by itself. A letter to the editor of *Down Beat* revealed that well over 400 sets had been sold in the San Francisco

Down Beat *ad, March 15, 1942.*

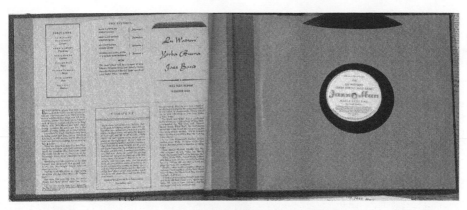

Jazz Man Album #1

and East Bay regions alone. Although sales were going well, Stuart had still not shipped any sets to dealers in the East. Despite wondering whether the initial encouraging sales were just a West Coast phenomenon, Stuart was selling more than even he had expected.

Stuart included testimonials from his friends from *It's All True* in advertisements for the Watters set. When Orson Welles heard the Watters band play "Memphis Blues," he intoned, "Where did you find a band that plays like that? It's wonderful!" *Jazz Information* editor Eugene Williams wrote to Stuart, telling him that the Watters discs were the best jazz band records he had heard in years. Despite this, Stuart had misgivings about the band's sound, and wanted improvements made for their next session, which he was already starting to think about:

There are a number of faults – the drum is dragging, the clarinet is playing the trombone part too much and lacks power to get out, the second cornet does not get up enuf to allow Lu to play, the bass is not enuf – too much ump-pa-pa-ump-pa-pa. And some other things. Myself, I think that they are pretty good but having heard the band so often, know that they could be much better. Helm would make them twice as good. His clarinet is that fine. By comparison, say with Commodore or HRS or Signature, etc., they are a thousand times better. This, I know, is no base to judge them on, but it makes me feel better.

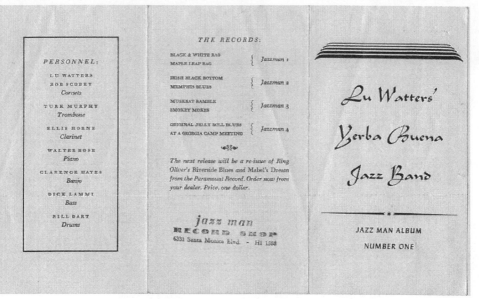

*Booklet for Jazz Man Album No. 1: Lu Watters' Yerba Buena Jazz Band
(From the author's collection).*

EVERYBODY knows that jazz music came from New Orleans; but nobody can tell you what happened to it. Until recently, only a handful of recordings were left to remind the listener that there was a "classic" style of jazz as created and played by King Oliver, Jelly Roll Morton and Louis Armstrong. Somehow the music got lost in the shuffle of swing bands and commercialism.

This album by The Yerba Buena Jazz Band is living proof that jazz, native American folk music, is still around, just as alive as it ever was, just as compelling, just as moving, just as honest.

When the band first opened at San Francisco's Dawn Club in 1940, their audience was small, for paradoxically, Americans found the music which was as American as the Mississippi River, to be unfamiliar to their ears.

But during the following year, as the band learned and progressed and played their hearts out, increasingly larger audiences came to listen.

And that's all this album is: eight young musicians playing what they call "honest jazz."

For their first recording date, the Yerba Buena Jazz Band picked eight fine tunes.

* Four ten-inch records. Price, $4.43. Released by Jazz Man Record Shop, 6331 Santa Monica Boulevard, Hollywood, California.

COMMENT

THEIR MAIN ACHIEVEMENT follows their main goal: to build a good jazz ensemble. As Lu often says, sometimes a bunch of utterly unknown players may unexpectedly happen to feel right and hit it off together, while many "all star" combinations never get together in the right spirit. So Lu's men are picked primarily for their ensemble musicianship. Solo ability is incidental, for it grows out of good ensemble. Turk Murphy can turn in a fine solo like Ory, Brunies or Jim Robinson. But like them, he excells in playing knocked-out tail-gate background with full, brassy tone. Lu Watters himself is an extremely able cornetist, who, like all good horn players, idolizes Louis Armstrong. Lu is an extraordinary person in many ways, and his ideas and tenacity are the backbone of the band. But it would take another whole article to tell about him; and it's the band that counts.

EUGENE WILLIAMS, in *Jazz Information*

December, 1941.

Georgia Camp Meeting was first published in 1897,but was popular for years before that. It was called "a characteristic March which can be used effectively as Two Step, Polka or Cake Walk."

The *Black and White Rag* is performed in the album as a piano solo by Walter Rose, accompanied by Bill Dart and Clancey Hayes. When Elliot Paul, the well-known author and critic, heard the test pressing, his eyes lit up and he shouted, "I'll be damned, that's the *Black and White Rag*, the first rag I ever played!"

As for Abe Holzmann's *Smokey Mokes*, another Cake Walk, its three strains have become familiar, either as marches or college songs.

Then there's *Muskrat Ramble*. Kid Ory, who composed it, said, "That Lu Watters band's the kind of band I wrote that tune for."

When Orson Welles heard Handy's *Memphis Blues*, with it's two beautiful melodies, he said, "Where did you find a band that plays like that? It's wonderful!"

Finally, what would a ragtime album be without a Scott Joplin or a Jelly Roll Morton tune? So they did *Maple Leaf Rag* and *Original Jelly Roll Blues*.

It took a lot of foraging through junk stores and dusty old book shops to dig up the sheet music for some of these numbers, but they did it; and here they are on records.

For the follow-up records he had been thinking about, Stuart wanted to pare down the band to Watters, Helm, Murphy, pianist Paul Lingle, Lammi, and a banjo and call the group the Cable Car Six. He also queried Russell about reissuing a King Oliver record made around December 24, 1923 that had been released on the Claxtonola label, a subsidiary of Paramount. Stuart thought that he might have an alternate take of the record and wanted to put it out on the Jazz Man label. He even advertised the fact, in a small flyer he had printed up for the shop's customers:

The next release will be a re-issue of King Oliver's "Riverside Blues" and "Mabel's Dream" from the Paramount Record. Order now from your dealer. Price, one dollar.

A month later, Stuart decided against the Oliver, as he wrote to Russell:

I've been caught! Seems several people own that Paramount Oliver and are ready for it. The same people own the Clax and know there are two masters. What now? Do you think the second master ever came out on Paramount? Or should I go ahead and do it and then tell the wondering ones that it was the Clax and a great mistake was made? I don't want to stick my neck out and have it cut off by a bunch of guys who own both the Clax and the Paramount

By March 16, Stuart was getting ready for a second session with the Watters band. He still had not heard from Russell about the test pressings he had sent him and was getting concerned about the musical quality of the first records.

You still have not given me any sort of a report on the Watters records. Don't be afraid, Pops, I can take it. I want to do another set right away so if you have any suggestions, send them with haste. This time I can use a bass with a more melodic brain and also take the bass drum away from that heavy-footed character Dart. The one thing wrong is that Lu is a hard headed bastard and won't let me use Helm. He's so much better than

Horne, there is no lookin' for Ellis. Helm, and you may quote this, is the best white clarinet in the country, and as Gene [Williams] *says, would scare Rap* [New Orleans Rhythm Kings clarinetist Leon Rappolo] *plenty. I really like him better than Rap because he has more power and gets around the horn more like J.D.* [Johnny Dodds]. *His tone is rough but tremendous. Between Turk and Helm, they can cover the entire Watters band. The main reason he is not in the band is that sad person Hayes, the colored hill-billy. He thinks he sings like Morton. Morton should be alive to hear that – he'd whip his head. Both Horne and Hayes are unhappy 'cause I wouldn't let Hayes sing on the records. If I can swing a deal with a local studio to use the band, I'm sure I can get Helm in on the job. All he needs is a chance to play. I want to make some six-piece records using him instead of Horne – one cornet and no drum – and this is the one chance.*

The second Watters sessions took place on two successive Sundays in March 1942, this time at the studios of radio station KFRC in San Francisco, then located at 1000 Van Ness Avenue. According to Turk Murphy, the band recorded in a large studio with the music transmitted by wire to acetate cutting tables at Photo and Sound Studios on Kearny Street, a mile-and-a-half away.

The first day of the session, March 22, was devoted to piano solos by Wally Rose. Stuart was unhappy with the December recording of "Black and White Rag" because the piano was poorly miked. So he had Rose re-record it, backed by Clancy Hayes on banjo and Bill Dart on drums. That day, Rose cut two other piano rags: Paul Pratt's "Hot House Rag" and Harry Lodge's "Temptation Rag." Pratt was an Indianapolis-based vaudeville pianist who made a few piano rolls under the name Paul Parnell. "Hot House Rag" was published in St. Louis in 1914, but had never been recorded. Turk Murphy found the sheet music for Rose, along with many other vintage rags, in a second-hand book store in San Francisco. Thomas Henry Lodge wrote many popular rags, but "Temptation Rag" (1909) was his must popular.

On both these numbers, two banjos were used, with Russ Bennett joining Hayes. The KFRC recordings were far superior to those made at the Picto Studios, so all subsequent pressings of Jazz Man 1 featured the later take of "Black and White Rag."

On the following Sunday, March 29, the Yerba Buena Jazz Band laid down 12 more tunes. Despite Stuart's misgivings, Ellis Horne played clarinet again as Watters continued to refuse to allow Bob Helm to play with the band. Stuart's other recommendations, however, were heeded. Drummer Dart eliminated the bass drum and Dick Lammi was replaced on tuba by Squire Girsback. Stuart was adamant about Clancy Hayes not being permitted to sing, so all 12 of the songs cut that day were instrumentals, with one remake ("Muskrat Ramble," which had been recorded the previous December. This take remained unissued.). In a letter to Russell dated April 1, Stuart said:

Ellis, Bob Scobey, Hayes, etc. are all sore as hell at me for not letting Hayes sing several vocals – but you should hear the guy! He sounds much better if you hold your nose and flap your tongue in undulations! As Paul Lingle says: "He's a 'nigger hill-billy.'"

Turk Murphy's lip was bleeding during the session and he was not at his best that day. Stuart was pleased when the test pressings came out, and told Russell that the band had "that busy background sound" that was evident on King Oliver's OKeh recordings from 1923.

A photograph taken at the recording session shows the brass section standing with their backs to the control booth window (a smiling Dave Stuart can be seen in the booth overlooking the studio). In the first session Ellis Horne's clarinet had been all but obscured by Watters, Scobey, and Murphy, so for the second session, Horne stood on a small platform ten feet in front of the rest of the band, directly in front of the microphone so as to balance better with the brass. Horne's clarinet was much better in the second session; in the first, he mainly stayed in the instrument's lower register, but

*The second Jazz Man recording session, KFRC radio studios in San Francisco, March 29, 1942.
L-R, top row: Turk Murphy, Lu Watters, Bob Scobey. Seated: Squire Girsback, Clancy Hayes, Bill Dart,
Russ Bennett, Wally Rose. Standing at far right is Ellis Horne. In the booth, Biff Leonetti (roommate of
band manager Augie Giretto) and Dave Stuart of the Jazz Man Record Shop.
(Courtesy the Archive of Recorded Sound, Stanford University).*

on the March 1942 recordings, he often soared into higher registers; his solo on "Tiger Rag" was one of the highlights of the session. Wally Rose played on a splendid grand piano, which would have been much too large for the cramped studios used at the 1941 session.

The songs chosen cut a wider swath than the older, ragtime-oriented songs of the first session. None of the tunes had been recorded in years, except for "Fidgety Feet" and "High Society," which had been cut by Bob Crosby's Bob Cats in 1938 and 1939. (The band did record a version of Crosby's "Dixieland Shuffle," recorded 4/13/36 on Decca 825, which they called "Riverside Blues.") No newly-written tunes were featured at this session; Watters would not begin recording his own songs until after World War II.

In a letter to Stuart, William Russell criticized the choice of songs at the first session, calling them "white, Tin Pan Alley, New York commercial rags and cakewalks that ridiculed the Negro people." Stuart took slight offense to this and responded by saying:

About the racially, socially, and musically conscious friends of yours –I asked several of MY friends if the tunes were wrong and the answers were all no. Perhaps the pinks in your section are "more" than they are here.

Regardless, the choice of songs in the second session included numbers written by blacks, including two by Jelly Roll Morton ("Milenberg Joys" and "London Blues"), two by Clarence Williams ("Terrible Blues" and "Cake Walking Babies"), and a cover of a Louis Armstrong Hot Five record: Luis Russell and Paul Barbarin's "Come Back Sweet Papa." Three of the records, Jazz Man 5, 6, and 7, were issued that spring, while the remaining six sides were held back until early 1943.

Sneering at Commodore's roster of members of the Austin High School gang (including saxophonist Bud Freeman and guitarist Eddie Condon), Stuart said that only clarinetist Pee Wee Russell was good enough to record for Jazz Man:

Yes – Pee Wee can play for me anytime, but that bunch with him are rather sad, don't you think? Freeman, drums, banjo players playing four-string guitars, etc., etc., no more! I'm cooked on them forever. Bill [Colburn] *says to let Pee Wee come along but to tell him to leave his friends at home.*

By the middle of April, Dave Stuart had orders for several thousand copies of the seven records that had been released, but was having trouble filling them due to the wartime demand for shellac. Jukebox operators were demanding copies by the hundreds, which threatened dealers' supplies. Stuart told Russell that the jukebox industry was doing better with the Watters Jazz Man records than with swing 78s by the Dorsey Brothers and Glenn Miller.

Through all of this, it is unknown what Marili Stuart's role was, if any, in the Watters sessions. Her job was to take care of the Jazz Man Record

Shop while Dave worked on promotion of the records. The first reference to her in Stuart's letters came on the day of the third Lu Watters session, which took place on April 24, 1942. Stuart didn't attend, but it appears Marili went on his behalf. Watters wanted the members of the band to enlist together, so that they could remain as a unit while serving in the army.

The war is working against the Watters band and records. I believe tonite will be the last date. Marili went up to hear them. I remained here to keep the shop going so that we may have enough money to pay for her trip north, so that, etc. Seems the Navy turned them down for several reasons.

Jazz Man

★ RECORDS ★

—————————— ★ ——————————

3 NEW RECORDS BY

LU WATTERS YERBA BUENA

JAZZ BAND

Jazz Man 5 { CAKE WALKING BABIES
              RIVERSIDE BLUES

Jazz Man 6 { TIGER RAG
              COME BACK SWEET PAPA

Jazz Man 7 { TEMPTATION RAG [*Piano Solo*]
              FIDGETY FEET

Price, $1.05 each. Now ready for immediate delivery.

First 4 records, also ready for immediate delivery:

JAZZ MAN 1. *Black & White Rag (Piano Solo)* and *Maple Leaf Rag*
JAZZ MAN 2. *Irish Black Bottom* and *Memphis Blues*
JAZZ MAN 3. *Muskrat Ramble* and *Smokey Mokes*
JAZZ MAN 4. *Original Jelly Roll Blues* & *At A Georgia Camp Meeting*

Released by JAZZ MAN RECORD SHOP

6331 Santa Monica Boulevard, Hollywood, California

Turk has very bad eyes and stutters. Bob Scobey is in the army, etc. The union also put its foot down on the idea of them playing in the Navy band and on a regular job.

The third Yerba Buena session almost didn't happen. According to Stuart, Watters had been arrested on a manslaughter charge for running over someone with his car, but had been inexplicably freed three days earlier. Stuart said that for the first time in months, Watters was sober. For some reason, the matter was kept out of the newspapers.

With Marili possibly in attendance, the Yerba Buena Jazz Band recorded eight songs, which included two Clancy Hayes vocals, "Careless Love" and an ancient novelty, "Auntie Skinner's Chicken Dinners," a hit for Arthur Collins and Byron Harlan in 1915. Had Stuart been present, he most certainly would not have permitted Hayes to sing. The other titles were more standard jazz songs, blues, and ragtime tunes. For some unknown reason, none of the records was issued. It's plausible that in view of the way Stuart felt about Clancy Hayes, that he decided not to release any of the records made that day, rather than put one of Hayes's hokey vocals on a label with the Jazz Man's name on it. Stuart designated the next series of master numbers in his catalog for the songs, beginning with MLB-132, but eventually replaced them with Bunk Johnson sides in June. These were the last records Jazz Man recorded of the Yerba Buena Jazz Band.

On June 12, Watters and his men went down to the induction center to enlist as a group, but only two, Watters and Murphy, were accepted, which ended any chance of the band staying together for the duration of the war. Murphy spent much of his hitch on the West Coast while Watters ended up in Hawaii, serving on the S.S. Antigua, eventually becoming a First Class Aviation Mechanist's Mate. When Bob Scobey enlisted too, the decimation of the Yerba Buena Jazz Band's powerful brass front line was complete. Watters would reunite the Yerba Buena Jazz Band after the war ended, but his days as a recording artist for Jazz Man Records was over.

The Watters recordings were the beginnings of what would be called "The San Francisco Style." For fans of traditional New Orleans jazz, it was as if their favorite music had been brought back from the dead. The stultifying and relatively sedentary swing recordings of Glenn Miller, Tommy Dorsey, and Benny Goodman bored them. The increasingly predictable and meticulously arranged charts left little room for spontaneity or freedom of expression. In comparison, the freewheeling, exciting, danceable, and rhythmic sounds coming from the Bay Area ignited a veritable firestorm of praise from collectors of traditional jazz recordings. Dave Stuart's Jazz Man Records became a sensation, and with the address of the Jazz Man Record Shop printed at the bottom of the record labels, Stuart received floods of mail and phone calls from jazz fans asking not only for copies of the Lu Watters records, but for original recordings by Louis Armstrong, King Oliver, and other pioneers.

It was clear that by starting his own record label, Dave Stuart finally realized his long-desired dream of recognition. But with World War II looming, and the Watters band gone, Stuart had to look elsewhere for his next releases.

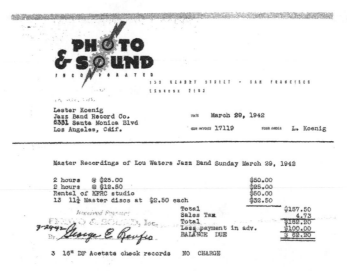

Invoice from Photo & Sound for the second Lu Watters session. Note that Lester Koenig is the addressee and not Dave Stuart (Courtesy Concord Music Group).

Chapter Nine

A Whole Lotta Bunk

Despite separating shortly after their marriage, Dave Stuart and Marili Morden shared a true and honest affection for the pioneers of jazz. Their devotion to the music extended to the performers who created it, and both became friends with many of the pioneers of jazz, not just famous names like Louis Armstrong, but obscure New Orleans musicians like clarinetist "Big Eye" Louis Nelson Delisle and trumpet player Henry "Kid" Rena.

One of these New Orleans pioneers was also one of the most mysterious. William Geary "Bunk" Johnson was the last link to the first generation of New Orleans brass bands during the days of the legendary Buddy Bolden. In his autobiography *Satchmo: My Life in New Orleans,* Louis Armstrong reverently intoned Johnson's name when he said "You really heard music when Bunk Johnson played the cornet with the Eagle Band." Although King Oliver played with a fire unequalled among New Orleans cornetists, it was Bunk Johnson's sweet tone that most impressed Armstrong.

In the late 1930s, Johnson was living an obscure life as a field laborer in New Iberia, Lousiana. For their book *Jazzmen,* Fred Ramsey and Charles Edward Smith tracked Johnson down with the help of Armstrong and William Russell. Believing Johnson to be one of the few performers of

Bunk Johnson, New Iberia, Louisiana, c. 1940.

early jazz still living, they began corresponding with him, gathering facts and stories that became an invaluable part of their book. Johnson's detailed and colorful accounts included playing with Bolden in the 1890s and about teaching Armstrong how to play cornet. (Armstrong was sensitive enough not to dispel this claim until after Johnson's death in 1949.) Through *Jazzmen,* Johnson became a legendary figure, courted by jazz historians all over the world. This increased attention resulted in Johnson embellishing and exaggerating his stories, so that one was never sure what was accurate and what was fabricated. In order to support his claims, Johnson reinvented a life for himself, saying he was born in 1879 when his actual birthdate was ten years later. (Johnson claimed to have played with Buddy Bolden from 1895 until 1898, but if he revealed his true birth year of 1889, this would have meant that he started playing with Bolden's unit at the age of 6.)

Johnson had not played trumpet since 1932, when his horn was destroyed during a knife fight in the small Louisiana town of Rayne. His teeth had been bothering him for years as well, but he was still interested in playing, a fact that made researchers salivate. Ramsey and Smith set about raising the money to have Johnson's teeth fixed, which cost $60.00. Through the efforts of the Lu Watters band in San Francisco, enough money was raised to buy Johnson a used trumpet and cornet from a pawn shop. In 1941, Armstrong visited his old friend in New Iberia and Johnson actually sat in with his big band, but no recordings were made.

In February 1942, Johnson was persuaded to record some unaccompanied horn solos for a young jazz enthusiast named Mark Karoley. Karoley had been sent a portable disc recorder by John Reid, who worked for RCA Victor. William Russell and Eugene Williams (editor of *Jazz Information*) decided to organize a formal recording session with Johnson and a small band of his choosing. *Jazz Information* had folded the previous November, but Williams was in the process of starting his own record label also called Jazz Information. They bought Johnson a new Selmer instrument to play at the session.

Back at the Jazz Man, Dave Stuart was counting down the days when he, like the members of Lu Watters' band, would enter World War II. The war wasn't going well for the Allies, with Germany taking France, Belgium, and now attacking England.

On May 19, Stuart received a letter from a destitute Bunk Johnson in New Orleans, asking for financial help on behalf of his niece. Through William Russell, Stuart had been corresponding with Johnson, and with the Watters band ready to break up, Stuart started thinking about recording Johnson and asked Russell if Johnson still had his lip. In a letter to Russell on May 20, Stuart said that he could only spare $15 to help Johnson, but also "put the finger" on Elliot Paul to contribute something. Stuart knew Paul was good for the money since he had recently sold a book he had written to MGM for $25,000. Stuart kept a tin can in the Jazz Man labeled "The Bunk Johnson Fund," into which customers would drop spare change from time to time.

A week later, Stuart wrote to Russell about his plans:

Looks like I'm into the air business soon, so I think I'll take a fast run to N.O. before I go. May be the last time, and I like the town. I'll write to you from there.

Johnson had written to Stuart, telling him that he was ready to record, and sent a six-inch homemade acetate to prove it. With both Stuart and Eugene Williams vying to be the first to record Johnson, the two decided that Stuart should have the honor in light of Jazz Man's more established distribution network. The Watters records were selling like hotcakes, so it was a natural and easy decision to have Johnson's recordings issued on the Jazz Man label.

Stuart invited Bill Colburn and KYA disc jockey Hal McIntyre to accompany him to Louisiana, leaving Marili in charge of the shop. They left town on June 1, arriving in New Iberia three days later. Although each had corresponded with Johnson for several years, none of the jazz enthusiasts had met him in person. Bunk greeted them on his front porch and before they knew it, he had volunteered to play a tune or two for the three jazz-starved researchers. Stuart recalled the moment in an article he wrote in 1962 that accompanied a Good Time Jazz LP reissue of the recording session:

This was what we'd come 2000 miles for, yet we followed him into the house with a certain trepidation. After all, he hadn't really played horn for a good number of years, and it was only recently that he'd been fitted with workable false teeth and a new trumpet. His cornet had been destroyed in 1932 and his teeth went soon after. Since then he had worked the rice fields, hauled cane, and taught music on rare occasions.

But it was bootless worry, chicken skepticism. Bunk took his horn from the case and rubbed the gold finish lovingly as he held it out for our inspection. He whipped the valves several times. Then he opened up on a slow blues that put tears in my eyes. Broke me up! Just thinking about it now makes my spine tingle all over again. He played his "head music" exactly as we'd dreamed he would. Rhetoric aside, it was altogether an amazing performance. Bunk played several more tunes and we talked for a couple of hours before he finally said, "I rise mighty early for work," and sent us off elated and limp.

The next day, Russell and Eugene Williams arrived, and the group decided to go to New Orleans to put a band together. Bunk would join them by bus the following Monday. The five spent the week looking for musicians to be in Bunk's band. The first person they settled on was trombonist Jim Robinson, who had recorded with Henry "Kid" Rena's Jazz Band in a session for the Delta label in August 1940. Robinson helped Bunk find clarinetist George Lewis, who was playing an instrument that was in horrific condition. Stuart later said:

George got out the worst beat-up, wired-together, rubber-band-action clarinet I've ever seen. The keys were loose, one was missing entirely, and the pad on the octave key was a ball of hardened chewing gum.

After Lewis serenaded them with "Over the Waves," Stuart went out and bought two Boehm system clarinets, and presented both to Lewis, asking him to choose the one he preferred. Not wishing to insult the generosity of his host, Lewis selected one of the instruments, even though he felt more comfortable playing his jury rigged model. (Stuart shipped the other one back to himself in Hollywood.) Lewis recommended a friend of his named Lawrence Marrero to play banjo, and the band was completed with Austin Young on bass, Walter Decou on piano, and Ernest Rogers on drums.

With the band in place, Stuart and his friends began looking for a recording studio. There were two established studios in town, but neither would allow blacks to record there. By Wednesday, June 10, the researchers, hot and frustrated, walked into Grunewald's Music Store looking for acetates to record on. The proprietor had 12 blanks in stock and offered the use of a home Presto recording machine. The next day, June 11, 1942, the group tromped upstairs to a third floor storeroom that had a piano and cut the historic session. Since Rogers, the drummer, worked in an iron foundry, he wasn't free until after three o'clock. Grunewald's closed at six, which meant they had less than three hours to record. With only a dozen acetates available to them, they knew that there would be no luxury of making second takes. Stuart recalled:

The storeroom was on the top floor of the clapboard building, and in the mid-afternoon heat, it was nothing if not a furnace. So we opened the windows to let in any breeze, and got honking horns, streetcar clankings, and the barking of dogs. And for one reason, none of this seemed at the time really disturbing: the thing was to record Bunk and George and the band and to hell with the nonsense.

Bunk had his own ideas about what he wanted to record—the historians were shocked when Bunk told them he'd like to record "Deep in the Heart of Texas." Terrified that a man who claimed to have once played with Buddy Bolden would record a current juke box hit, Stuart, Russell, and the others persuaded Bunk to do some of the tunes he played in the old days. To their relief, Bunk relented and the session began.

The microphone on the Presto machine was just large enough so that one or two instruments could be heard clearly, with the remaining musicians playing in the background. Bunk and Lewis played close to the mike and the rest of the band was arranged in an arc surrounding them. As they recorded, the sound spilled out onto the streets, attracting a crowd of curious people, wondering where the music was coming from, cupping their hands to their ears so they could hear better. The result was electrifying: traditional New Orleans jazz played by men who were there at its inception, the sounds of a rhythm-heavy New Orleans street parade; a blending of instruments in the best ensemble tradition. Even though they had never played together as a unit, the music was spontaneous, driving, infectious, and exciting, far from the primitive, rusty sound Stuart and his partners feared might result.

Nine of the twelve acetates were used that day, including false starts for "Pallet on the Floor" and "Ballin' the Jack" (accounting for the notation of second takes being issued). Five of the songs were traditional songs that everyone in the band knew. To these, Johnson added three of his own compositions, with head arrangements worked out during the session. One of the best titles recorded was "Moose March," a number Johnson had played in Mardi Gras parades at the turn of the century; named in honor of one of New Orleans' numerous secret societies.

The next day, the three remaining acetates were used to allow Johnson to reminisce about his early years as a musician. Gene Williams acted as the interrogator. His voice can be heard asking one question to start off each master:

"Bunk, tell us, where did you learn to play cornet?"

"Say, Bunk, give us a list of the trumpet players who learned from you, or got ideas from you."

"Say, by the way, Bunk, you didn't tell us about King Oliver yet."

On the interview records, Johnson talked about playing with Buddy Bolden and teaching Louis Armstrong to play cornet, both fabricated stories. Despite not containing a whole lot of useful information, getting Bunk Johnson's voice on disc, talking about people he knew that were only ghostly legends to record collectors, was riveting stuff. In 1958, Ralph Gleason transcribed the interviews, which were printed on the inner sleeve of Good Time Jazz's 1962 LP re-issue of the Johnson session.

After the session was finished, Stuart sent the acetates to Los Angeles for mastering. The transferring engineer initially thought that the recordings sounded so bad that he nearly discarded them. Although they were crude, the circumstances surrounding the session made the session all the more romantic. On June 30, Stuart wrote to William Russell:

I had the acetates dubbed so that a master could be made from them. The dubbing helped somewhat as it balanced the band a little. They really sound terrible by any modern standards, but sound good if played against the Delta album. There are four fine sides: "Moose March," "Weary Blues,"

"Panama," and "Storeyville [sic] Blues." The slow tunes are not as good. They fall apart too often. When Bunk puts his horn down, there is a lull in any of the sides. The way the mike worked, Bunk was the main one and the rest are really in the background. The rhythm section is rather messy. However, all in all, they sound real good, if the recording room, machine, mike, etc. are taken into consideration.

Apparently, Russell had cut one additional side of his own with Johnson, but in light of the fact that all 12 acetates were accounted for, it is uncertain when that disc was made, possibly from another session held after Stuart left New Orleans. Stuart hints at this in his letter:

How about the side you made. I was thinking–if it is still in good shape and a master could be made from it, I'd like to borrow it and back one of the talking sides (I have three) and put out a short edition of say 50 sets of the four sides. Except for a few out of place sounds, the talking sides are interesting. I believe there might be enough people in the country willing to buy the four sides just for Bunk's voice alone. What I thought I might do is to call them a limited edition and price them at $4 for the two records. This way it might sound quite ritzy and get the jerks around the country. So–if your side is in good shape and you'll let me borrow it, I'll have it dubbed, made into a master, and put it on the back of one record. For this service I will send you as follows: One (1) set of Bunk records (nine band sides–this is 5 more than I intend to issue), one set of the talking limited edition album priced at $4, and one of Bunk's cigar butts; a saving of an awful lot of money. V for Villie Johnson!

Stuart released five discs that summer. Jazz Man 8, 9, and 10 included "Down by the River," "Panama," "Weary Blues," "Moose March," "Storyville Blues," and "Bunk's Blues." Stuart decided to call the band "Bunk Johnson's Original Superior Band" (in honor of the Original Superior Orchestra, which Johnson played with from about 1908 to 1913) and added the phrase "Co-sponsored by *Jazz Information*" on the label to credit Gene Williams, who allowed Stuart to issue the sides on Jazz Man Records. Gene Williams started his own label that October, which was initiated with more recordings by Bunk Johnson.

In addition to the three Jazz Man 78s, Stuart issued the two special limited edition discs he mentioned to Russell in what became known as the "Bunk Johnson Talking Records." The interview constitutes three of the four sides on these discs, which were numbered Jazz Man Limited Edition No. 1 and No. 2, with artist credit to "Willie Bunk Johnson." Whatever Russell had recorded himself apparently was not good enough to release, so Stuart put Johnson's recording of "Yes, Lord, I'm Crippled" on the fourth side.

Left: *Jazz Man release #9 by Bunk Johnson's Original Superior Band. Right: "The Bunk Johnson Talking Record, Part 1." Johnson printed his name on one side of many of the copies pressed. Today, the Johnson Talking Records are exceedingly rare (From the author's collection).*

This recording was later issued on Jazz Man 17, backed with "Hot House Rag," a Wally Rose piano solo (with rhythm) that was left over from the second Lu Watters session. Fifty hand-numbered copies of the two Talking Records were issued, with many of them personally signed by Johnson. The labels of the talking records were changed from the usual red print to blue. It is likely that Stuart had a second pressing of the Talking Records made because some unnumbered copies have turned up. The remaining two sides from the session ("Pallet on the Floor" and "Ballin' the Jack") were issued in 1943 as Jazz Man 16.

In his letter to Russell, Stuart announced that he was learning celestial navigation, line of position, meteorology, and dead reckoning as part of a three-month course in preparation for his enlisting in the ferry command. His job was to transport bombers and officers to and from Europe. Time was of the essence, and Stuart wanted to make sure the Bunk Johnson records came out before he had to leave. Stuart was excited about the opportunity to help the war effort, but was equally relieved to finally rid himself of the Jazz Man Record Shop. By July 7, flight school was still proving difficult for him, and he hadn't had much time to work on the Bunk releases. Again he mentioned the disc Russell had recorded:

If your record is not in the best of shape, don't send it as I can use one of the other band sides. Gene remembers it as being slightly flat in a spot due to the recording [engineer] *placing his hand on the table. If not, and I can use it to back the talking records, shoot it out and I'll dub it.*

Bob asked that I do an article on the Watters band but I have little time [Bob Thiele was the editor of a new collectors publication called *Jazz*]. *Do you want to, or should I scratch something out for him? Probably you have enough to do without writing about that white outfit. I really believe it would have been better if no white had ever played a note.*

Stuart also received the second clarinet that he had purchased for George Lewis to play, which he had shipped ahead before he left town.

The clarinet from N.O. came and it is in fine shape. They forgot the mouthpiece so I sent for one and it finally came. Now I play like J.D.! [Johnny Dodds] *Another thing, Lewis is not as good as we thought, so go light about him. DON'T FLIP YOUR LID or you'll be sorry. He plays some awful riffs—right thru "Pallet on the Floor," and he gets some really sour stuff on some of the other sides. Still, he is probably better than Big Eye*

[Louis "Big Eye" Nelson] *yet, watch what you say or you'll have to retract it.*

Soon after, Stuart left Hollywood for Washington, D.C. to complete his training, leaving Marili in charge of the shop and supervising the release of the Johnson 78s. The event was big news in the jazz world; in its September 15, 1942 issue, *Down Beat* printed a story about the changing of the guard at the Jazz Man:

Wife Takes Over as 'Jazz Man' Joins Up

Los Angeles—Many a girl is stepping into a man's job these days but one of the most unusual cases bobbed up as Marili Stuart, wife of Dave (Jazz Man Records) Stuart, took over the complete operation of the Jazz Man Record company and the Jazz Man Record Shop, Hollywood rendezvous for collectors and jazz fans.

Husband Dave Stuart, who founded the Jazz Man Record Shop, and later the Jazz Man Record company for the issue of unusual jazz items, is in Washington, D.C., completing his schooling to become a navigator in the bomber ferry command. His future whereabouts will probably be a military secret.

Marili wants it known that the Jazz Man Record Shop will function as ever and that Jazz Man records will appear as long as shellac is available. At writing she was busy preparing for the first release of the Bunk Johnson discs, recorded by Stuart with a group of old time jazz stars rounded up in New Orleans. The records go on sale this month.

Down Beat, *September 15, 1942.*

Four days later, Marili wrote to Russell:

Dear Bill,

I suppose you know where David is now, if you looked at the latest Downbeat. *In case you didn't: Washington, D.C. I thought he had written to you about it. He's going to school at the moment, for the ferry command, navigator for TWA. So I'm caring for things here.*

The Bunk records are there by now, too. Orders are coming in fine, and I'm really rushed, because business has been good in the shop. The only number that is likely to be sold out is No. 10. ["Storyville Blues" and "Bunk's Blues"] *There'll be only 500 of them. But they aren't selling as well, either, so far. I'm not having any trouble getting records. They are a little slow in finishing orders because of government work, which comes first.*

The Bunk Johnson records on Jazz Man helped ignite a new career for the 53-year-old musician. He soon became an object of fascination to budding traditional jazz fans, much as Lead Belly was deified by the folk music community. Johnson went on to have a successful recording and performing career for the remaining seven years of his life. He died on July 7, 1949 at the age of 59. His controversial comments and fabricated stories were "de-Bunked" in later years as further serious research was made of his statements. Still, the Johnson 78s now increased Jazz Man's status as the pioneering record label of the New Orleans jazz revival, having now documented its chief progenitor (Watters) and a legendary group of pioneers from the past.

In her letter, Marili Stuart also informed William Russell that Kid Ory was back and happy to be playing again, working in a group in Los Angeles with Barney Bigard. She reported that the band was still rusty, except on familiar songs such as "Muskrat Ramble" and "High Society," and reminded Russell that more collectors of early jazz were springing up all the time, a sign of the increasing importance of the Watters releases. Marili was to keep her eye on Ory, for she knew this was another major pioneer from the golden age of jazz in the 1920s, a musician who had not succumbed to commercialism as had Louis Armstrong, his former band mate in Armstrong's legendary Hot Five sessions. So Marili kept in touch with Ory, and waited for his band to improve enough to warrant a recording session.

The growing interest in traditional music was still mainly a West Coast phenomenon; in a later letter, Marili wondered about "New York collectors" who had the capabilities of influencing so many people, yet devoted all their time to modernists like Duke Ellington and swing. "Imagine their fluffing off the Bunks!" she exclaimed.

With Stuart gone, Marili was now the face of the Jazz Man Record Shop. Although she was still legally married to Stuart, she was beginning to experience the difficulties of not only running the shop by herself, but managing the affairs of the record label as well. The beautiful 23-year-old entrepreneur soon would have help, in the person of a charming, charismatic visitor from the East, a man who would not only have a pronounced impact on her professional and personal life, but on the traditional jazz revival as well.

Members of Bunk Johnson's band, 1944. L-R: Jim Robinson, Bunk, Baby Dodds,
Lawrence Marrero, George Lewis, Alcide "Slow Drag" Pavageau.

Chapter Ten

The Crusader

When the United States entered World War II, many Los Angeles record collectors were drafted and Marili Stuart found her young customer base slowly drying up. In early 1942, a fascinating newcomer came to town. He was a dapper young man who had recently moved to Hollywood from Washington, D.C. Erudite, well-dressed, well-mannered, and with a charismatic way of speaking, the man was short in stature, yet made up for this with an encyclopedic knowledge about the history of jazz. His name was Nesuhi Ertegun.

Born in Istanbul, Turkey on November 26, 1917, Ertegun was the son of Mehmet Münir Ertegun (1883–1944), the Turkish ambassador to the United States. Mehmet Ertegun was trained in international law and spoke many languages, which enabled him to represent his country at the 1923 peace conference in Lausanne, Switzerland that resulted in Turkey becoming a republic. In 1934, he came to America to be his nation's ambassador to the U.S.

Both Nesuhi and his younger brother Ahmet (1923–2006) were educated by governesses. The brothers learned to love American music from their mother, who bought recordings by Josephine Baker, Mae West, the Mills Brothers, Bing Crosby, and Paul Whiteman. At 13, he became fascinated by American culture, took Ahmet to museums, and introduced him

102

Portrait of Nesuhi Ertegun, Washington, D.C., c. late 1930s
(The William P. Gottlieb Collection).

to American music. He liked adventurous composers like Igor Stravinsky and Erik Satie, but, at the same time, appreciated traditional New Orleans jazz, which soon became a passion. In 1952, Nesuhi told jazz historian Floyd Levin:

I first became aware of jazz in London in 1932 [at a performance featuring Cab Calloway]. *I had purchased Ted Lewis records in Switzerland when I was 12 years old, but I felt the full impact of jazz when I saw Coleman Hawkins introduced from the Palladium stage. We used to listen to Lew Stone's band broadcast every Tuesday evening on the BBC. Nat Gonella played lead trumpet and Al Bowlly sang the vocals. The Stone band played many of the Ellington tunes. When the Duke came to London in '33 with what most persons consider his "finest band," I was very impressed with the work of* [Johnny] *Hodges and* [Barney] *Bigard.*

In 1935, Ertegun saw Hawkins appear with Benny Carter, and by 1937, when he moved to Paris to study philosophy at Sorbonne University, he had already begun assembling an impressive record collection, which included original recordings by King Oliver, Duke Ellington, and the Mound City Blue Blowers. During the daytime, he studied. At night, he spun records by Django Reinhardt, Eddie South, Dicky Wells, and Coleman Hawkins.

By 1939, Nesuhi was burning with a desire to go to America, so when his father accepted a diplomatic post in Washington, Nesuhi and Ahmet went with him to spend the summer. Ahmet later said that when he found out he was going to America, he was thrilled because he thought that he would see nothing but cowboys, Indians, and jazz musicians.

When they arrived in Washington, the Ertegun brothers immediately went to a record shop, but the records they were looking for were not there. So they went to places where few white Americans would dare go, deep into black neighborhoods, looking for what were known as "race" records. They scoured small towns and cities in Virginia and North Carolina, and assembled a collection that included records by all of their heroes: King Oliver Gennetts, Hot Fives on OKeh, Ma Raineys on Paramount, and Bessie Smiths on Columbia. They bought anything, as long as their favorite names were on the labels. Condition did not matter. Many records were bought for pennies. Ahmet Ertegun later said:

We'd clean them up, put them in new jackets, and classify them. I could hear any orchestra and tell you whether it was white or black. You can't tell the difference anymore, but in those days, you could.

The Erteguns saw both sides of America at an early age: the elite, wealthy homes of Washington diplomats and the poverty-ridden ghettos only a few miles away. When the Nazis invaded Poland in September, the Erteguns were unable to return to Europe, so they stayed in Washington, with Nesuhi enrolling at American University.

Ahmet and Nesuhi Ertegun at the Turkish Embassy, Washington, D.C., c. 1940s.
(The William P. Gottlieb Collection)

In 1940, Nesuhi launched a series of jazz concerts, which were held at the Turkish Embassy. For the first concert, he went to New York and brought back Sidney Bechet, Vic Dickenson, Sidney de Paris, Wellman Braud, Art Hodes, and Manzie Johnson. Even the artists that performed at intermission—Joe Turner and Meade Lux Lewis—were stars. Unfortunately, the first concert was a financial flop, but Ertegun persisted, and continued staging the concerts for several more years, despite many neighbors complaining about black musicians invading their neighborhood. When Nesuhi hosted a concert featuring the folk/blues singer Lead Belly, he insisted upon allowing mixed audiences to attend. Washington was, after all, a Southern city, and segregation was still the order of the day. This didn't deter the Erteguns, who were always colorblind when it came to race relations.

By the age of 23, Nesuhi was a respected and knowledgeable authority on jazz history. He was invited to deliver a series of lectures at the Bookshop, a local book and record store located at 916 17th Street in

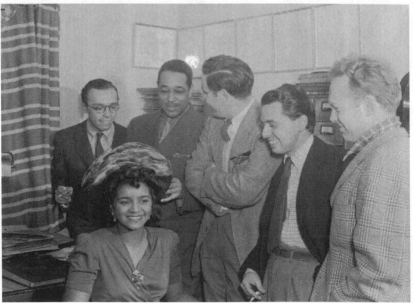

Photo taken in the home of photographer William P. Gottlieb, probably in late 1941. Standing, L-R: Ahmet Ertegun, Duke Ellington, Gottlieb, Nesuhi Ertegun, and the Jazz Man's Dave Stuart. Seated: an unknown protege of Ellington (The William P. Gottlieb Collection).

Washington. His second lecture, which took place on February 20, 1941, was announced in *Jazz Information* as a discussion of King Oliver, Louis Armstrong, and Chicago in the early 1920s. Ertegun was invited to parties and get-togethers and became a well-known and respected personality amongst the East Coast jazz community. He traveled around the country, listening to jazz, getting to know America's cities, and learning American customs.

On one occasion in 1941, he and Ahmet were invited to the Maryland home of William Gottlieb, a photographer who had authored the "Swing Sessions" column in the *Washington Post* since 1938. At Gottlieb's house, Ertegun met Duke Ellington and a 31-year-old Hollywood record shop owner by the name of Dave Stuart. Photographs memorializing the meeting were taken by Gottlieb's wife, although in a book of images published by Gottlieb in 1979, Stuart was cropped out of the picture.

It is not known what Ertegun and Stuart discussed, if anything, but it is possible that Ertegun told Stuart about a recent acquisition from a private collection: five piano solos recorded by Jelly Roll Morton in 1938. Morton had made the records while in the nation's capital for interviews conducted by folklorist Alan Lomax. Ertegun was looking for someone with an established label who would release the Morton sides, but at the time, Stuart was busy with his upcoming session with Lu Watters' Yerba Buena Jazz Band and his work on the faltering Orson Welles film. Nevertheless, the meeting could have been the genesis of Stuart's interest in the Morton sides for Jazz Man.

In January 1942, shortly after his Maryland meeting with Stuart, Nesuhi Ertegun visited the Jazz Man in Hollywood for the first time. As a student of art and architecture, he was no doubt charmed by the elegant Spanish façade of the shop on Santa Monica Blvd., but when he walked in, the erudite Turk was even more taken with the beautiful young woman who greeted him. It wasn't just Marili Stuart's looks that attracted him, although

807 1/2 N. June in West Hollywood. Nesuhi Ertegun rented the left side of this duplex. Building shown in 2009 (Photo by Cary Ginell).

that was certainly something in her favor. Ertegun found that Marili was a rarity: a sophisticated young woman who wasn't a "jitterbug." Not only was she a fan of New Orleans jazz, she knew all about the records that he had so passionately pursued. When she put a few 78s on the Jazz Man turntable, it was love at first spin.

When he returned to Washington, Nesuhi Ertegun could not get Marili Stuart off of his mind. There is no evidence that they communicated further during 1942, but there is little doubt that when Stuart left for flight school that summer and Ertegun subsequently decided to move to Los Angeles, that this was no mere coincidence. Marili was only one reason Ertegun was lured to the West Coast, the other being the temperate California weather. Afflicted with jaundice and asthma, and cooped up in the Turkish Embassy with his entire family, Ertegun needed to get his own place, and thought that the warm, dry California climate would be ideal to assist in his physical recovery. He hated the cold weather on the East Coast and didn't want to face another freezing Washington winter.

With the revival of New Orleans jazz instigated by Lu Watters and Bunk Johnson (both Jazz Man artists), Ertegun probably felt that Los Angeles was where he could pursue his professional goals. The 1942 edition of the Los Angeles City Directory lists "Nesuhi Ertegun, salesman" living at 807½ N. June in West Hollywood. (The building, an attractive duplex cottage, still stands.) According to Ertegun's fourth wife, Selma, Nesuhi found kindred spirits in the northern half of the house. The residents were like him: intellectual émigrés who loved arguing and playing bridge. In California, Ertegun could indulge his passion for tennis and ping-pong year-round, instead of just during the summer months, when the Washington weather was often hot and muggy. The dry California climate improved Ertegun's health and with his visits to the Jazz Man to talk music with Marili becoming more frequent, Nesuhi Ertegun saw much promise in his second home.

Ertegun's jazz lectures soon attracted the attention of Gordon Gullickson, who had been distributing a mimeographed auction list to jazz record collectors. *Jazz Information,* the first U.S. publication devoted to jazz 78s, had folded in November 1941, leaving a wide open market for Gullickson to tap. His new publication, which he called *The Record Changer,* made its debut on July 15, 1942. The first issue was one large page, folded up like a road map, which mainly featured listings of records for sale or trade, but as the monthly magazine developed, it expanded into a more traditional saddle-stitched pamphlet, with record listings augmented by articles and editorials about happenings in the world of traditional jazz.

Its second issue, dated August 15, 1942, once again consisted of only listings of records. Among the magazine's advertisers were Ahmet Ertegun, Ralph Gleason (who had not yet moved to San Francisco from his home in Briarcliff, New York), and Dave Stuart. By this time, Stuart was in Washington attending navigator's school for the ferry command, but he listed his address as 6331 Santa Monica Blvd. Ahmet Ertegun posted a short list of seven records he was auctioning, which included items by Coleman Hawkins, Fletcher Henderson, Cab Calloway, and Louis Armstrong. His address, 1606 23rd Street in Washington, was that of the Turkish embassy.

By the time the September issue came out, Stuart was no longer an advertiser, as he was now preoccupied, flying missions to Europe. He tried to keep up with what was going on at the shop, but as Marili wrote to Bill Russell in November, "He has been pretty busy flying around lately, and hasn't had much time to think about records."

The first non-auction-related article appeared in *The Record Changer* issue of November 15, 1942, which featured a drawing of Bunk Johnson on the cover. The column, by John Phillips titled "A New Attack on the Grading Problem," sought to streamline how records were described in the magazine. By the end of 1942, Gullickson began thinking about including more articles for *The Record Changer*. He immediately thought of Nesuhi Ertegun and the lectures he had given at the Bookshop before moving to California. After the December issue of the magazine came out, Gullickson expanded the format to include a regular column for Ertegun plus other features on records, record collecting, and traditional New Orleans jazz music, in addition to the usual auction listings.

Ertegun's columns began with the January 1943 edition. As his first subject, Ertegun chose the recordings of Lu Watters' Yerba Buena Jazz Band, which had been released on a brand new California label called Jazz Man Records. In his April column, titled "A Style and a Memory," Ertegun eloquently stated his case for traditional jazz, acknowledging that although times had changed and jazz had progressed, there was a certain wistfulness about the disappearance of New Orleans jazz from the music scene. Although pessimistic about the prospects for traditional jazz to return to the mainstream, Ertegun cited Lu Watters as the only important exception to his theory that "there is absolutely nothing in common between the values of New Orleans music and the values in which today's young musician believes." His glum conclusion:

It is possible that in the future that music will adopt certain forms which will be as rich and as satisfying as New Orleans music. But there will be no rediscovery of New Orleans music. It is impossible to resurrect it. Musically speaking, history does not repeat itself.

Ertegun had spoken prematurely, because as he was writing this, the Watters band's influence was gaining momentum, and with the Bunk Johnson records creating a stir, New Orleans jazz was indeed beginning its renaissance.

Gullickson found that having a writer living on the other side of the country was not as difficult a prospect as it sounded, and Ertegun proved to be a good choice, delivering monthly essays on his visits to musical locales around the country.

In the December 1943 issue, Ertegun wrote about American jazz in Paris, delving away from his usual treatises on New Orleans artists to praise Duke Ellington, Django Reinhardt, and Teddy Bunn, three musicians who were anathema to moldy figs like Dave Stuart. Introduced by editor Gullickson as "the young man who went west," Ertegun also wrote eloquently about the absence of racism toward musicians in France:

As race prejudice was naturally unknown in France, and as the Parisians have had a traditional respect for artists, the Negro musicians were always treated as such, and they never encountered any of the humiliations which they suffer here all too frequently. In Paris, they were all great artists, living in an atmosphere of esteem and admiration.

In January 1944, Ertegun was elevated from a contributor to a reviewer. *The Record Changer* announced that Ertegun, Tom Williston, and Gordon Gullickson would be judging literary submissions offered for publication, with an award of $10.00 going to the best article. In Los Angeles, Ertegun also continued delivering jazz lectures, much as he did in Washington. In the summer of 1945, he gave talks on the history of New Orleans jazz to members of the Pasadena Institute of Art, which included well-received demonstrations of ragtime by Seattle-based pianist Johnny Wittwer.

Like Dave Stuart, Marili Morden, too, had begun to tire of the day-to-day boredom of sitting around, waiting for customers to come in to the shop. Many of those who came in had to be told that the Jazz Man didn't stock the latest swing hits on the Hit Parade. Although she got to meet many of Dave Stuart's Hollywood friends, including Orson Welles, she was a young, vibrant, attractive woman and hated being cooped up in the dusty shop all day. Welles, a notorious skirt chaser, possibly increased the frequency of his visits because of Marili and they soon became good friends. He would often call and talk to her about projects he was working on.

With Stuart gone, Marili was imprisoned by the Jazz Man, no longer able to squire musicians around to clubs or go where she wanted to during the day. She also had the Jazz Man label to contend with, and with the popularity of the Lu Watters and Bunk Johnson records remaining strong, she had all she could do to keep up with orders from customers and record stores across the country. To break up the monotony of her day, Marili bought a half-hour of time on a local radio station, during which she played traditional jazz records, wrote her own scripts and plugged the Jazz Man Record Shop. *Down Beat* announced the weekly program in its issue of March 15, 1943 but did not indicate what radio station it was on nor how long the program would last.

It's likely that Marili and Ertegun became very close during these early months; how close we will never know, but even though Marili and Stuart were separated, they were still legally married, and despite their growing attraction for each other, Marili and Ertegun were most likely careful to conceal any sense of their relationship being anything but professional. Marili wanted her divorce from Stuart to be finalized, and with her feelings for Ertegun growing, she probably felt some degree of tension about their friendship, but for the time being, they kept their relationship discreet.

Some time after he began visiting the Jazz Man, Ertegun began

New Show Airs Only Jazz from Pre-swing Era

Los Angeles—What is probably radio's first platter programs devoted exclusively to authentic jazz music of the pre-swing era has been launched here by Marili Stuart, who has been operating the Jazz Man Record Shop since her husband, Dave Stuart, noted collector and authority on jazz, became a navigator in the ferry command.

Mrs. Stuart has bought the time (Wednesdays—12:30 to 1:00 p.m.) for sponsorship by the Jazz Man Record Shop and permits no other advertising. She writes her own scripts and does her own announcing.

First program was ushered in to the theme of *Doctor Jazz* by Jelly Roll Morton's Red Hot Peppers. Discs heard on the show included King Oliver's *Dippermouth*, *Terrible Blues*, by the Red Onion Jazz Babies; *Tiger Rag*, by the New Orleans Rhythm Kings; *Creole Trombone*, Kid Ory and his band.

Only new record heard on the program was *Fidgety Feet* as recreated in the New Orleans manner by Lu Watters' Yerba Buena Jazz Band.

Down Beat, *March 15, 1943.*

pitching the Jelly Roll Morton masters he had acquired to Dave and Marili Stuart. This probably occurred in the summer, when Dave Stuart was attending flight school in Washington. It is not known whether Ertegun contacted Dave or Marili about it, but in his November 24, 1942 letter to Russell, written from Washington National Airport, Stuart expressed his excitement over the Morton test pressings Ertegun had sent him. The week before, he had visited Gene Williams in New York, and while there, he attended a concert at Town Hall featuring Commodore jazz artists. Stuart sniffed derisively as he criticized the musicians' performances: Bud Freeman (who "blew his reeds out"), Hot Lips Page, Big Sid Catlett, and Zutty Singleton. The only person he had anything good to say about was Pee Wee Russell:

I went in such haste (that) I forgot to take the Morton tests. Really, William, he makes the others sound a little like tyros [a word that means "neophyte"].

Perhaps you've heard his "Honky Tonk Music" —sometime, B.W. If so, taint bad.

But—best of all is "The Creepy Feeling." This he made for the L. of C., so you've probably heard it. Still one of his best, I think. Also, I've another "Winin' Boy," but with more piano and better—possibly a little jive in a spot or two but awful good. Then, of course, "Finger Buster." All in all, they sound like four fine sides—equal to the Generals.

This was the last letter Stuart wrote to Russell until June 1943.

By now, Marili was running both the shop and the record label and with Stuart's blessing, she issued four of the five Morton sides as Jazz Man 11 and 12. The labels included the phrase "co-sponsored by Nesuhi Ertegun," the young jazz crusader's first credit on a phonograph record.

The Morton records were released in December 1942. An ad in *Down Beat*'s issue of December 15, 1942 announced the four previously unissued piano solos by Jelly Roll Morton, which were advertised at $1.05 each. Jazz music fans had been starved due to the ongoing strike launched on August 1 by American Federation of Musicians president James C. Petrillo, who banned all recording activity by union musicians, claiming that radio stations were playing phonograph records rather than hiring live musicians, and thus, cheating musicians out of millions of dollars of income. Many record companies, including the three majors: RCA Victor, Columbia, and Decca, frantically stockpiled recordings before the ban took effect, but by the end of 1942, their supply was nearly used up. The reissue business increased in popularity, and the four Morton sides became big news in the jazz world.

In 1943, Marili Stuart issued five more Jazz Man 78s. Releases 13, 14, and 15 were leftover sides from Lu Watters' second session in March 1942. Jazz Man 16 and 17 included three more sides from the Bunk Johnson session from June and Wally Rose's "Hot House Rag," featuring a reduced unit of piano, two banjos, and drums. Aside from these, no Jazz Man releases would be issued until the beginning of 1946. Marili Stuart did not have the knowledge to organize and supervise a recording session by herself and she needed a partner who could help her with the business. She looked more and more to the dapper, cultivated Turk for professional guidance and personal companionship.

From the author's collection.

Chapter Eleven

The High Priestess of Jazz

For Marili Stuart, life at the Jazz Man Record Shop during World War II had an unending sameness to it. Most of the record collectors she had come to know during the time she shared the shop duties with Dave Stuart had been, like her estranged husband, drafted. All that remained were

Marili Morden, mid-1940s.

the old-timers who sauntered in to pass the time of day and young teenagers just learning about jazz, who came in not just to listen to music, but to ogle the stunning young lady behind the counter.

Jim Leigh first encountered the Jazz Man in 1943 when he was 13. He grew up with the sounds of popular music in his house, his mother often singing him to sleep with whatever was popular at the time, including '20s and '30s favorites

like "My Blue Heaven," "Little Man, You've Had a Busy Day," and "Let the Rest of the World Go By." Leigh was, like most other teenagers during World War II, hooked on the weekly *Lucky Strike Hit Parade*, which played the latest big band hits by Glenn Miller and Tommy Dorsey. For his birthday, he had been given a copy of *American Jazz Music* by Wilder Hobson, which

116

introduced him to "real jazz"—music that wasn't heard on the radio. It intrigued him enough so that he became curious as to what it sounded like. Through an English record-collecting friend, Leigh heard his first "real jazz" records: selections by white musicians like Bix Beiderbecke, Miff Mole, Joe Venuti, Adrian Rollini, and Eddie Lang. One of his favorites was Red Nichols' Brunswick recording of "The Sheik of Araby," featuring a vocal and trombone solo by Jack Teagarden, which made Leigh recognize the relative values of "real jazz" and the false prophet: commercialism. When his friend pulled out a record on the Victor label by Jelly Roll Morton's Red Hot Peppers called "Doctor Jazz Stomp," Leigh began to understand the difference between white and black jazz.

He began ordering 78s from the Commodore Music Shop in New York, but in the spring of 1943, he rode the streetcar from his home in Santa Monica to the Jazz Man Record Shop in Hollywood. Nearly 60 years later, Leigh had vivid memories of the Jazz Man, but mostly, he recalled the sultry, sexy, but oh-so-serious Marili Stuart.

I remember the green Venetian blinds on the glass front door. You'd come in and there were tables with racks of 78s in stiff, tan cardboard sleeves. On the walls were enlarged photos of players for whose music I still have great affection and afición. The photos on the wall were of Kid

Interior shots of 6331 Santa Monica Blvd. (Courtesy Selma Ertegun)

Ory, Mutt Carey, Bud Scott, Buster Wilson, Turk Murphy, and Watters, as I remember.

At the back of the store, under the photographs, was a counter with a tall stool with Marili sitting on it, looking ineffably beautiful and unapproachable. Her husband David, the owner of the shop and founder of the Jazz Man record label, was away in those days, on such missions as flying VIPs to Dakar, but we didn't miss him. She was the only person I ever saw in there.

Dave Stuart, Gene Williams, and Bill Colburn were part of a kind of nexus of very knowledgeable guys who had spent time in New Orleans. They were the daddies of it all. But she was the crown princess. I don't know how much depth of knowledge she had, but she certainly knew more than I did, and if somebody told me that she was only 23, I would have been amazed. She was extremely soignée and very quietly dramatic. This was a young woman living in a sophisticated world of older men, doing her best to keep up with them.

As soon as I went in there, Marili told me about the Lu Watters records Jazz Man had released. You couldn't spend much time at the Jazz Man without becoming aware of—what to call it?—a prevailing taste, a preference, a complacency, an orthodoxy. There, in the smoky afternoon light, with the green shade half-drawn on the glass front door, and the collector's items sleeping in their sleeves, Marili might play a record (without comment), or she might read, or simply smoke. Questioned, she would answer civilly, with an air of noblesse oblige. Still, it didn't take us long to realize that on these premises, the New Orleans masters, living or dead, were the gods. Everyone else was just a musician.

Marili knew everything we wanted to know—or we believed she did. The Jazz Man had a sort of political correctness about it with Marili. You had a feeling that there was superior knowledge there, but she wasn't evangelical. If you asked her, she would tell you. When I asked her a question about a record, she would simply say "Yes." Then I would stammer, "But what I meant was, what does it sound like?" She wouldn't even look up. "I think you should listen yourself and decide." The closest she came was when she told me, "Don't buy that Bix Beiderbecke record when you can get three Bunk Johnson records for the same price."

She had a kind of primness about her. Very arousing, I have to say. And she was not unkind. She just didn't do you any favors. It wasn't peer pressure that made me a cigarette smoker but the example of Marili's constant smoking, in a tense adult silence to which I aspired.

Marili was never very forthcoming. I can't imagine what it would have been like living with her. I have gathered that in the right mood, that she could be quite wild. Her whole demeanor was judicious. She didn't give you the come-on. She didn't flirt. Maybe it was just a superior way of being flirtatious. Everybody in my age range was hopelessly, flat-out in love with her. Hopelessly was the key word. Her fires were banked but she wasn't out. I think she was extremely involved in being who she was.

When she was no longer involved in the shop, I lost interest. She was half the fun of the place. We got to be pretty good friends after a few years and she watched me grow up. I brought girlfriends in and she would check them out and let me know later what she thought of them. Her image was important to her. She was always conservatively dressed: dark clothes, dark skirt, dark sweater. I never saw her with her hair down.

Cartoonist Gene Deitch had just turned 20 when he first encountered the shop during World War II. It was there that he bought his first copy of *The Record Changer* and began devouring its contents. In December 1945, he joined Don Anderson as one of the magazine's staff artists, drawing cover illustrations, and introducing "The Cat," a visual impression of Krin Gabbard's "Jazz Nerd." Sixty-five years later, Deitch still drools with delight when talking about the Jazz Man and its musical as well as its feminine contents.

I was medically discharged from the U.S. Army in 1944, a year before the end of World War II. The shop was but a short walk from where I lived in West Hollywood. That was the shop I knew and was nursed on; the mother's milk of jazz flowed to me from that shop.

Marili was a fabulous looking woman. Very regal, like a duchess. So beautiful, so knowledgeable, and so remote. To me, she was the High Priestess of Jazz. I was an emerging New Orleans jazz fanatic, having been duly baptized by Marili. In a youthful burst of revelation, I entered her shop and proclaimed that I had just discovered "the real jazz" in a recording of Bob Crosby's Bob Cats. After a pause, during which Marili considered whether it was worth her time to straighten me out, she deigned to play me her rare copy of the Gennett label King Oliver Creole Jazz Band recording of "Dippermouth Blues." "<u>This</u> is the Real Jazz!" she said. Of course, she was right—to this day, the 1923 KOCJB has never been equaled, let alone surpassed. From that moment on, I was the most doggedly, or CATedly, pure N.O. jazz fanatic of them all.

She just barely tolerated me because I wanted to learn, and because I was a good customer. If that had been all, she would not likely remember me if she were alive today, but only because I later became "The Cat," and of course, for a while I was co-editor with Nesuhi of The Record Changer.

Of course, another regular visitor to the Jazz Man, whose presence Marili looked forward to, was Nesuhi Ertegun. Between his regular travels around the country, Ertegun spent much of his time in Los Angeles with Marili. Together, they did the town; going to nightclubs, listening to records, and enjoying each other's company. There isn't much doubt that when Marili's divorce became final in March 1944 that their friendship intensified, if it hadn't already. It was at this time that Marili Morden and Nesuhi Ertegun not only stepped up their personal relationship, but, with the help of Orson Welles, also revived the career of a New Orleans master.

Chapter Twelve

Orson Welles' Almanac

In early 1944, Orson Welles accepted an offer from Mobil Oil to produce his own radio variety program. He borrowed its format from *The Jack Benny Show,* which he had hosted when Benny came down with pneumonia during March and April of 1943. In the show, Welles played himself (as did Benny), surrounding himself with a cast of eccentrics, with names like Dr. Snakeoil and Prudence Pratt. Where Benny often made fun of his character's stinginess, Welles made himself the target of barbs due to his ever-increasing girth.

Orson Welles' Almanac originated in Los Angeles. During its six-month run, beginning on January 26, 1944, it was broadcast on Wednesday nights for the West Coast by the CBS network in front of a live audience. Welles was apt to do anything on the show, from trading quips with the likes of Groucho Marx and Lucille Ball to reciting esoteric factoids, commemorating historical anniversaries, and noting celebrity birthdays.

Originally, the show featured the music of a big band, led by Lud Gluskin, a well-known, but unexceptional band leader. In March, bored with the mundane sounds emanating from Gluskin's orchestra, Welles called Marili at the Jazz Man, and asked if she could round up a traditional New Orleans band that could play on his show. Within a short while, she called him back with the names of seven jazz veterans, all seasoned New

121

Orleans musicians who had been playing in the Los Angeles area. Welles was delighted with Marili's selections, which included a front line of three legends from the Crescent City: trombonist Kid Ory, trumpeter "Papa" Mutt Carey, and clarinetist Jimmie Noone.

Edward "Kid" Ory (1886–1973) was born in LaPlace, Louisiana, some 30 miles from New Orleans. Originally a banjo player, he switched to trombone when he was 14. Ory liked to brag that the legendary Buddy Bolden had offered him a job to play with his band, but that Ory's sister said that he was too young and declined on his behalf. In time, Ory was leading one of the most popular bands in Storyville, New Orleans' notorious red-light district. In the early 1910s, Ory was joined by Mutt Carey and bassist Ed Garland. In 1919, two years after Storyville closed, Ory moved to Los Angeles, and sent for Carey to join him. In 1921, under the name Ory's Sunshine Boys, Ory cut his historic session for the Spikes Brothers, which included Carey and Garland. In 1925, Ory went to Chicago, where he recorded in Louis Armstrong's famous Hot Five sessions. He played in Chicago until 1929, when he returned to Los Angeles. In 1933, unable to find work due to the Depression, Ory retired from music, working at his brother's chicken ranch, sorting mail in a post office, and gardening in his own yard. It was there, in 1940, that Dave Stuart found him and wrote an article about the pioneering musician, which appeared in the November 22, 1940 issue of *Jazz Information*. When Stuart met Marili Morden, he introduced her to Ory and the New Orleans musicians who were living in Los Angeles.

Ory became one of Marili's favorites. He was always good with a story, although it would be a few years before she could convince him to begin playing his trombone again. That happened in 1942, when clarinetist Barney Bigard left Duke Ellington's band to start his own group and asked Ory to join him. Bigard remembered that Ory told him he had been working as a cook and was currently sweeping out the city morgue for $12 a week.

Bigard's group, which included a young Charles Mingus on bass, played at the Capri night club in Hollywood. In 1943, Ory was invited by critic Rudi Blesh to play a radio broadcast at San Francisco 's Geary Theatre with Bunk Johnson. The New Orleans jazz revival was underway, instigated by Lu Watters' Jazz Man recordings of 1941 and 1942.

When Ory got the call from Marili about the Welles show, he jumped at the opportunity, and in no time at all, assembled a seven-piece unit consisting of some old friends from New Orleans: Carey, Garland, Noone, pianist Buster Wilson, guitarist Bud Scott, and drummer Zutty Singleton. Marili had been encouraging both Ory and Carey to resume their careers since she first met them in the early 1940s. According to columnist George Montgomery in *The Record Changer*, the band would never have gotten together had it not been for Marili's influence, counsel, and encouragement. In 1942, she convinced Ory that there was still a lot of music left in the old trombone that lay dormant in his closet at home, the same instrument that had accompanied Louis Armstrong, Jelly Roll Morton, Johnny Dodds, and King Oliver. Marili also persuaded a disconsolate Mutt Carey to pick up his trumpet and play again as well.

The band made its debut on *Orson Welles' Almanac* on March 15, 1944. Nesuhi Ertegun wrote about it in Art Hodes' *The Jazz Record*:

It was decided to have the band play one tune on the program; if the reactions of the listeners were favorable, then perhaps Welles could convince his sponsors to make the band a regular feature on his show. We went to the first rehearsal filled with curiosity, hopes, and excitement. The men began arriving in the studio; most of them hadn't seen each other for years. Noone, for instance, had not seen Garland since they worked together in New Orleans in 1916. The happiness of all of them to be together again after so many years was obvious.

Marili Morden recalled:

They were deeply engrossed in the routine they had worked out for

The All-Star Jazz Group, which Orson Welles called the Mercury All-Star Jazz Combination. His radio program, Orson Welles' Almanac, aired from March to July 1944. Back row, left to right: Ed Garland, bass; Buster Wilson, piano; Marili Morden; Papa Mutt Carey, trumpet; Kid Ory, trombone; Bud Scott, guitar. Seated in front: Jimmie Noone, clarinet; Zutty Singleton, drums.

"High Society" when Welles walked into the rehearsal studio. They showed a refreshing lack of concern at his appearance, and when he was introduced to Ory, who tends to be preoccupied during rehearsals, Ory asked "What was the name?"

The star of the program that night was actor Charles Laughton, who performed a scene with Welles from Shakespeare's *Julius Caesar.* (Laughton was Cassius and Welles played Brutus.). Then Welles introduced Ory's band. Speaking off the cuff, he rhapsodized about "the real jazz:"

Many of you listening have never heard it before. What you've heard are jazz ideas slicked up by commercial musicians. The whole thing started in the wide-open good time carnival city that was New Orleans before the last war. From that it spread to Chicago and all over the world and influenced all popular music. This is art for art's sake, if anything ever was—music musicians play for themselves for their own satisfaction, just because they like it.

Ertegun later wrote:

The audience applauded the New Orleans band five times as much as they did Welles and Laughton put together. It sounds incredible, but so it was. The program's signal man was gesticulating desperately, but it went on and on. In the next days, a wonderful thing happened: thousands of letters and telegrams started to pour in, telling without a single exception how much the music was enjoyed, and there was much clamor for New Orleans music. The sponsors, deluged by all this mail, and under the impact of Welles's powerful rhetoric, consented to keep the band on their show.

Several weeks later, Welles made an announcement on his program, underscored by Noone's clarinet:

Ladies and gentlemen, a couple of weeks ago, we brought together a group of the great men of jazz. And they played jazz, the real thing. And you loved it. You wrote us so many letters, asking for more, that we've decided to make our Jazz Combination—probably the only real jazz band left on Earth—a regular feature of this program. Tonight we are to hear the deathless "Muskrat Ramble." Kid Ory, who wrote the tune, will play his trombone. The clarinet is Jimmie Noone; Mutt Carey, trumpet; Buster Wilson, piano; Bud Scott, guitar; Ed Garland, bass; and Zutty Singleton, drums.

The band, billed as the All Star Jazz Group, was signed to a 13-week contract, which extended until July 12. Despite this, Welles continued to refer to the band on the broadcasts as the "Mercury All-Star Jazz Combination," and mentioned each musician's name in every broadcast. Welles became friends with each of the members of the band, and invited them to rehearse at his home for each broadcast.

During the show's run, the band (there was some disagreement as to whose band it was: Ory's or Carey's), played tunes that they could have played in their sleep: "Panama Rag," "Savoy Blues," "Tiger Rag," "Oh,

Didn't He Ramble," and "Royal Garden Blues," among others.

On the next program, Welles decided to explain to his listeners once again what he meant by "the real jazz:"

Now ladies and gentlemen, jazz isn't just brass and beat. Emphatically, it isn't what people usually call swing. Those of our listeners who are hearing real jazz for the first time, from the All Star Combination, which is a regular feature on this program, are advised to separate the different instruments by conscious effort of the ear. You won't miss tonight's solo by Zutty Singleton, who is almost certainly the greatest drummer alive. But listen for Jimmie Noone's clarinet, Kid Ory's trombone, Mutt Carey's trumpet, Bud Scott's guitar, Ed Garland's bass, and Buster Wilson's piano. The number is "That's A-Plenty."

Marili Morden, Jimmie Noone, and Nesuhi Ertegun, probably mid-1940s.
(Courtesy Selma Ertegun)

On April 19, Jimmie Noone died from a sudden heart attack. He was only 48 years old. Everyone, especially Welles, was devastated by the news. Half-heartedly, the band made the broadcast that night, with Wade Whaley substituting for Noone on clarinet. To honor his late friend, Kid Ory wrote a haunting elegy that Welles called "Blues for Jimmie." Six minutes before the end of the broadcast, Welles delivered an extemporaneous, poignant, and somewhat loquacious eulogy. With Bud Scott strumming quietly in the background to Buster Wilson's playing of Noone's signature song, "Sweet Lorraine," Welles stepped to the microphone:

One thing about this program we've been very proud of is the combination of notable jazz musicians it's been our good fortune to get together, and who've been playing real jazz and great music for us these last few weeks. Mutt Carey on the trumpet, Kid Ory on the trombone, Bud Scott on the guitar, Buster Wilson on the piano, Ed Garland, bass, and Zutty Singleton on the drums. Tonight, Wade Whaley is taking Jimmie Noone's place on the clarinet. Mister Whaley is a very fine musician, but he knows, as we all do, that no one will ever take Jimmie Noone's place. Jimmie was a guitarist, first of all, but the great Sidney Bechet started him on the clarinet, back forty years ago. That was in New Orleans, when Jimmie was about 10. Later on, when jazz men moved up the river past Saint Louie and on up north to Chicago, when recording got underway and jazz became a worldwide institution, Jimmie joined up with King Oliver's Creole Jazz Band and got to be the greatest clarinet player in the world. Jimmie played in many combinations and his own Apex Club Orchestra was responsible for some of the finest jazz ever transcribed; "Apex Blues," for instance, which was Jimmie's own composition. And "Sweet Lorraine"— that was his theme, remember? Buster Wilson's playing it now, "Sweet Lorraine."

Jazz was conceived in New Orleans. It was born there and it grew up there because life in New Orleans found so many reasons for brass bands. Funerals, for instance. The musicians here in this studio who are going to play for you pretty soon, and who all come from New Orleans, can tell you about funeral music in those days in the Creole City. They used to play at funerals and nobody ever thought it was out of place because jazz, like anything else that man makes out of his sincerity and passion, is holy dignified and always worthy of the occasion of death.

With this, Welles signaled for the band to stop playing underneath him. Then, with his voice hushed, he continued, almost whispering, pausing often during his words:

And so they're going to play some jazz for Jimmie Noone. Not for us. Not for themselves. But for Jimmie. You know, the last thing Jimmie told us was this: He said he sure wanted to come down here and play some blues tonight. That was yesterday. Jimmie had to leave before he could play the blues again. He went away to make beautiful music somewhere else with Buddy Bolden and Jelly Roll Morton, King Oliver, and the others; all his true-hearted brothers who made jazz for the glory of America...and who aren't with us anymore. That's all I have to say on the subject. What you're going to hear now is better than any funeral speech. All right, Mutt, and Bud, and Buster, and Ed, and Kid, and Zutty. Play "Jimmie's Blues."

When the band finished the song, Welles held up a hand so that the studio audience would not applaud. Then, still speaking quietly, he recited the 23rd Psalm. When he was done, Welles walked silently off the stage and went straight to his dressing room. The show was over. The audience remained motionless. For several minutes after Welles disappeared into the wings, nobody rose from their seats to leave. It was an extraordinary moment, and a testament to Welles's supreme mastery of the medium of radio.

In the May 1944 issue of *The Record Changer,* Los Angeles correspondent George Montgomery wrote an enthusiastic note about the Welles show, indicating the possibility of the group making records some time soon. The next month, this was followed by a notice announcing

Noone's passing. Barney Bigard took Noone's place for the remaining programs in the series.

On one broadcast, Welles recalled his juxtaposition of the music of New Orleans and Brazil, which he had intended to display in the aborted film, *It's All True,* with the following song introduction:

Earlier on this show, you heard a little samba. Now you're going to hear some jazz. Samba comes from the gay city of Rio de Janeiro and jazz comes from New Orleans, another gay city. Now your obedient servant is very smitten with both cities and both kinds of music; the cities are more alike than they're different. They both have a Latin and an African past and they share a common weakness for Carnival and Mardi Gras. Now I have a theory. And this explains why samba and jazz are closer relatives than any other kind of popular music in this hemisphere. Our New Orleans All Star Combination is going to help me prove my point this week by rendering that hot classic, "Sugar Foot Stomp."

Despite the success of the Ory band's appearances on *Orson Welles' Almanac,* CBS network executives thought that the regional broadcast would not be suitable for a national audience and canceled the program after the July 19 broadcast. Nesuhi Ertegun, however, saw an opportunity brought about by the public's reaction to the Ory unit, and with the demand for traditional jazz growing, decided to keep the band together and take them into the recording studio. But Kid Ory wouldn't be recording for Jazz Man Records.

Chapter Thirteen

Do What Ory Say

O*rson Welles' Almanac* was only one event that made 1944 a watershed year for the New Orleans jazz revival. The Lu Watters and Bunk Johnson recordings, both released during 1942, started the wave. When Watters and key members of his band were drafted, Johnson became the focus of the revival, and made a multitude of personal appearances, recording with the remaining members of the Yerba Buena Jazz Band, Sidney Bechet, and others. Johnson had become a well-known, highly respected elder statesman representing the origins of jazz in the Crescent City. It didn't hurt that Johnson heavily embellished and sometimes invented his many stories, which were colorful and highly entertaining. The jazz intelligentsia would not catch on to his charade until some years later.

In May 1944, the National Jazz Foundation was founded by Dr. Robert Goffin, an international lawyer and jazz reviewer for *Esquire* magazine. The first New Orleans-based jazz club, the NJF announced its intention to stage and promote concerts and competitions as well as to open a jazz museum in New Orleans.

Dave Stuart had come up with a concept similar to this nearly a year before, although like most of his ideas, it never came to fruition. In a letter to Bill Russell dated August 17, 1943, Stuart wrote about his latest brainstorm:

*I am working on a terrific—no other word will fit—really terrific deal
and if it comes thru I will have a batch of stuff to issue that will knock you
as flat as Colburn plays ocarina. Part of this deal means getting together a
group of people as sort of an historical jass society. Gene* [Williams] *and
I have been talking it over and have picked a few people such as Sterling
Brown, Orson Welles, Stokowski* [Stuart probably meant Igor Stravinsky]*,
etc. etc. If the thing will work, and you are interested, the three of us will
be the C's in C's. Gene and myself will toss in our records and so give the
society a good stock to begin with. The thing will be called The American
Jazz Society or something equally hightoned. Anyway, if what little I've said
sounds any good, let either one of us know and we'll tell you the rest.*

The major record labels were still concentrating on swing and
mainstream big band music, but many independent labels followed Jazz
Man's example by recording not only traditional musicians but younger
artists influenced by the revival. In June, New York-based Blue Note
Records announced a new subsidiary called Climax that would focus on
New Orleans jazz. Its first five issues consisted of 12-inch 78 rpm recordings
by George Lewis and His New Orleans Stompers. (Lewis had recorded with
Bunk Johnson on the Jazz Man sessions of June 1942.) Eugene Williams
continued releasing recordings he made of Bunk Johnson from 1942 on
Jazz Information. Meanwhile, William Russell was making new recordings
featuring Johnson, which he issued on his own American Music label.
John Steiner, who had acquired the Paramount catalog, began a series
of reissues of Paramount masters on his S.D. label, beginning with King
Oliver's 1923 recordings of "Mabel's Dream" and "Riverside Blues," the
two sides Dave Stuart had considered reissuing two years earlier on Jazz
Man. Other S.D. releases that came out during the busy summer of 1944
included vintage recordings by Jelly Roll Morton, Johnny Dodds, and Cow
Cow Davenport. Milt Gabler's Commodore label, which had previously
focused on more contemporary small group jazz from Chicago and New

York, began incorporating New Orleans titles by tradition-bound artists like George Brunis and Wild Bill Davison into its catalog.

At the end of 1944, RCA Victor and Columbia settled their dispute with the American Federation of Musicians and began a flurry of recording activity, joining the upstart independents by bringing back classic material by Louis Armstrong and Jelly Roll Morton. With the tide having turned in World War II, the end of the long war was finally in sight. In June, the Allies landed in Europe, establishing a foothold for the long, laborious drive to Berlin. Soon, the soldiers would be coming home, and record companies, anticipating heavy increases in sales, stockpiled jazz recordings for issue in 1945.

All of this activity made Jazz Man Records conspicuous because it was now the least active of any of the labels, despite its status as the pioneering label of the traditional jazz revival. Jazz Man's last live session had occurred two years before (the Bunk Johnson "talking records"). Its last releases were the four 1938 piano solos by Jelly Roll Morton and some sides left over from the Watters and Johnson sessions. But nothing had happened since.

Although Dave Stuart gave Marili the shop after their divorce, he retained ownership of the Jazz Man record label. In September 1944, when his two-year hitch with the Air Transport Command was up, he moved to New York, where he took up residence in Greenwich Village. His address, 68 Washington Square South, located on the site of New York University, was printed in an auction list advertised in *The Record Changer*. Although he still bought and sold jazz 78s, Stuart was, for all intents and purposes, out of the record business. He was now investing in and selling post-World War I German postage stamps that he had collected while with the ATC. Stuart kept in contact with Marili, however, who forwarded profits from the sale of Jazz Man records to him in New York.

When Stuart retained the record label after their divorce, Marili

Morden saw a drastic reduction in her income. She knew nothing about conducting a recording session, but had become familiar with the marketing and shipping side of the business. But Nesuhi Ertegun had a three-point plan, and in the summer of 1944, he began putting the first of these into action. Ertegun's first idea was to start a new record label of his own called Crescent, which would be devoted to New Orleans jazz. The name Crescent had a double meaning: New Orleans was well known as the Crescent City, but in addition, a crescent moon was a major feature on the national flag of Turkey, where Ertegun was born. He had a simple logo designed for the label, with "Crescent" written in Art Deco letters in silver print displayed on a forest green background. As with Jazz Man releases, the complete personnel and instrumentation were to be listed on every label. The Jazz Man Record Shop's name and address were added along the bottom rim, just as they had been since the label began. (By the time the first Crescent records came out, the shop had moved back to 1221 N. Vine St.)

The first, and, as it turned out, only Crescent releases were by Orson Welles's Mercury All Star Jazz Combination, which was renamed Kid Ory and His Creole Jazz Band. The band's first session was held in Hollywood in early August 1944, with Ertegun supervising. Five of the seven musicians from the Welles program returned: Ory, Carey, Garland, Wilson, and Scott. Jimmie Noone's role on clarinet was taken by Omer Simeon, who was permitted to leave Jimmie Lunceford's big band to record with his old friend Ory; they had last recorded together in 1926 on Jelly Roll Morton's "Doctor Jazz Stomp." Zutty Singleton was unavailable, so Alton Redd was brought on board to play drums.

By the time the session took place, the Ory band had spent five months rehearsing and playing together, so they were more than ready. The four sides they cut on August 3, 1944 consist of some of the most effervescent New Orleans jazz ever recorded. On the first number, Ory and Bud Scott's "Get Out of Here (and Go on Home)," the band played an extended ensemble passage before Omer Simeon took a fluid solo on clarinet. The swinging rideout chorus featured sharp, punchy off-beat rim shots by Alton Redd. The second side, "South," was the old Bennie Moten jazz standard. Ory's lament for Jimmie Noone, misspelled "Blues for Jimmy," was the third side, featuring a march-like tempo with a solo by Ory on trombone and Carey playing his trumpet into a bucket mute. The fourth and final song was Ory's "Creole Song," with Ory singing the French lyrics in his crackly voice, the band providing the call-and-response answers. (This recording is noteworthy in that it is the first vocal at a Jazz Man session.)

Crescent Records, Nesuhi Ertegun's tribute to New Orleans and his Turkish roots. (From the author's collection.)

Although Nesuhi Ertegun produced the Crescent sessions, Marili Morden was still listed as the label's owner. In the December 1944 issue of *The Record Changer,* the first Crescent records, numbers 1 and 2, were announced in a full-page ad taken out by Marili. The records, which were made available on January 1, sold for $1.00. The December ad also noted another change in address for the Jazz Man Record Shop, as it had moved back to 1221 N. Vine Street, the old address where the shop was located for a few months in early 1940. But this was only a temporary move. Nesuhi

Kid Ory and Papa Mutt Carey
(Courtesy the Frank Driggs Collection)

Ertegun had bigger plans for the shop, which necessitated acquiring a larger building. Although quaint and atmospheric, the Mexican hacienda at 6331 Santa Monica Blvd. was inadequate for Ertegun's next idea, which was to turn the Jazz Man into a distributor of records for the West Coast. Early in 1945, he and Marili formed Jazz Distribution, which would handle mail order sales of jazz 78s for customers in the western United States. To do so required a larger facility for inventory. Ertegun was eyeing a building nearby that could accommodate his plans, but it would not be available for some months, so he and Marili moved the shop back to Vine Street for much of 1945.

They also began running regular ads for the Jazz Man in *The Record Changer.* The first ad, which appeared to be hastily designed, was included in the May 1945 issue, and mistakenly included David Stuart's name, although Stuart had long since abandoned the shop to Marili. The next ad, which first appeared in the July issue, was in the form of a record label, with Marili

Left: 1945 advertisements displayed in The Record Changer. *Below: shop sticker affixed to in-stock 78s*
(From the author's collection).

Jazz Man

RECORDS

CATALOG
January
1945

Released by
JAZZ MAN RECORD SHOP
1221 North Vine Street
Hollywood 38

The following numbers are still available:

BUNK JOHNSON AND
HIS ORIGINAL SUPERIOR BAND

Bunk Johnson, *Trumpet;* George Lewis, *Clarinet;* Jim Robinson, *Trombone;* Walter Decou, *Piano;* Lawrence Marraro, *Banjo;* Austin Young, *Bass;* Ernest Rogers, *Drums.* RECORDED JUNE 1942.

Jazz Man 8	{ PANAMA / DOWN BY THE RIVER
Jazz Man 9	{ MOOSE MARCH / WEARY BLUES
Jazz Man 10	{ BUNK'S BLUES / STORYVILLE BLUES

JELLY ROLL MORTON
piano solos

Jazz Man 11	{ HONKY TONK MUSIC / WININ' BOY BLUES
Jazz Man 12	{ FINGERBUSTER / CREEPY FEELING

Price $1.05 each. Ready for delivery.

Jazz Man Records

presents:

LU WATTERS'
YERBA BUENA JAZZ BAND

Jazz Man 13	{ MILENBERG JOYS / DADDY DO
Jazz Man 14	{ LONDON BLUES / SUNSET CAFÉ STOMP
Jazz Man 15	{ HIGH SOCIETY / TERRIBLE BLUES

RECORDED MARCH 1942

BUNK JOHNSON AND
HIS ORIGINAL SUPERIOR BAND

Jazz Man 16	{ PALLET ON THE FLOOR / BALLIN' THE JACK

RECORDED JULY 1942

Price $1.05 each. Ready for delivery.

The following numbers are still available:

LU WATTERS'
YERBA BUENA JAZZ BAND

Lu Watters, Bob Scobey, *Cornets;* Ellis Horne, *Clarinet;* Turk Murphy, *Trombone;* Walter Rose, *Piano;* Clarence Hayes, Russ Bennett, *Banjos;* Dick Lammi, *Bass;* Bill Dart, *Drums.*
RECORDED DECEMBER 1941.

Jazz Man 1	{ MAPLE LEAF RAG / BLACK & WHITE RAG, *piano solo*
Jazz Man 2	{ MEMPHIS BLUES / IRISH BLACK BOTTOM
Jazz Man 3	{ MUSKRAT RAMBLE / SMOKEY MOKES
Jazz Man 4	{ ORIGINAL JELLY ROLL BLUES / AT A GEORGIA CAMP MEETING

Lu Watters, Bob Scobey, *Cornets;* Ellis Horne, *Clarinet;* Turk Murphy, *Trombone;* Walter Rose, *Piano;* Clarence Hayes, Russ Bennett, *Banjos;* Squire Girsback, *Bass;* Bill Dart, *Drums.*
RECORDED MARCH 1942.

Jazz Man 5	{ CAKE WALKING BABIES / RIVERSIDE BLUES
Jazz Man 6	{ TIGER RAG / COME BACK SWEET PAPA
Jazz Man 7	{ FIDGETY FEET / TEMPTATION RAG, *piano solo*

Price $1.05 each. Ready for delivery.

Four-page catalog distributed upon the Jazz Man's move back to 1221 N. Vine Street.
(Courtesy the L.A. Institute of Jazz)

indicated as "proprietor," and an assortment of expanded products the shop was now stocking, including books, magazines, and photographs, as well as reissues of hot jazz classics.

On November 11, 1944, Nesuhi Ertgeun's father died of a sudden heart attack at the age of 61. Mehmet Münir Ertegun had become the dean of the Washington diplomatic corps, and his passing stunned the Washington community, not to mention his family. Because the war was still on, Ertegun's body had to remain in the capital until preparations could be made to safely conduct it back to his homeland for burial. After more than a year, on March 22, 1946, the ambassador's body was finally conveyed, with great pomp and ceremony, back to Istanbul, crossing the ocean on board the *U.S.S. Missouri*. From April 5 to April 9, the crew of the *Missouri* participated in the funeral services.

After the funeral, the ambassador's wife returned to Turkey with her daughter Selma. Nesuhi had established a home in Los Angeles, but Ahmet was still living at the embassy; he was studying classical philosophy at St. John's College at the time and decided to stay in the United States, rather than return to Turkey. Ahmet wanted to get into the record business like his brother, but was having trouble getting a label started.

In the January 1945 issue of *The Record Changer*, Nesuhi listed five pages of jazz 78s for sale rather than shipping them to California. With his responsibilities at the Jazz Man increasing, he had no time to deal with record auctions, so he listed about 400 records at bargain basement set-sale prices. Many of the records were in substandard condition, so it is likely these were duplicates of items he already had in better grades. Most sold in the one-to-two-dollar range, with the highest priced item (a Cripple Clarence Lofton on Solo Art) going for $7.50. In the ad, Ertegun promised to ship all records by the end of the month.

The release of the first two Ory discs on Crescent was a major event in the traditional jazz world, warranting nearly three columns in *The Record*

CRESCENT
RECORDS

presents

KID ORY'S
CREOLE JAZZ BAND

Personnel

✫

KID ORY'S

CREOLE JAZZ BAND

✫

MUTT CAREY—TRUMPET
KID ORY—TROMBONE
OMER SIMEON—CLARINET
BUSTER WILSON—PIANO
BUD SCOTT—GUITAR
ED GARLAND—BASS
ALTON REDD—DRUMS

Crescent 1   South
              Creole Song

Crescent 2   Blues For Jimmy
              Get Out of Here

Price $1.00 each, plus taxes
Ready for delivery

✫

Released by

JAZZ MAN RECORD SHOP
1221 Vine Street
Hollywood 38, California

Changer. Reviewer Bill Riddle praised the two discs effusively, saying that for fans of New Orleans jazz, "these records are the answer to a prayer." Riddle compared the records to classic sides by King Oliver's Creole Jazz Band and Jelly Roll Morton's Red Hot Peppers, long considered the standard bearers of traditional jazz. He named "Creole Song" the best of the four sides, with an ensemble spirit "comparable to any which has ever been recorded." Riddle singled out Simeon's clarinet on "Get Out of Here" and Bennie Moten's "South," the first recording of the tune in New Orleans style. Riddle congratulated Nesuhi Ertegun and Marili Morden "for their courage and clear vision in picking the men they did for this session and for choosing as 'leader' of the little group such a man as Kid Ory, whose understanding of the music is certainly profound." He closed by saying "Let us hope that Mr. Ertegun and Miss Morden will find it possible to give us many more records like these in the future."

News about the Ory sides spread quickly, and on January 10, less than two weeks after the records were issued, *Time* magazine conducted an interview with Ory in Los Angeles. The article, titled "The Kid Comes Back," was published in the magazine's February 5, 1945 issue, marking the first national exposure directed to the New Orleans jazz revival (which had actually been going strong for three years, since the release of the Watters sides on Jazz Man). Marili (described as a "dark-eyed zealot") and Ertegun ("erudite, diminutive son of the late Turkish ambassador) were credited with Ory's Phoenix-like return to the limelight from his job working in the mail room of Los Angeles' Santa Fe railway station. The article also mentioned that 1,500 pressings of the two Ory discs had already been sold, a phenomenal total given such a short time had elapsed since their release. The records were colorfully described as "a mixture of Congo barrelhouse and Creole sauce...probably as close as anything ever put on wax to the spirit of old Storyville." The article concluded by announcing that an additional 1,200 copies of the two Crescent discs were being readied that week, and

Nesuhi Ertegun, Kid Ory, and Marili Morden examine 78s in a posed shot taken at the Jazz Man Record Shop, c. 1945 (Courtesy Jim Leigh).

that Ertegun and Morden were preparing a follow-up session that spring.

The high-profile article resulted in increased sales for Jazz Man's back catalog, and Marili quickly re-pressed the Watters, Johnson, and Morton releases, making sure to include the new Vine Street address on the labels. The Ory band, however, did not record for Crescent that spring, as was indicated by the *Time* article. Instead, Ory recorded four sides on February 12, 1945 for Dr. Fred Exner, a wealthy, Seattle-based jazz buff who had started his eponymous record label the previous September with a session featuring the locally-based Johnny Wittwer Trio.

Meanwhile, Dave Stuart was still ruminating about starting a new cooperative label with Gene Williams and William Russell. Stuart knew that Russell had recorded Bunk Johnson and other New Orleans artists and wanted to combine their catalogs so that they would have a monopoly on the Johnson sides each had stockpiled. On February 19, 1945, he wrote to Russell about his idea:

What about a thing like this. You, Gene, and myself toss in all our records, put up a few thousand and go for a sizable outfit. We would have some 30-40 records, all of which are better than any of Milt's items (the Watters being the worst), design a new label and start in. With this, there should be enough money on the income side to take care of you as you sit in New Orleans and do nothing but record "I Scream."

I have no idea what you are going to do. Bill C [Colburn] is on his way here now and may be able to tell me a little, but I'm sure you've the jass records in your lot. The difference between one of yours and "Moose March" is the difference between Dodds and Goodman, I get a little panicky thinking of those records just a sittin' there. They should be in every home. A Bunk in every pot.

So, I'm willing to go for any sort of a deal in the formation of a record group, and I'm sure Allied can take care of enough pressing on this end of the coast to cover the Western states, possibly the country. I don't know about your end of the country. Can you get pressing in quantity? Or can you get any at all? Too, I've a few dollars and Gene has a few. Probably enough to swing such a deal. You and Gene can have your pictures on every label like the Smith Bros.

Bill tells me that you are going to start out with about $3000 of Gene's. Ask Gene about the above thing, think it over and let me know. I'm sure the Watters will sell enough to pay for a lot of good things. I'll also toss in whatever is necessary, up to my limit, in money. At least we'd have a sizable company what with my Bunks, Watters, Mortons, and Gene's stuff, so that it wouldn't amount to a lot of little outfits as things are now.

Stuart was obviously aware of the splash Ertegun and Marili were making with the Ory sides and wanted to start a new label, since any further sales of Jazz Man items would only serve to promote the record store, which he had given to Marili after their divorce. His idea to combine resources with Gene Williams (Jazz Information) and Bill Russell (American Music) would make him the kingpin of the New Orleans jazz field once again. Throughout 1945, he continued prodding Russell on the idea of having all of the Bunk Johnson recordings on one label. It is apparent that Stuart and Marili still co-owned the label but stock was running low on Jazz Man items and Marili was not keeping up with orders, a fact that plainly irritated Stuart, especially since he wasn't even coming up with enough pressings to satisfy the wartime rationing set on shellac.

I am allowed 500 ten inch shellac a week, so if you have any 10" stuff I can get it done quite easily. The reason my stuff has not come out is because the shop is a little mixed up, as you've probably heard from Bill. Anyway, that's out as I've taken over myself from the ordering standpoint and the records are in shape. So, if you can scratch up any 10" items, or rerecord them at finer cuts, it will be easy.

Another idea whereby we can toss all of our records into one pool and have more than a lot of little names. The American Music deal is good as Gene and I had talked it over before. Think it over – the idea of having all the Bunks on one label along with the Mortons and the Watters (these will pay off as they still sell more than Bunk or Morton and put up enough money to record more things) would be a good thing as the catalog would read with a lot of fine things. The Climax records would add just that much more.

However, ship me the records as soon as they are ready. They're the best! No doubt of that. Played them for Marili the other night and she is a little taken, though the JM shop is on a bad kick with the Turk and Marili going strong.

Stuart's efforts, however, went nowhere. He wanted to take sales away from the Jazz Man Record Shop by convincing Allied Pressing to redirect its business elsewhere ("They like me and don't like the shop," he wrote.) But Ertegun was one step ahead of Stuart. He had already secured the services of the Bishop Presses in South Pasadena, to press the Crescent 78s. Bishop's ads promised "high quality phonograph records" and boasted of being caterers to independent jazz labels. On the first four Crescent pressings, the words "A Bishop Pressing" were stamped in raised letters over one label of the discs.

At this point, Stuart's letters to Russell stopped. He apparently had given up trying to start a New Orleans jazz cooperative and gradually lost interest in the venture entirely. He would not write to Russell again until 1953.

Nesuhi Ertegun didn't get the Ory band back in the studio until August 5, just over a year after the first Crescent sessions were cut. At this second session, Ory included all of the musicians from the 1944 session except drummer Alton Redd, who was replaced by Minor Hall. The August 1945 session featured three chestnuts: W.H. Tyers' "Panama," the ragtime era novelty "Under the Bamboo Tree," and W.C. Handy's "Careless Love." For the final title, Kid Ory provided a catchy tongue-in-cheek number called "Do What Ory Say," in which Ory sang the vocal in his craggy voice and Simeon provided another beautifully melodic chorus. Although not as electrifying as those from the first session, these sides were well-received when they were released in early 1946.

A third session was held on September 8, 1945, with the resulting records actually released before the sides from the August session. The band remained intact except for Simeon, who was replaced by another veteran of the Oliver and Morton bands, Darnell Howard. Once again, the session was dominated by numbers familiar to fans of the traditional jazz revival: W. C. Handy's "Oh, Didn't He Ramble," "Maryland, My Maryland," and Wilbur Sweatman's "Down Home Rag." For the fourth tune, Ory decided on a traditional rag that he had known for years but could not recall its title. For the purpose of the session, he named it after the year Marili Morden was born, "1919." These four sides, numbered Crescent 3 and 4, were released on November 15, 1945.

Just as those records were coming out, the Ory band went back in the studio to record what would be their final four tunes for Jazz Man. This time, Ory was persuaded to do "Ory's Creole Trombone," the first time he had recorded it since the legendary 1921 Nordskog session. Also cut that day were Scott Joplin's "Maple Leaf Rag," the Original Dixieland Jass Band's "Original Dixieland One-Step," and Artie Matthews' energetic stomp, "Weary Blues." By the beginning of 1946, eight Crescent discs by Kid Ory's Creole Jazz Band had been released, encompassing one of the finest collections of authentic New Orleans jazz ever recorded.

As Crescent 3 and 4 were being released, Marili Morden was in the process of finally moving the Jazz Man to its new home, a few blocks west of the stucco building on Santa Monica Blvd., this time on the south side of the street at 6420. This remained the home of the Jazz Man for the next eight years, longer than any location during its years in Hollywood. The address first appeared in a two-page ad in the November 1945 issue of *The Record Changer,* which promoted the first four Ory Crescent discs.

In the brief time since Marili Morden and Nesuhi Ertegun joined forces, they had taken the Jazz Man from a struggling, cramped record store with a stagnant label back to the top of its field. The New Orleans jazz revival had hit its stride, and the Jazz Man Record Shop was still leading the way.

Chapter Fourteen

6420

The Jazz Man Record Shop's new home on Santa Monica Blvd. was decidedly different from any of its previous locations. Although the exterior was not as exotic looking as the stucco structure at 6331, the new building was geared toward the serious collector.

Exterior of the Jazz Man Record Shop at 6420 Santa Monica Blvd., Hollywood, late 1940s.
(Courtesy Selma Ertegun)

Rare shot of the front room of 6420 Santa Monica Blvd. Nesuhi Ertegun goes over inventory with Marili Morden. (Courtesy Selma Ertegun)

Inside 6420, the shop was divided into two sections: a front room served as a reception area, with a long counter top separating it from a back room, where the rare 78s were safely stored on shelves, away from casual browsers. Patrons would enter to find an austere front area, decorated with enlarged photographs of jazz musicians, a coffee table, and a few chairs. Complimentary cigarettes were offered in a glass on the coffee table along with a guest book. Customers were not permitted to enter the back room and browse; specific requests would be communicated to Marili, who would then go into the back room (which was separated by a curtain) and retrieve the precious, fragile objects of their desire. A turntable was built into the counter in the front room on which the records could be played. Marili would audition customers' choices on it, always handling the records herself until a purchase was made. In the years to come, the front room/back room format of the shop remained, although as the shop's location changed, access to the back room was gradually permitted. Eventually, browser bins were added to the front room. But when the shop first opened at 6420, jazz records were treated as priceless antiques, to be presented to a customer upon request, hand delivered by the glamorous, but unsmiling Marili Morden.

Cartoonist Gene Deitch, who first frequented the shop in late 1944 when it was still at 6331 Santa Monica Blvd., recalled:

There certainly was NOT self-service in those days. No scruffy mortals were allowed to touch the rare records before purchase. Of that I am absolutely sure. I don't even remember any bins or shelves of new records that customers could browse through. "Don't Touch!" was the rule. Aside from the danger of breaking or cracking, even fingerprints were considered a major hazard. If you were looking for a specific disc, you had to ask Marili.

By this time, Deitch had begun drawing cartoons for *The Record Changer* featuring "The Cat," the bespectacled collector who represented nerdy, obsessive jazz purists. In the August 1946 issue, The Cat is depicted in the Jazz Man's front room, slouched dazedly in a chair as he tries to justify buying an exorbitantly priced 78 that is playing on the shop turntable.

It was at 6420 that the glamour and mystique of the shop was at its peak. The presence of the musically intoxicating collectibles in the back room—physically close, but monetarily miles away—made the Jazz Man as magical to jazz collectors as a Sotheby's showroom would be to aficionados of fine art and exotic antiques. With Marili perched seductively on a stool behind the counter, an aura of forbidden eroticism added to the shop's musical enticements.

Teenaged Jim Leigh had become a regular visitor to the shop and eventually, Marili inspired him to go to some of the local clubs and hear live music by the jazz legends playing around town:

Marili sent me out to Watts to hear Ory with his quartet. He was

"THE CAT"

"GAD!—I'D BUY THAT RECORD

IF IT HAD A TROMBONE CHORUS;—
IF IT HAD A VOCAL;—
IF IT WAS ON THE ORIGINAL LABEL;—
IF I HAD THE MONEY!"

Gene Deitch's rendering of the Jazz Man's front room.
(Used by permission of Gene Deitch)

very sweet to my friend and me when we went out there on the trolley. But Nesuhi said to me later, "Pops (he always called people Pops), if you want to know what a French peasant is like, just get to know Kid Ory." I didn't realize what he meant at the time. But when I was in S.F., I used to go down and hear Ory. After so many times, they'd come down to say hello to you. One night, I said, "I'm a trombone player" and he said, "Really? You know, I've got a nice old trombone you might like." And I thought, "Gee, I get a chance to buy a trombone from Kid Ory." So I said, "How much you want for it?" He said, "Oh, I could let you have it for $50." The next time I got paid, I came in there and he had the horn with him. It was an absolute wreck. The slide didn't work at all. I said, "The slide seems kind of stiff." I'm 6'5" and Ory was about 5'7." He kind of smiled and looked up at me and said, "Oh, you put a little oil on that, it'll slick up just fine." For the *same amount of money, I bought one from Turk Murphy and played it for years. So Ory screwed everybody. He screwed everybody in his band.*

Ory was playing at the Club Hangover in S.F., and after many, many years, Ed Garland discovered that Ory had been holding out money on the band, ever since the beginning. Somehow or other, they put it together and caught Ory red-handed. Garland knocked Ory off the bandstand and he fell down among all the crates and empty bottles. But Ory got right back up there and finished his set. These guys were roughnecks and crooks. Ory would screw anybody if he had the chance to.

Marili warned me not to spend too much time with Bill Colburn. He was the first person I ever saw smoking a joint. When I was 15, he took me up to the green room and let me meet Ory. It took me years to figure out why the waitresses would bring me in, sit me down, and give me a Shirley Temple. I'm sure he was selling them dope. It just makes sense. He really had this kind of stealthy quality about him. He didn't seem to care about

Bill Colburn (left) with Eugene Williams, in front of the Jazz Man at 6331 Santa Monica Blvd., early 1940s. (L.A. Institute of Jazz).

anything other than New Orleans jazz. He was a friend of Stuart's and Gene Williams. They all knew each other. They were the cognoscenti.

On February 25, 1946, shortly after the move to 6420, Marili Morden and Nesuhi Ertegun were married, in a small ceremony in the town of Santa Ana, about 30 minutes southeast of Los Angeles. For whatever reason, word about the marriage was kept secret for six months. Selma Ertegun, Nesuhi's last wife, speculated that the delay was because Nesuhi had lost his diplomatic passport when his father died and was unable to travel abroad.

News of the marriage first emerged in August in *The Record Changer* and *Clef* magazines. The note in *The Record Changer* fell under the heading "For Whom the Bells Toll Dept.," erroneously announcing that Ertegun and Morden had married "a year ago." *Clef's* notice was somewhat more positive, noted in a box adjacent to an article Marili wrote about New Orleans jazz under her new married name. Under the title "Congratulations, Marili," the announcement noted that the marriage "caused confusion and gasps of surprise the world over" and that the two had been married "for some time." Collectors who knew both Marili and Ertegun were probably not shocked since they had run the Jazz Man together for more than a year. Some young collectors, such as jazz critic and producer George Avakian, already suspected that there was more to their relationship than just business.

I first heard of the shop while I was in the army, and when I was discharged on the West Coast in February 1946, I finally was able to visit the shop and meet Marili Morden, who I assume was divorced from Dave Stuart by then. She was living with Nesuhi Ertegun. They made an attractive and enthusiastic couple.

The shop was quite small and so was the stock, which was thoroughly selective. There is no question that the shop was responsible for the rise of traditional jazz on the West Coast. I am always astonished at the indifference in the East toward the movement; I often felt that Nesuhi and I were the only Easterners who understood and appreciated the importance of Lu Watters and Turk Murphy, a real hero who carried the torch for decades afterward.

Even Kid Ory did not fare as well in New York as he should have, particularly as he had an engaging personality, as did Turk.

By 1946, not only had the New Orleans jazz revival exploded, but the Los Angeles record store scene was growing as well. No longer was the Jazz Man the only game in town. Other stores were now thriving, sparked by increasing interest from G.I.s returning from World War II. New labels were issuing records by artists previously recorded by Jazz Man. In February 1945, Seattle radiologist Fred Exner inaugurated his own eponymous record label by recording ragtime pianist Johnny Wittwer and recordings made by Kid Ory in Los Angeles in February. Since Ory did not have an exclusive agreement with Jazz Man, he was free to make records elsewhere. The Exner pressings were promised for release by June. William Russell's American Music label was announced in April, with a series of recordings made by Bunk Johnson in New Orleans as its first releases. Capitol Records announced a series of 40 sides documenting the history of jazz, including new recordings by New Orleans pioneers Nappy Lamare and Zutty Singleton. In the summer, John Steiner revived the old Paramount label, beginning a series of reissues featuring 1920s recordings by blues maven Ma Rainey. In 1946, independent labels featuring New Orleans jazz included Disc, King Jazz, Jubilee, Swan, Century, Pacific, Mirror, and Tournament. Older labels, such as Commodore, were also releasing discs, both new and reissues, of New Orleans-geared material, including a series of piano solos by Jelly Roll Morton.

Back from the war, Lu Watters had reunited the Yerba Buena Jazz Band and returned to his old haunt, the Dawn Club, with a gala opening on March 1, 1946. (Ertegun had reviewed their first performance in the April edition of *The Record Changer*.) On April 15, Watters began a series of recording sessions for his own West Coast label, which would continue until the following February.

The Jazz Man was also getting competition from new collector-oriented record stores that had opened up. The first of these was the Tempo Music Shop at 5946 Hollywood Blvd., which advertised both jazz and folk music, a large stock of collectors' items, and "authentic imports." A small ad for this shop appeared in the September 1945 issue of *The Record Changer.* A year later, the Music Den, at 2133 Sunset Blvd. toward downtown Los Angeles, opened with an auction listing in *The Record Changer*.

Late in 1946, a young collector and photojournalist named Ray Avery (1920–2002) moved from Golden, Colorado, to Big Bear Lake, California. Avery would become a much-admired photographer of jazz performers as well as a respected collector of jazz 78s. In February 1947, Avery opened the Record Shack at 11800 Wilshire Blvd. in Los Angeles. Specializing in mail orders, this store advertised not only jazz records, but swing, popular, and classical items as well. By 1948, it was advertising itself as the "Southern California Headquarters for Vinylite Jazz Re-Issues." On June 1, 1948, Avery moved the shop to 7227 Beverly Blvd. and renamed it the Record Roundup. His next move was to 1630 La Cienega Blvd. Avery's best-known store was Rare Records in Glendale, which he operated until the 1990s.

In September 1948, another Los Angeles jazz venue opened, run by New York émigré Louis Lewin, whose Lewin Record Outlet at 5401 Hollywood Blvd. advertised "the best in jazz, swing, popular, and all your old favorites."

Record shops specializing in jazz were now popping up all over the country, not just in Los Angeles. In San Francisco, the return of Lu Watters inspired a new shop in Oakland. The Yerba Buena Music Shop, located at 5721 Grove Street, was run by another female entrepreneur, Vivian Boarman (1914–1982). The store distributed not only the new Watters records on the West Coast label but recordings on Exner and other independent imprints as well, including out-of-print items. The Jazz Man, which started out as California's only collector's shop, now had plenty of competition.

Ad for Jazz Distribution *and blurb for the Jazz Man Record Shop in the May 1946 issue of* The Jazz Record.
(Courtesy Steven Lasker)

CRESCENT
RECORDS

"THE BEST IN NEW ORLEANS JAZZ ON HIGH FIDELITY RECORDINGS"

Announces

Two Sensational New Records
by

KID ORY'S CREOLE JAZZ BAND

CRS 5   Do What Ory Say *
         Careless Love *

CRS 6   Ory's Creole Trombone
         Original Dixieland One-Step

Mutt Carey, Trumpet; Kid Ory, Trombone; Darnell Howard, Clarinet; Buster
Wilson, Piano; Bud Scott, Guitar; Ed Garland, Bass; Minor Hall, Drums.

*Omer Simeon, Clarinet.

Also Available

KID ORY'S CREOLE JAZZ BAND

CRS 1   South — Creole Song
CRS 2   Blues For Jimmy — Get Out Of Here
CRS 3   Maryland — Oh Didn't He Ramble
CRS 4   Down Home Rag — 1919

LIST ONE DOLLAR EACH PLUS TAXES

Order From Your Dealer—He Has Them or Can Obtain Them From

JAZZ MAN RECORD SHOP

6420 SANTA MONICA BOULEVARD   HOLLYWOOD 38, CALIFORNIA

Ad for Crescent Records releases in the August 1946 issue of The Jazz Record.
(Courtesy Steven Lasker)

Nesuhi and Marili Ertegun addressed some of these new competitors by promoting their new company, Jazz Distribution. A full-page ad in the April 1946 issue of *The Record Changer* advertised two new releases on the Circle label by drummer Baby Dodds. In May, this was followed by two reissues by blues singer Bertha "Chippie" Hill.

The last of the eight Kid Ory Crescent releases were announced in November 1946. Shortly after this, Nesuhi Ertegun purchased the Jazz Man record label from Dave Stuart. Stuart had remarried and was moving to Paris to start a business buying and selling antique books. In January 1947, Ertegun redesigned the Jazz Man label to match Crescent's forest green color. The old Jazz Man logo (now printed above the center hole instead of on either side of it) and label details remained, but the new records were pressed on lighter, quieter material than the noisy, heavier original issues. Lu Watters was more popular than ever, having resumed his regular gigs at the Dawn Club in downtown San Francisco. The Watters sides on Jazz Man 1 through 7 were the first releases announced on the newly redesigned label. These were followed by other releases by Watters, Bunk Johnson, and Jelly Roll Morton.

A few years later, Ertegun struck a deal with Tom Cundall, a traditional jazz fan living in London, to issue selected Jazz Man titles on 78s in England, where the New Orleans revival had now spread. Cundall used the Jazz Man label design and masters, but changed the color scheme of the label to silver print on a bright yellow background. In place of the shop's address, Cundall printed his own (146 Broadhurst Gardens, in West Hampstead). At least three releases have been identified: Jazz Man 1 and 2 by Lu Watters and Jazz Man 22 by Kid Ory's Creole Jazz Band.

After acquiring the Jazz Man label from Stuart, Ertegun saw no further need to continue the Crescent label and retired it, after issuing eight discs by Kid Ory. Ertegun's first new releases on Jazz Man were three discs of piano solos by Seattle-based ragtime pianist Johnny Wittwer (1920–

Jazz Man

RECORDS

Available For Immediate Delivery

Lu Watters' Yerba Buena Jazz Band

JM 1 MAPLE LEAF RAG
BLACK & WHITE RAG (Piano Solo)

JM 2 MEMPHIS BLUES
IRISH BLACK BOTTOM

JM 3 MUSKRAT RAMBLE
SMOKEY MOKES

JM 4 ORIGINAL JELLY ROLL BLUES
AT A GEORGIA CAMP MEETING

JM 5 CAKE WALKING BABIES*
RIVERSIDE BLUES*

JM 6 TIGER RAG*
COME BACK SWEET PAPA*

JM 7 FIDGETY FEET*
TEMPTATION RAG (Piano Solo)

Lu Watters, Cornet; Bob Scobey, Trumpet; Turk Murphy, Trombone; Ellis
Horne, Clarinet; Wally Rose, Piano; Clancy Hayes, Russ Bennett, Banjos;
Dick Lammi or Squire Girsbeck*, Tuba; Bill Dart, Drums.

LIST: $1.00 EACH, PLUS TAXES

YOUR DEALER HAS THEM OR CAN GET THEM

FROM

THE JAZZ MAN RECORD SHOP
6100 Santa Monica Blvd.
Hollywood 38, California

Nesuhi Ertegun's redesigned Jazz Man label, January 1947.

The British edition of Jazz Man, early 1950s.

1993), which were issued on Jazz Man 18, 19, and 20. Announced in June 1947, the Wittwer sides were recorded in San Francisco in December 1945. Wittwer had most recently played as an intermission pianist at a Kid Ory gig held at Ace Cain's Café in Hollywood in May.

Pianist Johnny Wittwer with Dick Lammi, bass, c. 1945.

Ertegun made regular talent scouting trips to the Bay Area, and although Lu Watters now had his own label, Ertegun became good friends with Watters trombonist Turk Murphy, who would start his own band later that year.

A few months later, Ertegun re-pressed the eight Kid Ory Crescent discs on Jazz Man, utilizing the catalog numbers 21 through 28. (These corresponded to the old Crescent catalog numbers 1 through 8.)

In August 1947, Ertegun was announced as the new editor of *The Record Changer.* The magazine's publisher, Gordon Gullickson, wanted to take advantage of the West Coast's domination of the New Orleans jazz revival, so for the next several months, Ertegun and art director Gene Deitch assembled the editorial material for each month's issue in Hollywood and then shipped it to Washington for publication. In working on the magazine, Deitch was often invited up to the Erteguns' apartment, located over the record shop at 6420.

I was eventually enough accepted by this ethereal couple to be invited to their upstairs apartment hideaway for an occasional dinner, and was hypnotized by its exotic atmosphere, with what then would be called pornographic artwork on the walls... more properly, erotic graphics. In those days, they could have been arrested for that stuff!

Portraits of musicians decorate Nesuhi Ertegun's living room in this photograph. Note the turntable with a Jazz Man 78 on it. (Courtesy Selma Ertegun)

By then, I was working with them on promotion of the shop, and did at least two or more full-page ads featuring my drawings of the shop, with caricatures of both Marili and Nesuhi.

The first ad appears in the August 1947 issue. In keeping with the elegance of the shop's front room, the ad was titled "For Cats of Distinction" and explained that Jazz Man Records were found wherever smart collectors gather. Deitch's drawing shows the immaculately dressed "Cat" lounging in a chair, gripping a 78.

Ertegun's regular editorial column was headed by a Deitch drawing of a windup Victrola spelling out Ertegun's name in abstract geometric shapes. By this time, Deitch had become heavily influenced by the work of legendary illustrator Jim Flora, who worked for Columbia Records in the early 1940s. Deitch's Jazz Man drawings often featured the scattered, shapeless blotches, stars, and squiggles that Flora called "plewds and briffits," which Deitch used to signify the Cat's "fervid, fanatic brain."

Ertegun's first editorial proclaimed an end to the magazine's printing of "obscurantist quarrels between critics." He also encouraged an expansion of the magazine's previous concentration on traditional jazz, announcing that "intelligent praise of all kinds of jazz," including bebop, would be forthcoming.

The September issue furthered Ertegun's loosening definition of jazz. The inside front-cover ad for the shop announced a more "broadminded" policy of now stocking records by forward-thinking jazz men like Benny Goodman and Dizzy Gillespie, but none yet by swingmeister Tommy

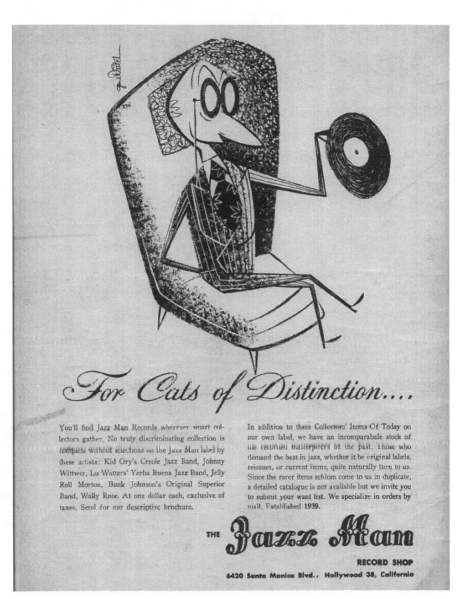

(Used by permission of Gene Deitch.)

Dorsey. (Deitch's illustration shows the Cat telling a collector to straighten his tie before entering the Jazz Man, but advises him not to ask for Dorsey records.)

Ertegun had followed his plan wisely. Dave Stuart ran the Jazz Man as an eclectic business, focusing solely on a narrow range of traditional jazz recordings. His wife, Marili Morden, shared his love for New Orleans jazz, but was also a fan of blues artists like Bessie Smith and her protégé, T-Bone Walker. Although Ertegun also favored traditional jazz, and wrote articles and lectured about the subject often, he was not blind to the more contemporary developments of the music that began showing up after World War II. After marrying Marili, Ertegun decided that in order to survive against the competition of the new stores popping up in the Los Angeles area, he needed to expand the scope of the Jazz Man's stock. Although Jazz Man Records recorded nothing but traditional jazz, Ertegun had been expanding his own personal horizons about other forms of jazz, including the hot new trend, bebop. This knowledge would pay off in later years, after he left the Jazz Man and went to work for his brother Ahmet at Atlantic Records.

In his editorial, Ertegun described his return to the Bay Area (via California Route 99) to revisit the region's jazz scene. By this time, the Dawn Club had been shuttered due to an insurmountable tax debt, and Lu Watters had subsequently opened his own club, Hambone Kelly's, across the bay in El Cerrito, just north of Berkeley. The region was bubbling with musical activity by a variety of bands, which included two schizoid groups called the Frisco Jazz Band.

While in the Bay Area, Ertegun visited the Yerba Buena Music Shop in Oakland, and joined Turk Murphy at Oakland's Rey Theatre (driving there in Murphy's Airflow Chrysler) where they saw the 1929 Photophone short *St. Louis Blues,* starring Bessie Smith. On the way to the theater, Murphy told Ertegun that he had designed and built a special three-level bandstand for the group to perform on at Hambone Kelly's. The club's

"All right now—straighten your tie, try to look like an old collector, and for heaven's sake don't ask if they have any Tommy Dorsey!"

We're really very broadminded about jazz, whatever you may have heard. Of course we carry King Oliver and Kid Ory, but we carry Benny Goodman and Dizzy Gillespie, too. And for all we know, some of our best customers buy Tommy Dorsey (but not from us). You don't have to be an old collector to deal with us because our years of experience enable us to offer all our records at set prices; you won't be competing with experienced buyers because it's first come, first served. It isn't necessary to get all dressed up to

buy a record from us, either. Just put on any old thing and write us a note, enclosing your want list. Our mail order department will take care of your needs promptly and efficiently. Shipments are sent by Railway Express, carefully packed and fully insured, COD orders preferred, no packing charges. So if you're interested in jazz books, magazines, photographs or records, (new, used, originals, reissues), the Jazz Man Record Shop is just what you're looking for. Established 1939.

THE **Jazz Man**

RECORD SHOP

6420 Santa Monica Blvd., Hollywood 38, California

The following pages show four ads drawn and designed by Gene Deitch during his association with Nesuhi and Marili Ertegun and the Jazz Man Record Shop. The ads appeared inside the front cover of four successive issues of The Record Changer *(September - December 1947) and include Deitch's caricature of Nesuhi Ertegun (Used by permission of Gene Deitch).*

"AH SMOKE *Jazz • Man's* . . .

. . . AND AH'VE SMOKED
EM FOAH YEAHS!"

AH LIKE THAT FINER, THAT MILDER, THAT NATURALLY AGED . . .

JAZZ MAN MUSIC

Yes, experts agree that for a mellower, a finer record in every way, look for the JAZZ MAN label. More students, more business men, more housewives are discovering for themselves that Jazz Man Records add that important lift to their listening pleasure. They are easier on your ears, too, say 7 out of 10 specialists. Better shellac, deeper grooves, finer artists combine to produce a rounder, firmer record which brings the best in jazz right into your own home. So after a hard day, light up your phonograph and spin a Jazz Man.

THE JAZZ MAN RECORD SHOP
6420 Santa Monica Boulevard • Hollywood 38 • California

THE CAT

"GAD! AND WITH THE ORIGINAL COBWEBS STILL INTACT!"

Time was when a trip to the nearest junk man or salvage shop was rewarded with a stack of old Okehs and Gennetts. But those good old days, like all good old days, had their disadvantages too. How many valuable items were passed up because pseudonyms were unrecognized? How many thousands of records were ploughed through to turn up one cracked Boyd Senter? How many cratchety old custodians thought that you ought to buy the whole lot of 10,000 discs at the original list price just to get the few you wanted? How many dollars were spent for bad records on the chance that they might be worthwhile?

You don't have to go through that any more, and you can still get those rare items you want. Fine clean copies

of rare items are in stock here at all times. You don't even have to leave your easy chair to add to your collection. All you have to do is write us a letter, enclosing your want list. We'll do the rest. Our packing is perfect, and at no extra charge. Our grading is precise, and guaranteed to satisfy you. Our mail

order service is available to all jazz collectors anywhere in the United States, Canada, South America, Sweden, Switzerland and South Africa, among others. We have happy customers in all these countries. Why not let us show you that the good old days couldn't compare with the present?

THE *Jazz Man*

RECORD SHOP
6420 Santa Monica Blvd., Hollywood 38, California

"H'm! Maybe I shouldn't give Sam an original Morton; he only gave me a reissue last Christmas!"

previous tenant had been stripper Sally Rand, who had decorated the club's walls with phosphorescent murals of nudes. Murphy explained that though the murals were painted over several times, at night, the nude images could still be seen, so the opening of the club was delayed another week, until June 13, 1947.

Ertegun's reign as editor for *The Record Changer* gave the magazine a decidedly West Coast slant. In October 1947, Marili wrote an article called "Collecting Hot: 1927–1947" in which she discussed how collectible jazz records were acquired. In the article, she traced the history of scholarly studies of jazz, which began in the late 1920s. She cited four jazz authorities existing as of 1928, which included college professors at Harvard, Princeton, and Yale. According to Marili, "junking" began in the early 1930s, thanks in part to nostalgic articles about early jazz in *The Saturday Evening Post* and *Esquire*. She then detailed the pioneering jazz record stores: New York's HRS and Commodore shops and, of course, the Jazz Man in Hollywood. *The HRS Rag,* the first American jazz magazine for collectors, began in 1938, followed by *Jazz Information* in 1939.

The December 1947 issue of *The Record Changer* included a Deitch drawing of The Cat in the front room of the Jazz Man, musing over his Christmas list, while a bug-eyed Ertegun watches. Opposite the cartoon was an ominous announcement stating that Gordon Gullickson had sold the magazine to advertising manager Bill Grauer, Jr., who moved the magazine's offices to New York City, eventually phasing Ertegun out entirely. (With the February 1948 issue, Ertegun's title was changed to West Coast Editor.) Even more ominous for traditional jazz fans was a feature article by Tadd Dameron titled "The Case for Modern Music: An Originator of Be-bop Tells How It Started and What It's All About."

In the meanwhile, noise relating to a pay dispute between James C. Petrillo's AFM and the record industry was reaching a cacophonous level. Petrillo, who had previously paralyzed the record industry with a long, drawn-out strike during World War II, was now planning another. A strike on recordings featuring union musicians was to take place on January 1, 1948, and record companies were scrambling to get to studios to start stockpiling recordings as they had done six years earlier. Nesuhi Ertegun followed suit by scheduling two last-minute sessions for Jazz Man. The first took place in Hollywood on Christmas Eve, 1947, featuring four sides by Pete Daily's Rhythm Kings, a popular Los Angeles revival group led by its trumpet-playing leader and including clarinetist Rosy McHargue. The band, which featured the traditional five-man lineup of the Original Dixieland Jazz Band (cornet, clarinet, trombone, piano, and drums), had been enjoying an uninterrupted run at Club Hangover on Vine Street since the previous August. Daily's band played orchestrated arrangements by McHargue rather than the freewheeling, improvised sessions of the more traditional bands. Daily and McHargue made sure to include obscure and attractive tunes, which made for a refreshing change from the same old standards played by many other bands. The Daily session resulted in two more 78 rpm singles, which were released as Jazz Man 29 and 30. McHargue wrote a rousing instrumental in honor of the Erteguns' shop called "Jazz Man Strut." The other titles were "Sobbin' Blues," "Yelping Hound Blues" (which McHargue took from a Louisiana Five record) and the Original Dixieland Jazz Band standard "Clarinet Marmalade." In the July 1948 issue of *The Record Changer,* George Avakian raved about the Daily discs, calling them "top-drawer Dixieland by one of the best white Dixieland groups jazz has ever known."

One week later, Ertegun went to San Francisco to supervise a session by his pal Turk Murphy, who had recently left Lu Watters' band to start his own group, the Bay City Stompers. The session took place on New Year's Eve, one day before the Petrillo strike would begin. Murphy's first effort as a band leader included six titles, four of which were issued as Jazz Man 31 and 32. The band featured other expatriates from Watters' groups,

Pete Daily's Rhythm Kings at Club Hangover on Vine Street, 1948. Left to right: Warren Smith, trombone; Pete Daily, cornet; George Defebaugh, drums; Skippy Anderson, piano; Rosy McHargue, clarinet.

The Erteguns have drinks with Pete Daily's Rhythm Kings in a break between sets at Club Hangover, c. 1948. Left to right: Warren Smith, Nesuhi Ertegun, Rosy McHargue, Marili Ertegun, Pete Daily, George Defebaugh, and Skippy Anderson (Courtesy Selma Ertegun).

Turk Murphy

including Bob Scobey on trumpet, Bob Helm on clarinet, Burt Bales on piano, and Harry Mordecai on banjo. The Murphy band was noteworthy for the absence of a drummer, however, the recordings pulsed with rhythm and drums were not missed. The four titles included Papa Charlie Jackson's "Shake That Thing," W.C. Handy's "Yellow Dog Blues," Clarence Williams and Clarence Johnson's "Kansas City Man Blues," and a Murphy original, "Brother Lowdown." In his autobiography, Murphy recalled that the session ran smoothly:

I think there was some cause for hurrying these records through in order to beat the deadline. We did a couple more tunes besides what was issued. We did "Willie the Weeper" for one, but Nesuhi Ertegun, who ran the session, didn't like the tune "Willie the Weeper," so that wasn't up for issue. There was another tune which I can't remember; there were six tunes in total.

I remember when the four sides came out. It really electrified people in the Bay Area. It was a departure from what we had been used to with Lu Watters, and yet everybody in the group had worked with Lu at Hambone's. It was lighter, with no bass, it was a lighter sounding band and this was what you might say the format of our band has been ever since. Because, economically speaking, we couldn't go on with an eight-piece band that Lu Watters had specified. There is no way you can work with that many pieces.

We went the opposite way and worked with five and got a plausible sound. It was partly the way Bales played piano at that time. If you listen carefully to the record, you will find that Bales was playing a very full piano.

Like the Daily discs, the Murphy sides on Jazz Man garnered a rave review from *The Record Changer.* Murphy, like Watters, was lauded for songs performed in the traditional style, and his own composition, "Brother Lowdown," was highlighted as the standout side of the four.

The April 1948 issue of *The Record Changer* included another Gene Deitch Jazz Man cartoon, this time featuring a caricature of a school-marmish Marili Morden, angrily glaring at the Cat, who is peering over stacks of Louis Armstrong OKehs, inquiring, "Is that ALL the Louie's you have?" The ad was repeated in the May issue, but that was the end of Deitch's series of Jazz Man ads and also Nesuhi Ertegun's reign as editor of the magazine.

(Used by permission of Gene Deitch.)

Also in that issue, Ertegun wrote his first article about a non-New Orleans musician: a profile of saxophonist Benny Carter. By the next month, Bill Grauer's transformation of the magazine was complete, with record reviews of mainstream performers like Peggy Lee and Les Paul sharing space with beboppers Dizzy Gillespie and Sonny Berman, as well as the usual releases of traditional New Orleans stylists.

In 1947, Nesuhi Ertegun's brother Ahmet borrowed $10,000 from his family dentist and, with partner Herb Abramson, started a new label which he called Atlantic Records. Ahmet had already tried, and failed, with two New York labels, Quality and Jubilee, before starting Atlantic. Its earliest recordings included a mixture of releases of modern jazz (Boyd Raeburn, Eddie Safranski), blues (Joe Morris, Tiny Grimes), and vocals (Bob Howard, Melrose Colbert). The AFM strike interrupted its progress, but coming out on the other side of the strike, Atlantic scored with its first national hit: Stick McGhee's rocking blues hybrid, "Drinkin' Wine Spo-Dee-O-Dee." On the West Coast, Nesuhi and Marili Ertegun were still managing the shop, but the Jazz Man label was stagnating. After the two last-minute sessions of 1947 by Pete Daily and Turk Murphy, Jazz Man Records would remain dormant for more than two years. There would only be one more session with Ertegun at the helm.

It is not known why the ambitious Ertegun did not do more recording sessions during this period. In addition to managing the shop and the label, he was now teaching "A Survey of Jazz" two nights a week at UCLA, the first accredited college course on jazz in the nation. (In late 1948, the Yerba Buena Music Shop's Vivian Boarman taught a similar course at the University of California at Berkeley, but it is not known whether or not it was accredited.)

In addition, the record industry itself was changing. The 45 rpm and 33 1/3 long-playing record formats were battling each other for their share of the marketplace, but Jazz Man did not get involved, preferring to stay with the increasingly antiquated 78.

Major changes were in store for the Jazz Man as the 1950s began, but little did anyone realize how those changes would affect the lives of Marili and Nesuhi Ertegun.

About The Author

Nesuhi Ertegun has been interested in jazz since 1932. Of Turkish birth, he has traveled all over Europe and the United States in search of jazz and authentic information on its origin and development. He has heard in person just about every important musician of two continents, from Duke Ellington in London in 1933 to Lu Watters in San Francisco in 1946.

Ertegun has contributed to several jazz publications, gave a course on jazz in Washington, D. C., has lectured in many other cities. Last summer he spoke on the historical background of jazz at the Pasadena Institute of Art.

Chapter Fifteen

Bootleg Blues

In the spring of 1949, a new traditional jazz group burst onto the Los Angeles music scene. In 1945, Ward Kimball, an animator and trombonist who worked at the Walt Disney Studios in Burbank, began leading informal noontime jam ssessions with other employees from the animation department. Eventually, the musicians were hired for a dance, calling themselves the San Gabriel Valley Blue Blowers. On New Year's Eve, 1948, they showed up at Roy Harte's Drum City on Santa Monica Blvd. (not far from the Jazz Man), dressed in bright red shirts, black pants, white suspenders, and wearing firemen's helmets. Bob Kirstein, a writer at Paramount Pictures, told a fellow writer about the band, and when the group was soon engaged to play a dance at a country club, Kirstein and his friend were there. The friend turned out to be Lester Koenig. After hearing the band play, Koenig decided to start his own record company, which he called Good Time Jazz. Kimball's group was called the Firehouse Five Plus Two in honor of Kimball's affinity for antique fire engines.

The first Good Time Jazz session took place on May 13, 1949, with four titles recorded. The September issue of *The Record Changer* was dominated by the Firehouse Five Plus Two, the back cover ad featuring a whimsical drawing by Ward Kimball. The inside front cover featured an ad for Rampart Records, Good Time Jazz's new East Coast distributor. Inside

Lester Koenig

Back cover of The Record Changer, *September 1949.*
(Used by permission of Richard Hadlock)

were a five-page story and a rave review by George Avakian of the group's first two 78 releases. Avakian called the FF+2 "the happiest band I have heard in a long, long time."

Before long, Good Time Jazz was dominating the traditional jazz marketplace. By the end of the year, it had amassed 10 single releases, including four by Turk Murphy. These were augmented in 1950 by 22 more. One year after its debut, Good Time Jazz had 32 singles on the market, as many as Jazz Man had released in eight years.

Koenig also took advantage of the new technology that resulted in Columbia Records pioneering the 33 1/3 long-playing record (1948) and RCA Victor the 45 rpm disc (1949). In addition to 78 rpm releases, Koenig issued 10-inch LPs as well as 45 rpm singles and extended play records. While Jazz Man stubbornly stuck to its 78 rpm catalog, Good Time Jazz, skillfully and masterfully directed by Koenig, was outdistancing not only

Jazz Man, but every other label producing traditional jazz on all three speeds.

In addition to dominating the traditional jazz market, Koenig started his own distribution firm, California Record Distributors. Beginning in 1951, Koenig signed 13 independent labels, including Jazz Man, to exclusive deals throughout Southern California.

During the time Koenig issued his first 32 discs, Jazz Man produced just two. On April 29, 1950, a group led by veteran clarinetist Darnell Howard (1895–1966), cut four sides at a studio in San Francisco. Darnell Howard's Frisco Footwarmers featured three former members of Lu Watters' band: Bob Scobey on trumpet, Clancy Hayes, who had switched from banjo to guitar, and Squire Girsback, now playing string bass instead of tuba. The band was rounded out by pianist Burt Bales, who had played with Watters after the Jazz Man sessions, trombonist Jack Buck, and drummer Gordon Edwards. The four sides were all New Orleans standards: W.C. Handy's "St. Louis Blues," Tony Jackson's "Pretty Baby," Shelton Brooks' "Some of These Days," and the King Oliver/Louis Armstrong classic "Dippermouth Blues." On the latter record, Nesuhi Ertegun made his vocal debut, yelling out the ubiquitous "Oh, play that thing!" prior to the final rideout chorus. The session was the last supervised by Nesuhi Ertegun for Jazz Man.

Ertegun was growing more and more disaffected with the Jazz Man Record Shop. No longer the only collectors shop in town, the Jazz Man was losing customers to well-heeled, better-serviced rivals like Lewin's Record Outlet and Ray Avery's Record Roundup. The Dixieland revival had been given a shot of adrenalin by the success of the Firehouse Five Plus Two and with Good Time Jazz and other labels flourishing, Jazz Man was being left behind. Even the reissue business was dominated by other labels, brazen pirate companies that were dubbing rare, vintage 78s onto inexpensive plastic and vinyl pressings without obtaining permission from the owners of the masters. *The Record Changer* blamed this development entirely on

Trombonist Julian Lane (left) and drummer Monk Hazel (right) visit Marili Ertegun at the Jazz Man Record Shop, 6420 Santa Monica Blvd., c. 1949 (Courtesy the New Orleans Jazz Club Collection at Louisiana State Museum).

the major record companies, which had "shirked a responsibility" to reissue their own valuable masters, leading to the proliferation of bootleg labels such as Biltmore, Creole, and Jazz Classics. One label, in brash defiance of the majors, even called itself Jolly Roger after the notorious flag displayed on pirate ships. (In a startling and controversial development, it was revealed in the November 1951 issue of *The Record Changer* that Jolly Roger's pressings were being manufactured by none other than RCA Victor itself, the sworn enemy of disc piracy.)

Another independent label, Folkways Records, was formed in 1948 by Moe Asch, a New York-based record producer who had started two previous labels, Asch and DISC. Focusing on folk, ethnic, and spoken word collections, Asch believed that the public had the right to hear music that the major labels refused to issue on their own. As a result, he released an LP of dubs from RCA Victor's out-of-print *Dust Bowl Ballads* by Woody Guthrie. When RCA refused to reissue it themselves or grant Folkways a license to do so, Moe Asch and Guthrie agreed that the recordings should be made available anyway, so Asch released them on a Folkways LP. Despite discovering the piracy, RCA permitted Asch to continue selling the records without penalty.

In 1951, Folkways released a 10-LP set called *History of Jazz*, edited by *Jazzmen* author Frederic Ramsey. Volume 3 of the series (FJ-2803) presented music from New Orleans and included "Down by the River" by Bunk Johnson's Original Superior Band, which had been issued on Jazz Man 8 in 1942. When the Folkways record came out, the Erteguns were furious, since Asch had not even bothered to contact them to get a license or ask permission to issue the track.

In the May 1951 issue of *The Record Changer,* a letter from Marili Ertegun appeared in the "Let That Foul Air Out" column, reserved for letters to the editor. In her letter, Marili annnounced that Jazz Man was suing Folkways for using the Johnson master without permission. She went on to say that Folkways was using records still available on the parent labels, citing Jazz Man's Bunk Johnson side (which was still in print) as well as another track by Kid Rena on Rudi Blesh's Circle label:

This record has been in print ever since it was first issued in 1942. One of the biggest distributors in New York handles Jazz Man records and we have distributors in other principal cities. We stand ready to supply stores and individuals in any area where they cannot easily get our records

Marili Ertegun with trumpeter Joseph "Sharkey" Bonano, behind the Jazz Man at 6420 Santa Monica Blvd., c. 1949 (Courtesy the New Orleans Jazz Club Collection at Louisiana State Museum).

locally. It is therefore obvious that any of our Jazz Man records, including the Bunk in question, is readily available at all times to any customer who wants them. It follows therefore that we are not guilty of withholding any of our records from anyone who might want to purchase them. Therefore, what service is Folkways Records and Service Corporation doing for anyone but themselves?

Marili adamantly made it clear that Folkways' intent was "to exploit for gain at no cost to themselves the fruit of the thought and labor of others." A similar letter was printed from Blesh, who joined the Erteguns in a two-headed lawsuit against Asch.

In an editorial in that same issue, *The Record Changer's* editor-publisher Bill Grauer, Jr. concurred with Marili and Blesh:

Until recently, the private re-issuers were very carefully limiting themselves to material that was not in the current catalogues. Almost all of their sides were comparatively rare items. But it has now come to our attention that there are exceptions to this honorable rule. We now seem faced with a situation in which currently available jazz records have been picked up by a firm other than the original producer and being included on an anthology-type release.

Whether or not this is legal we frankly do not know. However, we do feel, as does Mrs. Ertegun, that this kind of practice, if allowed to go unchecked, could precipitate an utterly chaotic situation in the entire recording industry. It could be of inestimable harm to the jazz world in particular.

If we are to have a continuing recording program carried on by the little companies, like Circle and Jazz Man, who almost literally starve to keep the art alive, these labels must at least have the knowledge that they will be protected against competition of this sort.

By the time the June issue of *The Record Changer* came out, cooler heads prevailed and the matter appeared to be settled. In an editorial titled

"More Bootleg Blues," Grauer revealed that neither Circle nor Jazz Man was pursuing legal action against Folkways and that Moe Asch had offered a cash settlement to the Erteguns for the Johnson side, which they accepted. According to *Down Beat,* the Erteguns were "very pleased and believed that an important precedent had been established as far as fighting the evils of bootlegging was concerned." In addition, Folkways promised that the pirated material would be discontinued and to never again lay a hand on the Jazz Man catalog without permission. (Despite this assurance, the Johnson side remained in FJ-2803, even through subsequent repackagings.)

Rudi Blesh, who had not been consulted when the Erteguns settled with Folkways, had no choice but to settle also. An incensed Grauer, however, was not satisfied. He admonished the Erteguns for not challenging Folkways' actions in court and selfishly settling their case themselves. In settling with Asch, Grauer claimed that the Erteguns legalized and thereby condoned Folkways' actions. But *The Record Changer* maintained its defense of upstart "reissue" labels pirating what they considered to be abandoned masters by the major record companies and continued running advertisements and printed reviews of releases by the pirate labels.

The bootlegging firestorm did have a positive effect, however, on the major labels. Columbia Records stepped up its long-dormant reissue program by releasing a four-disc series documenting Louis Armstrong's classic recordings of the 1920s, produced and annotated by George Avakian. In a few years, RCA Victor initiated its own reissue label, which it called "X," and mined its own vaults for previously out-of-print recordings and alternate takes.

As for the Erteguns, the entire bootlegging debacle only added to the stress they were feeling as they slowly drifted apart. More and more, Nesuhi involved himself with his outside activities; he was now teaching two jazz courses at UCLA while Marili continued to run the shop. Each wanted out, and in 1952, they would get their wish.

Chapter Sixteen

A Street of Mixed Emotions

Unlike many of the record collectors who frequented the Jazz Man, Nesuhi Ertegun had interests other than traditional jazz. He listened to classical music, was a devotée of paintings and Surrealist art, enjoyed visiting art galleries, discussing subjects such as philosophy, oriental tonality, and politics, and watching and playing sports, especially table tennis, a game in which he was extremely accomplished and competitive. After ten years of running the shop, Marili had grown from a 22-year-old ingénue into a 32-year-old woman. By now, she was burned out, and it was taking a toll on her mental well-being and her marriage. Her ambitious husband, however, felt stifled because of his obligations to his wife, the shop, and Jazz Man Records.

In 1951, Lester Koenig, who had been a writer and assistant to film producer William Wyler at Paramount Pictures, was blacklisted after refusing to testify before the House Un-American Activities Committee. By that time, Koenig had become a close friend to both Marili and Nesuhi, and with Good Time Jazz flourishing, Koenig, now ousted from the film community, set his sights on his record business as his primary means of support. He started a new label, Contemporary Records, to issue modern jazz and bop recordings. But Koenig still coveted the pioneering sides made by Lu Watters and his Yerba Buena Jazz Band. When he fronted Dave

181

Stuart the money to pay for the Watters sessions, Koenig retained a share of ownership of the masters. After the Watters sides became popular, Stuart was able to buy Koenig out. Now Koenig wanted the masters back, and during 1951, he and Ertegun began discussing a buyout of not only the Watters sides, but the entire Jazz Man catalog. The Erteguns saw Koenig as a means to help them escape the drudgery their lives had become because of the shop.

The deal was struck on November 26, 1951. Koenig agreed to pay the Erteguns $5,500.00 for the 68 issued masters and any alternate takes belonging to Jazz Man Records. A cash down payment of $1,000.00 would be delivered to the Erteguns on January 15, 1952, followed by monthly payments of $500.00 until the amount was paid in full. A special note was made to include an unissued recording of "The Pearls" by Jelly Roll Morton and eight unreleased masters each by pianists Don Ewell and Freddy Shayne. The agreement did not assign ownership of the Jazz Man label to Koenig, only the masters it had recorded, although any existing Jazz Man 78s would not be sold nor distributed. In addition, the Erteguns passed on to Koenig royalties relating to the licensing of Jazz Man titles to three foreign labels: British Jazz Man, Blue Star in France, and Gazell in Sweden.

On January 10, 1952, Nesuhi and Marili formally separated. Nesuhi moved out and rented a comfortable house at 810 ½ N. Orlando Avenue in West Hollywood while Marili remained in the apartment above the record shop at 6420 Santa Monica Blvd. It is not known whether their separation was caused by an emotional distancing of the couple or was merely a reasoned, business-like dissolution relating to the sale of the Jazz Man label.

On January 15, five days after their separation, the Erteguns sent out a letter to customers, distributors, and others on their mailing list, notifying them that Good Time Jazz had acquired all of the masters in the Jazz Man catalog. The letter stated the two catalogs were closely related, presenting an "unbroken story of jazz on the West Coast from 1941 to the present." It

JAZZ MAN RECORD SHOP

6420 SANTA MONICA BLVD. :: HOLLYWOOD 38, CALIFORNIA :: HILLSIDE 1588

January 15, 1952

Dear Friend,

One of the major events of recent years in the field of jazz and records is the sale recently concluded by which the rapidly-expanding Good Time Jazz label acquired all the masters in our own Jazz Man catalogue.

We are particularly happy to see our records issued by GTJ since the two catalogues are closely related, and together present an unbroken story of jazz on the West Coast from 1941 to the present. It was the Watters band in '41 which started the great jazz revival of the Forties, and in turn re-awakened interest throughout the country in such great original New Orleans musicians as Kid Ory and Bunk Johnson, both of whom can be heard at their best in the new Good Time Jazz catalogue, with records made in the period from 1943 to 1946.

It is interesting to note that GTJ's President, Lester Koenig, recorded the famous Jazz Man Lu Watters sides in 1941 & 1942. He has always had a great personal fondness for these records, and plans to re-record them, taking advantage of modern progress in audio-engineering to give them a new and exciting sound.

As these records and other masters by Jelly Roll Morton, Johnny Wittwer, Pete Daily, Turk Murphy and Darnell Howard are issued on all three speeds by GTJ, we are sure you will be anxious to hear and own them, particularly since alternate masters, previously unissued, will be used wherever possible.

Our best wishes go to GTJ for their continued success - meanwhile there is one thing we want to make perfectly clear; while we have sold Jazz Man masters, we still own the Jazz Man Record Shop. Every label that records jazz is represented in our stock, from the majors to the most obscure companies. We stock all the reissues and we have a constant supply of out-of-print originals coming in. We have a fast and efficient mail order service, and local customers will find the store open from noon to 8 P.M. every day except Sunday. You are, as always, welcome to browse to your heart's content.

Sincerely yours,

THE JAZZ MAN RECORD SHOP

Marili & Nesuhi Ertegun

P.S. We stock all the records in the enclosed GTJ catalogue.

Letter to Jazz Man customers and friends, announcing the sale of all Jazz Man masters to Lester Koenig of Good Time Jazz. (Courtesy Concord Jazz) also described Koenig's intention to "re-record" the Watters sides, "taking advantage of modern progress in audio engineering to give them a new and exciting sound." Within a few months, the old Jazz Man sides, cleaned up and remastered, began to appear on quiet vinyl 78s on the Good Time Jazz label. The first 10-inch LPs followed, led by an eight-song reissue of the vaunted Lu Watters sides from December 1941.

        As part of his deal with Koenig, Ertegun agreed to leave the Jazz Man to become Good Time Jazz's promotion and advertising manager. It is possible that Ertegun did not leave the shop immediately and for an undetermined period of time, he helped Marili while also working for Koenig. Some time later that year or early in 1953, Koenig lured Dave Stuart back to the States from his home in Paris to work for Good Time Jazz as well. Stuart's letters to William Russell, which had ceased after his attempt to start a consortium label failed, resumed in November 1953. Stuart had returned to California to supervise the restoration of the Bunk Johnson sides. His letters contained his usual bravado and confidence as he delighted in getting back into the record business:

        Now we are about to reissue that music, all cleaned up and put on tape and transferred to an LP so nice and bright you won't recognize it. "Moose March" and "Weary" and "Panama" and "Bunk's Blues" and "Storyville Blues" and "Down by the River" come on to make your hair stand on end just remembering. And the first two will blow you down, dear Willie. They can't catch the Old Man—never.

        My story is I'm now working for GJT. It's fun. I thought I had the game beat and didn't have to work, but somewhere I must have goofed because I must, and since I must, this couldn't be nicer.

        On August 28, 1952, Marili filed for divorce, using the same attorney who she hired when she divorced Dave Stuart. The divorce papers report that Nesuhi Ertegun, "disregarding his promises and duties of a husband, and in violation of his marital vows and obligations, has treated plaintiff with great and extreme cruelty;" however, there is no evidence that shows that Ertegun had been anything but the gentleman he always was in his public as well as private affairs. Ertegun did not contest the divorce, and on October 1, it was granted. Although Ertegun magnanimously turned over the shop and the Jazz Man record label to his wife, there were no masters left. All existing recordings, issued and unissued, now belonged to Good Time Jazz.

After her divorce, Marili returned to using her maiden name and began looking for a buyer for the shop. It wasn't long before she finally found one.

Albert Eugene Van Court, Jr. was born on February 19, 1922 in Oxnard, California, about an hour's drive northwest from Hollywood. At the time of his marriage, his parents, Albert Van Court, Sr. and the former Miriam Vail, were living in Pasadena. The 1930 census shows that the senior Van Court was an investment banker. During the boom years of the 1920s, the Van Courts took several cruises to Europe and one to Hawaii. They were also well-known for being judges in various dog shows all across the country.

Albert, Jr. attended school at the Catalina Island Boys School, followed by the Phillips Academy in Andover, Massachusetts, and in 1941, graduated from Princeton University. He enlisted in the Navy and served for two years in the Mediterranean and Pacific theatres. When he was released from active duty, he served as an aide and flag lieutenant to Vice Admiral Jesse B. Oldendorf. After his discharge, Van Court enrolled at Harvard University's law school, where he met Patricia Prescott of Holyoke, Massachusetts. The two were married there on September 28, 1946 and planned to make their home in Cambridge while Van Court continued his studies. The marriage, however, did not last long, and the two were divorced in 1948.

Sometime before 1952, Van Court moved to Los Angeles. Nothing is known about how he found the Jazz Man or what his relationship was with Marili Morden, but at some point between the Erteguns' divorce in August 1952 and the middle of 1953, Van Court purchased the shop and the Jazz Man record label. After selling the Jazz Man, Marili left the record business, never to return.

When Van Court took over, he hired a manager to run the Jazz Man while he looked for a less expensive location for the shop. According to Don Gray, then a 20-year-old on the hunt for jazz records, the manager's name during this period was "Red," but he could remember nothing more about him. All Gray knew was that during the six years Van Court owned the Jazz Man, he never managed the shop himself and rarely even appeared on the premises.

The Jazz Man stayed at 6420 Santa Monica Blvd. until the spring of 1954. Meanwhile, Van Court began planning an ambitious schedule of recording and licensing that would result in more records issued on the Jazz Man label in a year's time than had been released in the previous ten.

In 1950, Capitol Records acquired the KHJ radio studios, which were located next door to the Paramount Pictures lot on Melrose Avenue, and opened their own recording studios on the site. Van Court's first recording session took place there on October 26, 1953. The session featured a band led by New Orleans clarinetist George Lewis, who had recorded with Bunk Johnson for Jazz Man back in 1942. Lewis's band featured other veteran musicians, including Avery "Kid" Howard on trumpet, Jim Robinson on trombone, Alton Purnell on piano, Lawrence Marrero on banjo, Alcide "Slow Drag" Pavageau on bass, and Joe Watkins on drums. Although Lewis had made many records since his recording debut with Johnson in 1942, most of his recordings had come from either live concerts or makeshift sessions in empty New Orleans dance halls. For Van Court, this was a valuable opportunity to capture a New Orleans legend in the best possible circumstances, and he and co-producer Wayne Lockwood made sure to allow

George Lewis' Ragtime Band, which recorded for Jazz Man in October 1953.
L-R: Alton Purnell, piano; Alcide "Slow Drag" Pavageau, bass; Lawrence Marrero, banjo; George
Lewis, clarinet; Joe Watkins, drums; Avery "Kid" Howard, trumpet; Jim Robinson, trombone.

Lewis to select the repertoire and direct the band. Lewis, too, was excited to be recording in a professional studio with state-of-the-art equipment and came prepared with some of his best songs.

For the first time, a Jazz Man session was mastered on magnetic tape. The old-fashioned method of cutting records on lacquer discs not only produced inferior sounding masters, but limited their duration to the three-and-a-half-minute capacity of a 10-inch 78 rpm record. With tape, extended recording time was possible and three of the eight sides cut that day exceeded five minutes in length.

The session began tentatively, as an hour was spent positioning the musicians in the studio so that the mike placement could be balanced. The first two songs, "Panama" and Joe Darensbourg's "Lou-Easy-An-I-A," required several takes each due to the musicians' nervousness. Alton Purnell kicked off each song with a brief piano introduction, which helped get the band members going. After this, the band proceeded without any further difficulties.

The third number, the classic flag waver "Ice Cream," got everyone's juices churning in an exciting five-minute-and-forty-five-second jam. Jelly Roll Morton's "Doctor Jazz" was next, taken at a more leisurely tempo

than is usually heard, with a vocal by drummer Joe Watkins. Watkins then sang a rousing version of the spiritual "Ain't Gonna Study War No More," which was listed as "Down By the Riverside." (Lewis had recorded an instrumental version of this number with Johnson at his first Jazz Man session.) Following these two numbers, the band played the requisite New Orleans favorite, "When

George Lewis

the Saints Go Marching In."

The next song proved to be one of the most extraordinary, emotional recordings in the history of jazz. While Lewis and his band were rolling through the session, seated quietly in the back of the studio was veteran blues and jazz singer Monette Moore. Moore had been invited to sing a vocal version of Lewis's signature tune, the evocative "Burgundy Street Blues." In 1944, Lewis was working on the New Orleans docks when a heavy container fell on his chest, almost crushing him. Fortunately, he was rescued in time and convalesced at his home on Burgundy Street in the

French Quarter. When he was well enough to begin playing clarinet again, he asked two of his friends, Lawrence Marrero and Alcide Pavageau, to bring their instruments along and play with him. Joining them was William Russell who brought a portable disc recorder. The trio began improvising on a slow blues melody that Lewis wrote, which Russell named "Burgundy Street Blues." Nearly ten years later, Lewis, Marrero, and Pavageau were together again in Hollywood to record the song, but Lewis wanted some lyrics to go with the melody. Lewis and Marrero provided Moore with notes on what they wanted her to sing, but she had no time to rehearse before the session. Tentatively, she approached the microphone, and while Lewis softly played the melody in the background, accompanied only by his friends Marrero and Pavageau, she spoke, rather than sang, these nostalgic words about a New Orleans of long ago:

The blues were born in New Orleans
They're in the heart of each one that you meet.
Yes, the blues were born in New Orleans
They're in the heart of each one that you meet
Why, they make you laugh and sing, and you'll cry
All the way down Burgundy Street.

You know, on Toulouse and Burgundy
Things may seem to you just a little bit wild, just a little bit wild.
That's on Toulouse and Burgundy
Where, to you, things may seem just a little wild.
But each and everyone is having their fun
Like it should be done, even down to the smallest child.

Now, there's St. Peter Street, Orleans, St. Ann, and then Dumaine.
Yes, beautiful Dumaine.
Let's go back again, St. Peter Street, Orleans, and St. Ann,
And then Dumaine.
Where sometimes joy gives away to sadness
And you'll find many hearts are filled with pain.

Then there's the corner near the Caldonia Club
Where parade bands start and end.
Then on down to Slow Drag's hangout
I mean, sides tumble in.
Yes, near the Caldonia Club
Parade bands start and end
Don't forget Slow Drag's hangout; it's fun, as sides tumble in.
That's what you find when you walk down Burgundy Street.

St. Philip and Burgundy, 'round the corner to St. Claude.
You'll find a small church where one can stop
And rest and thank the Lord
Now as you make the rounds up and down
You'll meet girls with charm and grace
And for the time of your life, whatever you do
Don't forget Johnny Matassie's place
That's the life you'll find
When you walk down Burgundy Street.

Now it's a street of mixed emotions,
Stamps a mem'ry on your heart you'll never lose.
(sings) No, you'll never lose.
Yes, it's a street of mixed emotions
(sings) Stamps a mem'ry on your heart you'll never lose,
So, when you've stayed away too long
Come back to me where you belong
(sings) And we'll walk Burgundy Street with the blues.

As Lewis's last clarinet note faded away, Capitol Records' recording engineer Gene Becker pushed back his chair in the recording booth, opened his studio mike, and said to the musicians, "It's the living end. You'll never do it again. It sends chills down my spine."

The session then ended with the traditional New Orleans spiritual, "Just a Closer Walk With Thee," with Watkins singing the vocal and "Kid"

Monette Moore, one of only two women to have recorded for Jazz Man Records.
(Courtesy the Frank Driggs Collection)

Howard providing spoken obbligatos. Thanks to the extended capacity of recording tape, the band had time to record the traditional second line arrangement of the song, beginning with a slow drag, which was usually played in funeral processions on the way to the cemetery, and concluding at a stepped-up Dixieland tempo, just the way it was played on the way back.

Moving quickly, Van Court got two discs pressed within a few weeks of the session. On November 18, a 78 rpm single of "Doctor Jazz" and "Down By the Riverside" was issued. Van Court decided not to continue the Jazz Man's previous numbering system, which had ended with issue 34 (by Darnell Howard's Frisco Footwarmers), and began a new series that started with 101. The design of the label remained the same, with the green background and "Jazz Man" printed in the Annabelle Matinee font in silver print. But in addition to the standard 10-inch disc (whose price was reduced from $1.00 to $.89), Van Court also released a 12-inch 78, featuring two of the longer songs from the session: "A Closer Walk With Thee" and "Lou-Easy-An-I-A."

But Van Court wasn't done. On Christmas Day, Jazz Man announced the release of its first long-playing record, which was optimistically titled "George Lewis' Ragtime Band, Vol. 1." (Volume 1 would prove to be a misnomer as there would be no further editions.) The LP included six songs from the Lewis session, with Wayne Lockwood writing the liner notes. Although the labels of the two 78 rpm releases displayed the address of the shop, the ten-inch LP only listed a post office box in Hollywood.

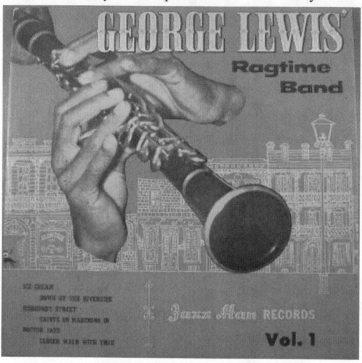

The first Jazz Man 10-inch LP (From the author's collection).

Whenever asked, Lewis said that the Jazz Man session of October 1953 was the best one of his career. With his first session, neophyte producer Albert Van Court continued the legacy of historic sessions recorded on the Jazz Man label. In 1954, other records would follow, and Van Court looked forward to even more successes in the future. But the next 12 months would see the glory years of the Jazz Man as a national force on the traditional jazz scene come to an unexpected and abrupt end.

Chapter Seventeen

Farewell to Hollywood

On March 6, 1954, an article in *Billboard* magazine appeared titled "Talent Array Set by New Jazz Man Diskery on Coast." The article went on to say that "Jazz Man Records, a new Coast indie specializing in the Dixie jazz field, organized here recently with an impressive talent roster to kick off their first wax." No mention was made in the article of Jazz Man's previous rich history under the leadership of Dave Stuart, Marili Morden, and Nesuhi Ertegun. Mentioned as the heads of the label were Albert Van Court, Howard Payne and Bill Hawley, with Rhodes Cook announced as A&R director and Larry Goldberg handling national sales and distribution. Central Record Sales was named as the label's distribution center in Los Angeles and Chatton Distributing Company in Portland. The list of artists slated to record for the label included Pete Daily, Ben Pollack, George Lewis, Octave Crosby, Johnny Lucas, Don Ewell, and Jerry Fuller. (Of these, all except Pollack and Fuller eventually made records for Jazz Man. The Ewell sides remain unreleased.) The *Billboard* article erroneously mentioned that the first Jazz Man release, "Make Love to Me" and "Swanee River," by "Pete Dailey (sic) and His Chicagoans" was already on the market. (The George Lewis session had been released in December.)

In 1954, Jazz Man released eight 78 rpm singles, six ten-inch LPs, and one 45 rpm extended play (EP) disc. Under Nesuhi Ertegun, Jazz Man

193

never took advantage of the new 33 1/3 and 45 rpm formats, but Van Court realized the popularity of these on labels such as Good Time Jazz and set about planning the phasing out of 78 rpm singles on the Jazz Man label in favor of the more durable and increasingly popular formats. LPs were introduced by Columbia Records in 1948 as a means to present uninterrupted long forms of music (i.e. classical). Producers of jazz soon discovered the advantages of the longer-playing format and before long, jam sessions and the *Jazz at the Philharmonic* live concerts began to be issued on 10-inch LPs.

Van Court's next session took place on January 25, 1954 (some sources show January 1) at the Capitol Records studios in Hollywood. Four sides were cut by New Orleans pianist Octave Crosby, who led a group similar to George Lewis's, minus the banjo. Crosby (1898–1972) began his career in 1922 with trumpeter Herb Morand (later with the Harlem Hamfats) and organized his own band shortly afterward. One of the four tunes Crosby recorded for Jazz Man was "Paddock Blues," named for the Paddock Lounge on Bourbon Street, where Crosby served as house band leader.

Crosby had come to Los Angeles with "Papa" Oscar Celestin, who was making his first engagement outside of New Orleans. (Celestin died soon after, in December.) The band that recorded for Jazz Man included Alvin Alcorn on trumpet and Albert Burbank on clarinet, two of New Orleans' most highly regarded musicians. Rounding out the session were Clarence and Spencer Williams's jazz standard, "I

Octave Crosby

Ain't Gonna Give Nobody None o' This Jelly Roll" (simplified on the label as "None of My Jelly Roll") and two flag-wavers: "Gettsyburg March" and "Ting a Ling."

For the next Jazz Man release, issued on April 12, Van Court licensed recordings by pianist Johnny Wittwer and Kid Ory's band which were recorded by Seattle physician Fred Exner for his eponymous record label. (Wittwer and Ory had both previously recorded for Jazz Man.) Van Court issued eight sides from the sessions on a 10-inch LP, which was titled *World Famous Exner Kid Ory–Johnny Wittwer Sessions* (LJ-332). Dr. Exner himself wrote the liner notes. The songs on the LP were the first Jazz Man recordings that were not also issued on Jazz Man 78 rpm single discs.

The Wittwer tracks were trio sides cut at radio station KOL in September 1944, featuring clarinetist Joe Darensbourg and drummer Keith Purvis. The Ory sides were recorded at the C. P. MacGregor studios in Hollywood in February 1945. In a somewhat confusing presentation, Van Court chose to alternate the Wittwer and Ory sides on the record rather than feature one group on one side and one group on the other, as was the custom.

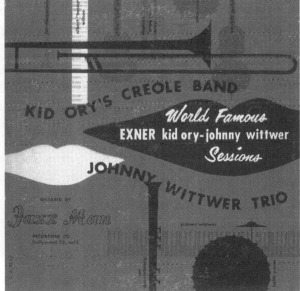

Jazz Man's second 10-inch LP (From the author's collection).

In March, Van Court printed up his first catalog, which announced current releases and forthcoming issues from two sessions held in February. (The two Exner sessions by Wittwer and Ory were inexplicably left out.) The catalog was basically a flyer, folded in half, with one side featuring the listing of releases (current and forthcoming), and prices and a policy statement on the other. The flyer indicated the phasing out of 78 rpm releases, as Jazz Man's emphasis would now be on 10-inch long-playing discs (priced at $3.85) and 45 rpm extended-play ($1.47) or single (89 cents) releases. In addition, the flyer showed signs that Jazz Man was going to broaden its focus beyond traditional New Orleans jazz. In a statement on the back page of the flyer titled "Notes on the Future," Van Court spelled out his ambitious plans for the label:

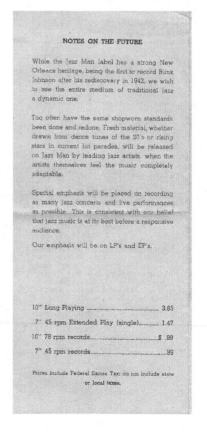

ARTISTS' LISTING

The catalogue is arranged by artists, in alphabetical order.

OCTAVE CROSBY'S ORIGINAL DIXIELAND BAND—A fixture for many years on piano with Papa Celestin at the Paddock Lounge, Crosby recently (Jan. 1954) brought the Celestin band to Southern California for its first engagement outside New Orleans. These recordings feature the outstanding trumpet of Alvin Alcorn and clarinet of Albert Burbank, considered by many authorities the top men on their instruments in New Orleans today.

(102)	None of My Jelly Roll
	Gettysburg March
	10" 78 rpm

(103)	Paddock Blues
	Ting-A-Ling
	10" 78 rpm

PETE DAILY AND HIS CHICAGOANS—One of the biggest sellers in the traditional jazz field while with Capitol records, Pete cut his Jazz Man session in February. In the minds of the band themselves these new sides should command all the attention given such hits as "I Want to Linger" and "South." Particularly outstanding is "Swanee," arranged by the old Bob Crosby trombonist Warren Smith.

(104)	Closer Walk With Thee
	Quaker Town
	10" 78 rpm
	(Available April, 1954)

(105)*	Make Love to Me
	Swanee River
	10" 78 rpm

* Indicates availability on 45 rpm single

(The Lucas and Daily Singles will be combined on LP May 1954)

GEORGE LEWIS' RAGTIME BAND—Rated by *Look* the most authentic Dixieland band in the country, George has carried on with the original members of the Bunk Johnson group of the early 40's. Though often recorded, the band freely admits that their Jazz Man sides are their finest. Highlights are original lyrics for George's now famous Burgundy Street Blues, composed jointly by George, banjo man Lawrence Marrero and Monette Moore; and George's personal favorite, the spiritual standard, "Closer Walk With Thee."

LJ 331 (LP)	
	Ice Cream
"A" Side	Down by the Riverside
	Burgundy Street
	Saints Go Marching In
"B" Side	Doctor Jazz
	Closer Walk With Thee

(101)	Doctor Jazz
	Down by the Riverside
	10" 78 rpm

(501)	Closer Walk With Thee
	Lou-Easy-An-I-A
	12" 78 rpm

JOHNNY LUCAS AND HIS BLUE BLOWERS—A member of the original Firehouse Five, Johnny has been a feature performer in Southern California for some time. Such big names as Jess Stacy and Matty Matlock join him for these recordings with each number a personal selection by the artist featured on it. The complete spontaneity of this session has drawn the highest praise from both disk jockeys and critics.

(106)	Loveless Love
	Lazy River
	10" 78 rpm

(107)	Hindustan
	High Society
	10" 78 rpm
	(Available April, 1954)

The catalog listed the recently released recordings by George Lewis' Ragtime Band and Octave Crosby's Original Dixieland Band, as well as forthcoming releases by Pete Daily and His Chicagoans and Johnny Lucas and His Blueblowers.

Daily last recorded for Jazz Man on Christmas Eve, 1947. Since that time, he had made records for Decca, Jump, and Capitol, and was one of the most popular Dixieland band leaders in Los Angeles. Since May, he had been holding court at Astor's in the San Fernando Valley.

Daily's Chicagoans featured an entirely different lineup, with pianist Skippy Anderson as the lone holdover. A notable addition to the instrumentation was a bass tuba, played by Bernie Miller. Since the release of the first Lu Watters sides in 1941, the tuba had been de-emphasized in favor of the string bass, but Miller gave Daily's sound a powerful, rhythmic thrust. Also in the band were former Bob Crosby Bobcat Warren Smith on trombone, clarinetist Jerry Fuller, banjoist Lenny Esterdahl, and drummer Hugh Allison.

The Daily sides were issued on April 12 on two 78 rpm discs: Jazz Man 104 and 105. The spring catalog indicates that Jazz Man 105 was also available on a 45 rpm single, although no known copies have turned up. What was issued, however, was the first, and as it turns out, the only 45 rpm extended play record issued by Jazz Man, consisting of all four Daily sides. Again, Jazz Man labels listed a post office box rather than the shop's address.

Despite Van Court's promise in the catalog to avoid "shopworn standards," the four Daily sides were all old tunes: David Berg and Alfred Solmon's 1916 "There's a Quaker in Old Quaker Town," the spiritual "Just a Closer Walk With Thee," Stephen Foster's ancient "Swanee River," and "New Tin Roof Blues," based on the old New Orleans Rhythm Kings classic. Of the four tunes, "Quaker Town" swung the most, with a joyous and rousing rideout ensemble chorus. "Tin Roof Blues" had recently been

The only Jazz Man 45 rpm release, by Pete Daily and his Chicagoans (From the author's collection).

retrofitted with lyrics by Bill Norvas and Allan Copeland and renamed "Make Love to Me." A hit vocal recording of the song by Jo Stafford was riding high on the juke box charts in early 1954, so Jazz Man issued Daily's version by its new title, even though it was recorded as an instrumental. (On the 45 EP, it was called "New Tin Roof Blues.") In its September 8 issue, *Down Beat* gave the disc three stars and wryly pointed out that "this is proof that there's one west coast school of jazz for which Shorty Rogers doesn't arrange (yet)."

Jazz Man's next session came later in February with four sides by Johnny Lucas and His Blueblowers. Lucas (1917–2001) was born in Minneapolis, but moved with his family to California in 1920. As a child, he contracted rheumatoid arthritis, and as a result, was unable to walk or bend his arms at the elbow. But Lucas stubbornly refused to view himself as being disabled and became a jazz musician, sketch artist, writer, and jazz historian. (His frequent articles in *The Record Changer* were credited to "John Lucas.")

Lucas started out playing drums and marimba, but switched to trumpet when he was in his twenties. In order to play, he designed a trumpet with an extended leadpipe connected to the mouthpiece, which enabled him to play with his arms outstretched. It was an odd sight, but the contraption worked, and Lucas soon was leading his own student band at Pasadena City College called the Blueblowers. He attended Stanford University but quit to work in the military defense industry during World War II. Later, he worked for the *East Pasadena Herald* as a writer. One of his hobbies was to make pen-and-ink sketches and use them on Christmas cards.

After his discharge in 1945, Lucas met animators Ward Kimball and Clarke Mallery at a Halloween party. When Kimball and Mallery formed the Firehouse Five Plus Two, Lucas became the group's original trumpet player, and played at their first session in May 1949 for Good Time Jazz. Shortly after, he formed his own band, using his old group's name, the

Johnny Lucas

Blueblowers. His place in the FF+2 was taken by cornetist Danny Alguire. Lucas would lead the Blueblowers for more than five decades.

Johnny Lucas's Blueblowers included veteran clarinetist Matty Matlock, former Benny Goodman pianist Jess Stacy, Pete Daily banjo player Lenny Esterdahl, trombonist Mike Hobi, bassist Bob Stone, and former FF+2 drummer Monte Mountjoy. The four tunes recorded by the band were, like the Daily sides, jazz standards, including Hoagy Carmichael's "Lazy River," "Hindustan," "Loveless Love" (sung by Lucas in Spanish as well as English), and "High Society." The latter song was the only Jazz Man record to feature a flute, played by Matlock. (The solo in the trio was originally written for flute but had become associated with the clarinet.)

The Lucas sides were issued on Jazz Man's last two 78 rpm releases, numbers 106 and 107. The four Daily sides were combined with the four Lucas sides to make up the third Jazz Man 10-inch LP (LJ-333), which was released in May.

In November, three more 10-inch LPs were released, constituting a combination of original recordings and reissues of previously released material. LJ-334 was again a divided issue, consisting of eight sides made by Pud Brown's Delta Kings and Rosy McHargue and His Ragtimers. Titled *Dixieland Contrasts*, the LP was the first evidence of Jazz Man changing directions and offering styles other than New Orleans jazz.

The four Brown sides, made for the tiny West Craft label on October 10, 1951, featured an all-star lineup of musicians who had made their mark in the swing world, including brothers Charlie (trumpet) and Jack (trombone) Teagarden, pianist Jess Stacy, drummer Ray Bauduc, and the leader on tenor saxophone, an instrument not yet heard on a Jazz Man record.

The McHargue sides had been recorded on April 8, 1952 and were originally issued on the Jump label. Although in the traditional jazz vein, the four songs were an eclectic group of obscure titles, including an ancient Tin Pan Alley novelty ("They Gotta Quit Kicking My Dawg Around"), an early Irving Berlin rag ("That Mysterious Rag"), and a McHargue original

Rosy McHargue & his Ragtimers, recording for Jump Records, Radio Recorders, 7000 Santa Monica Blvd., Hollywood, April 8, 1952. L-R: Ray Leatherwood, bass; George Defebaugh, drums; Rosy McHargue, clarinet; Bob Higgins, cornet; Moe Schneider, trombone; Earle Sturgis, piano (Courtesy Dan Levinson).

Pictured above are three 78 rpm labels of recordings licensed by Albert Van Court for reissue on Jazz Man 10-inch LPs in 1954. On the lower right, Jazz Man 10-inch LP label LJ-335, featuring pianist Marvin Ash. (From the author's collection)

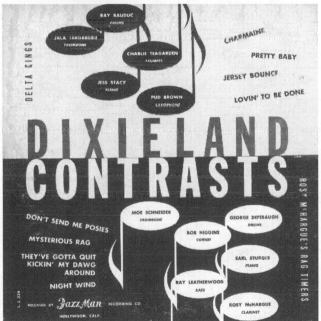

Jazz Man LPs LJ-333 and LJ-334, issued in May and November 1954, respectively (From the author's collection).

("Night Wind"). "Don't Send Me Posies" featured a vocal by Rink Leslie, the girlfriend of the producer of *The Dixie Showboat*, a television program the band was appearing on at the time. (Leslie joined Monette Moore as the only women to ever record for Jazz Man.)

A review in *The Second Line* gave grudging praise to the McHargue sides, calling them "good clean jazz," but said that "the commercial singing arrangements (are) aimed at selling (to) people other than archaic maniacs." *Down Beat* made no bones about its distaste for the McHargue sides, the anonymous reviewer calling them "some of the worst recordings I've ever heard." The review went on to say that two of the songs were "tongue-in-cheek but all four come through as caricatures. To whom are these supposed to sell? Rosy can really blow; why waste him on this sort of nonsense?" *The Second Line* called the Pud Brown sides a "surprise package," comparing them to music by Jimmy Dorsey or Chicago jazz rather than West Coast. Again, *Down Beat* was harsher, labeling Brown's tenor "tasteless." The magazine went on to liken the album cover art to "special sales day at the supermarket."

LJ-335 featured eight solos by the highly respected ragtime pianist Marvin Ash (1914–1974), which were recorded at Capitol on September 14, 1954. Born Marvin Ashbaugh in Lamar, Colorado, Ash came to Los Angeles after World War II where he helped open Club 47 (named for the L.A. Musician's Union) on Ventura Blvd. in Studio City. A series of popular recordings followed on the Jump and Capitol labels, and Ash found steady work with other local musicians like Nappy Lamare and Rosy McHargue. Ash had worked with the men in Pud Brown's Delta Kings, so it's possible there was some connection between the Ash LP and the sides Van Court licensed from West Craft. Ash's encyclopedic knowledge of ragtime did not disappoint, and his Jazz Man LP offers some obscure classics, ranging from George Rosey's cakewalk "A Ragtime Skeedadler's Ball" to Scott Joplin's rarely heard "Searchlight Rag."

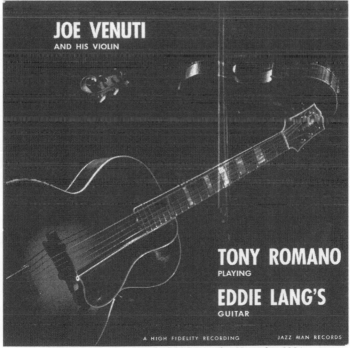

Jazz Man LPs LJ-335 and LJ-336, issued in November 1954.
(From the author's collection)

The final entry in the triumvirate of 10-inch LPs Jazz Man issued in November 1954 departed from early forms of jazz entirely, a spontaneous Hollywood studio date featuring legendary jazz violinist Joe Venuti (1904–1978) and guitarist Tony Romano (1915–2005). The two musicians had been introduced to each other by songwriter Johnny Mercer in 1937 during the filming of *Garden of the Moon*. Venuti and Romano would play together regularly for 40 years until Venuti's death. After Venuti's previous guitar-playing partner Eddie Lang died in 1933 following a botched tonsillectomy, Lang's widow gave her husband's Gibson L-5 prototype, which had been designed by Lang, to Venuti, with instructions to pass it on to Romano. Mrs. Lang heard echoes of her husband's playing in Romano's work and wanted him to have the instrument.

The Jazz Man session was made possible by the urging of Johnny Bradford, a mutual friend to Venuti and Romano. There was no set list of songs planned; Venuti merely suggested a tune and took off, with Romano

Joe Venuti, mid-1930s

Tony Romano, 1935

following along, anticipating every sudden change of mood Venuti threw at him. The session was cut in October 1954 at Hollywood's Gold Star Studios, with studio co-owner Stan Ross engineering. The eight sides cut that day included a sumptuous version of "Autumn Leaves" (with Romano humming along with the melody), a deliciously vibrant version of the Irving Caesar/Vincent Youmans classic "I Want to Be Happy," and a Venuti/Romano original called "Joy Ride," that saw Venuti play in his "Four String Joe" style, in which he loosens the hairs on his bow so that he can play all four strings simultaneously. The final number of the session, "Angelina," was an elegiac Albanian street song that featured an unbilled guest artist: Venuti's own (unnamed) optometrist, who joined the duo on mandolin.

The album cover (LJ-336) features images of Venuti's violin and Lang's Gibson in an impressionistic photo by Charles Potts. Albert Van Court, Jr. wrote the liner notes. The record was the last Jazz Man release. After that, the recording and distribution activity of the label abruptly ceased.

In its 13 years of existence, Jazz Man Records spearheaded the New Orleans jazz revival of the early 1940s and then presided over its boom years in the late 1940s and early 1950s. If not for the label, it is likely that the Jazz Man Record Shop would never have attained the status it achieved since its start in 1939. Jazz Man Records was dead, but the Jazz Man Record Shop would live on for another 30 years.

The location of the Jazz Man Record Shop during much of 1954 is unclear. Through 1953, Los Angeles city business directories still listed the shop's address at 6420 Santa Monica Blvd. The June 1954 telephone directory, however, showed the shop's location as 1538 Cassil Place, which was located in a residential neighborhood. The phone number, HO4-1588, was the same one the shop had used since 1947, so it is possible an alternate address was listed for the store, which was now owned by Albert Van Court. In that same June 1954 directory, however, Jazz Man Distributing

Company was still listed at 6420 Santa Monica, although with a different phone number.

To further the confusion, an advertisement for the Jazz Man in the July-August issue of *The Second Line* shows the shop's address as 532 Alandele Ave., in another residential neighborhood. In the November 1954 issue of *The Second Line,* a full-page ad showed a third address at 7511 Santa Monica Blvd., although in that same issue, a record review of the Pete Daily/Johnny Wittwer 10-inch LP shows the address to still be on Alandele. The ad implies a relationship between the shop and Omega Electronics, a distributor located at 520 Fifth Avenue in New York. In addition, this ad provides the first evidence that the Jazz Man was expanding beyond just being a shop for jazz collectors, announcing that in addition to traditional jazz, it would provide "anything else you may wish, whether it be "Beethoven or Brubeck, Scherazade (sic) or Sh-Boom."

The Jazz Man wasn't there long, however, because by the time the November 1954 issue of *The Record Changer* came out, the magazine's auction listings showed another new address for the shop. For the first time in its existence, the Jazz Man left Hollywood, materializing in an area toward downtown Los Angeles at 2689 W. Pico Blvd. It would remain there for more than 13 years.

The suddenness of the Jazz Man's disappearance from the Hollywood scene, in addition to the abrupt cessation of activity by its record label, is a mystery with no clear-cut answer. Van Court's ambitious plans had gotten off to an impressive start, but by the end of 1954, the label vanished and Van Court shunted the shop off to one of the least desirable neighborhoods in Los Angeles. To many of its former customers, it appeared that the Jazz Man Record Shop had disappeared off the face of the earth.

Down Beat *ad, June 30, 1954*

Chapter Eighteen

Lost in the Fifties

In 1954, 18-year-old Don Gray was looking for a place to buy the records he had been hearing on KFWB's *Strictly from Dixie* radio program, hosted by Frank Bull and Gene Norman. Gray was born in 1936 in the city of Bell, located a few miles southeast of downtown Los Angeles. While still in his early teens, he started listening to jazz, buying records, and visiting local music stores in Riverside, where his family had moved:

What got me going were radio shows. I remember there was one called Turn Back the Clock *with Andy and Virginia Mansfield on KFI. A lot of stations were playing older records by people like Paul Whiteman and Red Nichols. I was interested in what was called Dixieland or stuff from the traditional jazz revival: the Firehouse Five, Pete Daily, that's what interested me. And they were playing these old, old songs, so I started wondering where they got their stuff from. I soon found out they were playing tunes by King Oliver, Jelly Roll Morton, and the other black bands from the '20s. Well, back then, there weren't any record shops that carried that stuff. The 10-inch LP reissues on labels like X and Riverside hadn't come out yet.*

Anyway, in the early '50s, the only shop I heard about was on the Strictly from Dixie *show. Benson Curtis was the DJ who played all this old stuff and I was hooked. On that show, Curtis would do a commercial and say, "Get all of your records at the Jazz Man Record Shop." This must have been in late 1953 or early '54 and I wasn't driving yet, but somehow, I found the address and I got my mom and dad to take me down to Santa Monica Blvd. to the Jazz Man.*

When they found the place and dropped me off, it was kind of like a newsstand—it was right off the street. You went in the side door and there was a long table with records behind it. It wasn't a very big place. No browser bins in the front. There were some LPs on the wall, but that's about it. There was one other guy there, a tall fellow named Harvey, and I said, "Gee, this is the shop?" I asked a bunch of dumb questions and the guy behind the counter, who I only knew as Red, got some records for me that I bought for about a buck apiece.

About a year later, I was driving now, but the shop was no longer on Santa Monica. I used to go to the Strictly Jubilee *festivals and the programs had ads for the Jazz Man, so I found out it had moved to some place out on Pico Blvd. I didn't know my way around L.A. but I knew that Pico Blvd. was actually 13th Street, so I just went to downtown L.A., found 12th Street, went past it to Pico, turned right, and drove and drove and drove until I found the shop.*

The fellow running the shop was a mild-mannered, unassuming

This ad from the October 15, 1954 program for the Dixieland Jubilee Festival is the earliest published mention of the Jazz Man in its new location on West Pico Blvd. (Courtesy the L.A. Institute of Jazz) type named Jerry Weiss. When Gray got there, he also recognized the guy from 6420 Santa Monica who he knew only as Harvey, whose last name he discovered was Newland.

The new location was at 2689 West Pico Blvd., a few miles from downtown Los Angeles. Gray soon found out that Weiss ran the store while a friend of his named Perry Pugh went out and hustled up records to sell in the shop. A bespectacled would-be cornet player who was fond of Bix Beiderbecke, Weiss worked the counter, answered questions, and handled transactions in the shop. The Jazz Man was no longer a purveyor of exclusive, collectible jazz records, nor did it cater to the elite of Hollywood. Now, it had become just another used record store, with browser bins in the front room as well as in the large back room, where Weiss kept his personal collection of jazz 78s.

Unlike all of its previous owners, Albert Van Court, Jr., rarely showed up at the shop at all. By now, he had divested himself of the Jazz Man label, which he sold to Everest Records. Van Court had no interest in the shop itself and was simply paying Weiss and Pugh to run it for him. Occasionally, Van Court would drop in and talk to the customers, but few people ever knew who the owner of the shop was.

Within a few years, Weiss left and Harvey Newland took over as co-manager along with Pugh, leasing the shop from Van Court. Slowly but steadily, the shop built up an inventory of tens of thousands of old 78s. Pugh got them by buying up collections and going to Salvation Armies, Goodwill stores, and thrift shops, often paying a penny apiece for records of all types.

It was here, at 2689 West Pico, where collectors like Don Gray came to meet other collectors, have a beer or two, and buy or trade records from their collections. Although Pugh was more of a dealer, Newland and Weiss were big collectors, and would often trade records from the Jazz Man stock for 78s they wanted for their own collections.

In the mid-'50s, a collector from San Diego named Ken Swerilas also hunted down the Jazz Man:

I first learned about the shop from Arcade Music, which was a juke box outlet in San Diego. They had thousands of 78s, which they would get from places that had a lot of duplicates from juke boxes. One time I asked the owner if he knew of any other place that had old 78s and he told me about this place in Los Angeles called the Jazz Man. Well, in the 1950s, Los Angeles was a long way to drive. There weren't any freeways back then, so it was an all-day kind of trip.

So one time, my wife and I went up there and we met Jerry Weiss, Perry Pugh, and Harvey Newland. It happened to be on a Saturday, which Harvey described to me as being known as "Old Fogies Day." I walked into the shop and I remember seeing a turntable with a red label spinning around on it. I really liked the music I heard so I asked Harvey who the artist was. When he said that it was Louis Armstrong, I couldn't believe it. I had never heard Armstrong play that way before. I liked strictly country music at that time. That's all I listened to. To me, Louis Armstrong was "Blueberry Hill" and "Home," and songs like that that I didn't care for. Jazz was bebop to me back then.

Well, I liked the record that was playing so I asked Harvey what the record was and how much he wanted for it. The record was "West End Blues" and it was going for 30 dollars. Now, in 1954 that was a lot of money. I was living on the G.I. Bill at that time, which paid me 150 dollars a month. That's all I had for me, my wife, and to raise my child with. So 30 dollars was like 3,000 dollars to me. When I told him I had to pass, he said that I should go down to the Salvation Army or Goodwill and that if I had a lot of patience, I was liable to find a record like this for ten cents. So that started my really heavy duty record collecting. I went to every Salvation Army and Goodwill store between Los Angeles and San Diego. And from then on, I became a regular customer of the Jazz Man Record Shop.

It was this kind of hearsay that kept record collectors "discovering" the Jazz Man. After the record label was sold and the shop moved out of Hollywood, the Jazz Man lost its national presence. Other than ads placed in the annual *Dixieland Jubilee Festival* program, there was no regular advertising. If you were a Los Angeles record collector or knew one, you would have been hard-pressed to find whether the shop still existed. Despite the fact that it was only a few miles from Hollywood, the rundown neighborhood where it had moved was substantially different.

After Jerry Weiss left, Newland and Pugh cut back the hours the shop was open for business. Since each had a regular day job, neither could afford to manage the shop during business hours. By 1959, the Jazz Man was only open weekdays from 5:30 to 9:00 p.m. and on Saturdays from 10 a.m. to 9 p.m. It was during this time that Saturday became the day when collectors would show up. Many spent the entire day playing or trading records, socializing, and downing a few beers. Unfortunately, neither man appeared to have the shop's best interests in mind. Pugh was mainly concerned with making a buck on his own deals, while Newland padded his own collection and sold valuable records he scrounged for his own personal auction list. As a result, the shop's inventory got progressively smaller, with most of the desirable records gone. Still, the shop's stock was large enough—its advertisements estimated "over 20,000 records"—to impress a young teenager named Jim Cooprider, one of many who started collections in the 1950s.

A friend of mine in high school was interested in Bix Beiderbecke and told me about the shop, so I decided to give it a try. When I first walked in there, it blew my mind because I had never seen that many records in one place in my life. When you walked in, the classical music was on the left and I could smell the pungent odor of hot wax because the front of the shop had a southern exposure and the sun shone on the classical stacks. I would ride the bus in from South Gate, catch the "J" car to 10th St., and ride it all the way to Pico. I got five or six dollars in allowance every week, so I would hang out by the dime table. I would always find something: Boston Pops, early swing. I was just starting out.

By the middle of 1959, Van Court became concerned that the shop had become more of a clubhouse for Pugh and Newland at the expense of the business. He didn't like the fact that the shop was closed for most of the week. By this time, even the posted hours were not dependable. Sometimes Pugh and Newland wouldn't show up at all. Collectors were never sure when the shop would be open, even on Saturdays. So Van Court began looking for someone who could operate the shop full-time, and who could put his own interests aside in deference to shop business. The man he chose to run the shop would do so for nearly a quarter of a century.

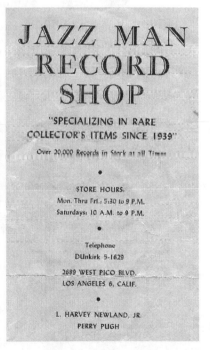

Ads for the Jazz Man during the late '50s show the gradual disappearance of Jerome Weiss from the shop and the reduction of business hours. By 1959, the shop was only open evenings and Saturdays (Courtesy the L.A. Institute of Jazz).

Chapter Nineteen

The Record Finder

Donald Calvin Brown was born in the small town of Dixon, Illinois, on May 11, 1923. Although all of the owners of the Jazz Man Record Shop started out as record collectors, none was as passionate about the hobby as Don Brown. In an article he wrote for *Joslin's Jazz Journal* in 1982, he recalled growing up as a record collector in the Midwest:

Dixon was a larger-than-average cornfield of some 15,000 souls some 42 miles south of Rockford. I began collecting jazz records in 1937 or '38 when I should have been interested in waltzes or, at the outside, records made by members of the WLS Barn Dance *crew out of Chicago. But jazz? Even my mother thought I must have been dropped at the hospital at some time or another.*

By 1938, record stores were franchised. One would carry the Decca and Columbia product, another the Victor and Bluebird sides. My Decca/Columbia/Vocalion outlet was Ray Miller's Music Store. He was a wonderful cat; or at least I thought so, because he tolerated my one or two dime purchases each Saturday. Mr. Miller carried a private stock for me, or so it seemed at the time. Under his counter, beneath those guitar strings, picks, and harmonicas, was a shelf. The ten-inch shipping carton under there was a gold mine (and would be today, also). But, as I say, in a Midwestern town of 15,000, jazz wasn't a staple item. Miller evidently received one each of

Don Brown, age 20, Dixon, Illinois, 1943 (Courtesy Darlene Brown).

every record issued by Vocalion (and others). And in this box, the juice of the orange. When I'd arrive after collecting my paper route, I'd stop at the music store and he would put the box on the counter. From its contents, I could choose new, unplayed Vocalions or Deccas of Cootie Williams, Barney Bigard, most anything then available. And at ten cents apiece! I still have most of those.

A little later, when Columbia, Victor, and Decca began reissuing the album sets ("Chicago Jazz," Bud Freeman, "Gems of Jazz"), I found that I could special order the records and album covers for fifteen cents less than the complete set. And, hell, I couldn't play the album cover, but in two weeks, I could buy three more goodies out of that under-the-counter box.

I used this same approach on Howard Hall's Radio and Phono Shop just around the corner. He was the Victor/Bluebird man and never had anything to do with jazz. Finally, he accepted my special orders, got the records shipped out from decadent Chicago, and I got to hear those Frankie Newtons and Panassié sessions coming out on Bluebird. This place didn't have the friendly atmosphere that was so enjoyable at Miller's. It was strictly business; place your order, buy the records, pick up a catalog supplement, and leave.

As a sidelight to Howard Hall's emporium, I remember one highlight that failed. My father and Mr. Hall were both members of the same Sunday school class, and Dad, having some kind of church meeting at our house one night, invited Mr. Hall to bring over one of those new phonographs he was selling: the RCA "Beam of Light" unit that (supposedly) didn't use needles. For once, I was eager to attend something connected with the church elders and waited for the demonstration of the latest in phonographs. But that night, no matter what Mr. Hall did, the damned thing wouldn't work! And to this day, I've never seen one actually working.

But even non-working, it sure beat the heck out of my radio-phonograph combination from Sears-Roebuck. Still, my unit stood up well to that onslaught of vile jazz! I'd saved nickels for a year or so, stuffing them into a quart jar with a slot in the top. Finally, I was able to write to Mr. Roebuck for a phonograph (with an A.M. radio, and Dave Garroway's jazz show thrown in) for ten bucks. And that improved my sound system of my grandmother's wind-up Victrola.

My first jazz record and that wind-up go hand-in-hand. I used to order records from an ad in the classified section of Down Beat. Send one dollar to Paramount, Box so-and-so, Wilkes-Barre, PA, and receive 12 of the latest records. Twelve for a buck. That even beat Miller's price, although I soon learned there were a lot more "latest" records than jazz. My dad's favorite turned out to be an almost white Vocalion of "It Makes No Difference Now" by the Light Crust Doughboys. He used to say, after I'd play it, that it was the best record I had.

One of the shipments from Wilkes-Barre turned me on to jazz. I still have the disc in just about the same condition as it arrived. Maybe E-minus, but loud. It was Louie's Decca of "I've Got a Heart Full of Rhythm" backed with "Alexander's Ragtime Band." And, as I said: it was loud, and sort of grew on you musically.

Like most school kids, I didn't like to get up in the morning for school. But now, I had, in my wind-up, a wake-up system that wouldn't quit. I tied a string to the off-and-on lever of the phonograph, wound it, and loaded it with my Louie record. When mother yelled the third time, I yanked the *string by my bed, the phono across the room started, and in three minutes, the horrible sound of the needle grinding at the run-off grooves forced me to get up and shut it off. And when you're up…*

In those days, few had cars, and Dixon had no thrift shop of any kind. The nearest ones were in Sterling, 12 miles away, and Rockford. I don't believe more preparation went into those distant visits than today's three-week tours of the Greek isles. Those trips were made by Greyhound, and completed (round-trip) within the day.

Rockford was overwhelmingly large, and I didn't get everywhere I really wanted to go. Sterling-Rock Falls (separated by the Rock River) was more accessible. And Sterling had a couple of thrift stores and an Eldorado: a juke box place full of records at 10 cents each, 12 for a buck. I still can remember those Decca Champions gleaming in the piles, but in those days, if it wasn't listed in the 1938 Delauney Hot Discography, you didn't pick it up. Oh, the gems I must have passed up!

With the advent of World War II, the record-buying public was supposed to turn in a record for each new one they bought. And the records turned in were usually those 10 years old or more. After all, you couldn't part with that "new" Harry James Columbia!

Mr. Miller again came to my rescue. Underneath his roll-top desk in the back of the store was a bushel basket. Into this now-rare item went all those worn old discs that were turned in. And Brownie had access to them for a nickel apiece. Now, at a nickel, you could experiment, right? You invested five cents into something called "Empty Bed Blues" (even though it had the same song on both sides) or maybe even that old band called the Original Dixieland Jazz Band. Who cared if the condition was only V or less. It was a jazz record, wasn't it?*

Don Brown's love affair with the music of Duke Ellington started in 1937, when he saw Ellington's orchestra perform at the National Guard Armory. A gifted writer, he completed a correspondence course in fiction writing from Writer's Digest in Cincinnati. In the late 1930s, show business jobs were non-existent in Dixon, so Brown earned money as a salesman at a local shoe store. Next came a stint as an office boy for the Illinois Northern Utilities Company. (Brown reported wryly that "all executive positions were filled.") In February 1942, he was drafted ("a command performance") and from then until November 1945, Brown served as a classification specialist, or, as he put it, "I made military misfits out of confused civilians," serving in England, France, and Germany during World War II. While stationed in Oklahoma in September 1944, Brown married Frances Darlene Nodine (known to everyone as "Dar"). Their marriage was a happy one that would last more than 40 years until Brown's death.

After his discharge, Brown worked at an aimless series of jobs while trying to decide what he wanted to do for a living. From December 1945 to March 1949, he resumed work for Illinois Northern Utilities as a photographer. In his spare time, he did obligatory commercial photo work, shooting weddings ("never again") and babies ("ditto"). At the age of 25, noting the expansion of television broadcasting in the United States, Brown decided to pursue show business as a career and enrolled in a television production course at the American Television Institute in Chicago. There he majored in television writing and acting, staging productions on a closed circuit television network. After graduating in December 1950, Don and Darlene followed another student to San Antonio, in the hopes that the student would give him a job. Darlene Brown remembered:

When we got there, the guy said to Don, "How much would you pay me to work for me?" Television was brand new and all the people who ran it were trained in radio. They didn't want to hire anybody who knew more than they did. So we stayed in San Antonio for about three months and then we came out to Los Angeles.

The Browns arrived in the spring of 1951 and lived in Hollywood for a while before moving to an apartment at 803-D Princeton Street in Santa

Monica. During his first three years in Los Angeles, Brown freelanced as he struggled to gain a foothold in the city's nascent television industry. He garnered experience by volunteering as a radio and television broadcaster for the Los Angeles City School System. Along the way, he wrote a script that was used on local radio station KMPC, wrote for *The Jerry Colonna Show*, and secured numerous acting and producing jobs on several series heard on KMPC, KFSG, and KPOL. His television work included acting as assistant producer for *In God We Trust*, a regular religious program on KTLA Channel 5, and co-starring in a live drama on KTHE. At one point, he developed a homespun children's show that he thought would sell, but the producers told him that the Nielsen ratings showed that kids were watching cowboys and space programs and refused to take a chance on this kind of a show.

In January 1954, Brown got a job as an account executive, copywriter, and janitor for the Lott Advertising Agency in Santa Monica. From then until April 1956, he handled a variety of jobs necessary to run a small advertising agency: contacting clients, handling mail order duties, and writing book jacket blurbs for the agency's subsidiary vanity publisher.

In March 1956, Brown started publishing *Cobweb Corner's Record Finder*, a publication that was offered to record collectors for the purpose of auctioning and trading records and music ephemera. (The name was shortened soon after to *The Record Finder*.) The first issue was a single two-sided sheet that he mailed to 50 names he found in an old issue of *The Record Changer*. He made copies on an ancient Edison-Dick mimeograph machine with a broken automatic feeder arm, which required him to manually shove each page into the machine and turn the crank to get the mechanism going. In a matter of months, Brown found his "pushing finger" extended an inch or so, but his mailing list ballooned to a thousand copies. *The Record Finder* eventually became an institution and Brown published it until 1977 ("Poorest stapling job in town," noted one comment he received

```
COBWEB CORNER          EDITOR-PUBLISHER  DON BROWN          VOLUME 1

RECORD FINDER             803-D Princeton, Santa Monica       NUMBER 1
                                   California

DEAR FELLOW COLLECTOR:

You now hold the first issue (tiny, we admit, but we'll grow quickly) of
COBWEB CORNER'S RECORD FINDER.  In my own 18 years collecting, buying and
selling records, I've felt the need for a monthly subscription auction list.
Individual lists cost money but with RECORD FINDER we can dispose of surplus
records and advertise our wants inexpensively.  And into COBWEB CORNER'S RE-
CORD FINDER will go all my love and knowledge of records and my advertising
background.

We're sending out this issue with our compliments.  We're proud of it and
the idea behind it and want to share it with you.  We know you'll use its
services and also show it to your collecting friends.  So here's the idea:

Future issues of RECORD FINDER will be larger, possibly 5 pages or more,
legal size.  For the nonce, it will be mimeographed.  Later we'll use off-
set - then there'll be photos, articles - and all the rest.  But this will
be our market place; we can Auction, Sell or Trade our records, sheet music,
piano rolls, photos, "items" and just lovable "junk".

A year's subscription of 10 issues (June/July and August/September will be
bi-monthly) costs only $2.  And, until April 20th, deadline for the May is-
sue, you'll get a listing for 6 records ABSOLUTELY FREE with your subscrip-
tion remittance.  Thus you'll have a chance to try out the RECORD FINDER's
effectiveness.

THE RATES:     Subscription  (10 issues)                    $2.00
               Record Listing (Either Wants or Disposition)  .15 per line
                  (Name and address FREE)
               Special Auction Rate Listing                  .10 per line
                  (Name, address and box number FREE)
               Display copy (2" wide)                       $1.50 per inch
                                                                    of depth
```

First edition of Don Brown's Record Finder, *March 1956. Brown published it by himself until 1977.*

about his publication).

    I actually ran into a used book store owner on 8th Street around Alvarado one time back in the '60s who actually collected those issues. I couldn't believe it. In my own files, I had one copy that was returned to me as "undeliverable" which was my file copy, but he had collected six or seven years worth of it. I thought that the most useless thing in the world is yesterday's auction list, but he was collecting them.

    Within a year, I found myself embroiled as the innocent third party in squabbles between record collectors on grading, shipping (or the lack thereof), and those of collectors submitting bids and then not honoring them.

I also discovered one advertiser who pulled more scams in the three months I allowed the subscription to run then I have heard in all the years since. This "collector" actually conned unsuspecting individuals into shipping records to that address so the advertiser could "determine what payment would be made." Evidently, most records were unacceptable because neither the advertiser nor the records were ever heard from ever after.

For four years, I blundered along, occasionally adding a jazz 78 to my own collection by submitting a winning bid or making some sort of trade deal. The classic trade deal probably was an experience involving an almost mint copy of a record by the Dixie Washboard Band. I was to receive it as payment for running an ad, which I felt was fair enough. That was, until I opened his shipping carton. There it was, in all its red wax glory, exactly as graded, except in 180 tiny pieces, each the size of a jelly bean. But it retained its shape perfectly. Not one shard was out of place as it nestled in its bed of crumpled newspaper.

I made some wonderful contacts, but I also learned a few things. For one, I realized that I never "won" a record on an auction. If I got the disc, it was because I offered more than anyone else for it. In other words, I technically overpaid. Think about that! I also discovered that, to some, a badly recorded acetate constituted a test pressing. Others would advertise "hot solos throughout" on a record that had no solos whatsoever. But I was learning. Not getting any smarter, but learning!

Meanwhile, Brown's efforts to get a toehold in the broadcasting industry continued to sputter. From September 1956 until January 1959, he worked as an editor and publicist for Roux-Woods Publications, which supplied weekly television logs to a variety of publications on the West Coast. Brown's job was to compile the logs, write publicity columns, select photos, and proof all copy. In the fall of 1958, he and Darlene bought a small house at 12537 Indianapolis Avenue in West Los Angeles. Brown announced the move in *The Record Finder* in his usual facetious manner:

Well – we made it! The wife, the cat, 5000 records and myself moved... and moved... and moved. Next time I start collecting anything, it's going to be cotton or feathers, or maybe just air.

When his editing job ended, he still had a mortgage to pay, and with nothing promising in sight, Brown searched unsuccessfully for work. In the middle of 1959, he reluctantly accepted a job that, although it didn't pay a lot, was at least closer to his heart: managing the Jazz Man Record Shop.

An unidentified record collector, a fistful of money at the ready, shows his frustration at the Jazz Man's limited business hours in this gag photo. This would all change when Don Brown took over management of the shop in 1959 (Courtesy Darlene Brown).

Chapter Twenty
Resurrection

By the middle of 1959, Albert Van Court, Jr. decided the Jazz Man Record Shop needed an overhauling. Ever since he purchased it from Marili Morden in 1954, the shop had proved to be nothing but a headache and not much of a money maker. The move from Hollywood to Los Angeles was a cost-cutting measure accomplished to save money on rent, but by 1959, Harvey Newland and Perry Pugh only opened the shop weekday evenings and Saturdays. The shop had basically become a clubhouse where they kept their own collections and whiled away the time with other collectors. The stock of premium records in the shop had dwindled over the years with few replacements being added. Any good records Newland and Pugh found would invariably find their way into their own personal collections rather than to help support the shop. This left the Jazz Man stagnating and dying.

Van Court felt that the shop needed fresh blood, so in May, he offered Don Brown the job of manager. Brown had become a familiar and respected presence at the Jazz Man; *The Record Finder* had earned him a reputation for being honest, savvy, and knowledgeable about the record business. It didn't take long for Brown to accept the offer:

Van Court wanted me to go in originally as the manager. But I wasn't going to go in and tell Perry Pugh and Harvey that I am their new boss because I knew that they knew a helluva lot more about it than I did. I didn't know anything at all about the retail business. So I told him, "Look, I'm not

225

going to tell these guys this. I've known them for years. So either I buy it and run it my way or forget it." And he didn't forget it, I'm sorry to say.

Van Court and Brown agreed that Brown would manage the shop on a trial basis and then, if everything worked out, after six months, he would be offered the option of buying the shop outright. Since arriving in Los Angeles a decade earlier, Brown had made little headway into the entertainment business. With their finances limited, Don and Darlene decided that a regular paycheck as manager of the Jazz Man would give them the stability they needed to pay the mortgage on their new house. After taking over, Brown immediately expanded the hours of the shop, opening it promptly every weekday morning at 10 a.m. In examining the remaining stock in the store, he recognized that many valuable records had inexplicably disappeared. In later years, Brown always suspected that Perry Pugh was responsible for taking most of the store's valuable records for himself. With the store's inventory down to around 30,000 78s and only 21 LPs ("the dogs of the lot"), Brown began scouring Los Angeles thrift stores, Salvation Armies and junk shops, and began rebuilding the inventory.

Late that year, Van Court was so impressed with what Brown had done to turn the Jazz Man around that he offered to sell him the business. Van Court was not wanting for money, but he was interested in continuing the shop's legacy and knew that in Brown, he had found a caretaker who not only had a passion for old records, but the knack and business savvy to be a capable owner. They struck a deal in December 1959, with Brown agreeing to purchase the shop and all of its contents for $500.00 ($300 for the records, $100 for the fixtures and other miscellaneous equipment, and $100 for the name of the business). Darlene Brown recalled helping her husband make the commitment to buy the Jazz Man.

When Don told me about the possibility of owning the shop, I was all for it. I knew it would be hard, but he knew he could run the shop himself. Van Court was the landlord and was very wealthy, so he didn't need the

BILL OF SALE

KNOW ALL MEN BY THESE PRESENTS: That **Albert Van Court, Jr.**

the part **y** of the first part, in consideration of the sum of **$500.00**, Dollars,

lawful money of the United States of America, to **me**

in hand paid by **Donald C. Brown** the part **y** of the second part,

the receipt whereof is hereby acknowledged, do by these presents, sell unto the part **y** of the second part **his**

executors, administrators and assigns **All stock in trade, fixtures, shelving, counters, racks, mimeograph machine, furniture, phonographic equipment, supplies, phonographic records (approximately 30,000), Good Will and the name of Jazz Man Record Shop plus all other assets of the business known as Jazz Man Record Shop same being located presently at 2681 West Pico Blvd L. A. 6, California   Albert Van Court, Jr.** do **es** for **his**

And

heirs, executors and administrators, covenant and agree, with the part **y** of the second part, **his** executors,

administrators and assigns, to warrant and defend the sale of the said property, goods and chattels, unto the part **y** of the

second part, **his** executors, administrators and assigns, against all and every person and persons whomsoever

lawfully claiming or claim the same **I**

IN WITNESS WHEREOF, have hereunto set **my** hand

the day of 19

Albert E. Van Court Jr.

BILL OF SALE — WOLCOTTS FORM 505   64487

Bill of sale, turning the Jazz Man over to Don Brown (Courtesy Darlene Brown).

money. He just wanted to get rid of the shop.

Gary Hammond, who met Don Brown during his time as manager, recalled that Pugh and Newland did not have the shop's best interests at heart:

I got to know Perry Pugh a little later on after I started coming regularly to the shop. Perry never really wanted to do anything that required any serious effort. Prior to Don taking over the shop, I was told by a variety of people that he and Jerry Weiss managed to make off with an awful lot of records in the place. I knew Harvey Newland better than Jerry or Perry, but I didn't really know him in some ways. Harve worked there on a part-time basis and lived in South Los Angeles. He was more interested in collecting records or just being around records, so whatever time he put in to running the shop was comparatively minimal. Harve was a straight shooter. He wouldn't have creamed the stock in the store like Jerry and Perry did and was pretty much a good guy.

Don Brown recalled wryly:

The only really choice record I found was a Clarence Williams black Columbia in the sink in the back room that was used for a toilet.

On December 31, 1959, Perry Pugh sold his remaining interest in the Jazz Man to Brown and Van Court for $75.00. It is possible Newland also sold his share in the shop, although no documents have surfaced regarding his ownership other than his name on a business license along with Van Court's. The next morning, New Year's Day, Don Brown officially took over as owner of the Jazz Man Record Shop.

It was a very strange day. I stood around the old shop from 1:00 until 4:30 waiting for this guy to meet me so I could close up the shop. I wanted to get in and get out quickly. When he finally showed up at 4:30, I said "Where've you been?" and he said "I had to watch the Rose Bowl game." Important things come first, I suppose. And then Harvey came in and found these two strange individuals inside his store, and that was a very strained thing. I felt like I didn't even belong on the face of the earth at the moment.

In the beginning, I really didn't know what to do. Thank goodness for Graham Lang, because he led me by the hand and showed me the wholesalers to go to and what to do. Gray was a guy who usually came in on Thursday. He knew a whole lot about World War II aircraft. But if it hadn't have been for Gray, I would have been totally lost and didn't know what to do. As proof of this, I figured that since the shop was still being run and it was still called the same thing, that I didn't need a new business license. Well, it turned out that I did. But I didn't find that out until the following October when I went in to renew my business license and the police permit we had to have then and they said, "Well, are you this guy?" And I said, "No, I'm me." "Well, how long have you been running it?" So now, not only did I have to buy a license and a police permit for that current year, but I had to buy it for the next year, too. So I discovered that my expenses were doubled on that trip to

City Hall. That's one reason why I eventually moved out of L.A., just to get away from that stupid police permit.

After learning how to run the business by himself, Don Brown decided to beef up his stock of LPs in addition to 78s, since new LPs were constantly coming on the market, creating a reason for customers to return to the shop to see what was new. The LPs moved more quickly than did the 78s, which often stayed on the shelves, unexamined, for years at a time.

When I got there, it was, more or less, a hangout for collectors when Perry and Harvey were running it, rather than a going business. But the shop had a following, a reputation, and the possibility that it might be rebuilt into something worthwhile. I knew absolutely nothing about running a business, records or otherwise. At first, I didn't understand the distribution system. My knowledge of jazz was adequate because I'd studied and listened since 1937. Country music was, to me, "hillbilly." Rhythm-and-blues was "rock 'n' roll," and shouldn't exist. Sweet bands were still "Mickey," and personalities and I were strangers. But again, listening to the experts, I brain-picked and learned. By avoiding direct answers to unfamiliar questions, I drew out more information. Soon, I talked "their" music and began to understand it. The stuff wasn't as bad as I imagined it; in fact, a lot sounded pretty good.

The early '60s saw the end of 78 production and brought a rebirth of traditional jazz, now on long-plays. This provided a good source of music to stock the shelves, and also brought in stashes of old 78s that "took up too much room." I remember one man distinctly. Inwardly I bitched as he entered the shop, a shoebox under his arm. "Another Knapp shoe salesman," I thought, and readied my best no-sale report for him. Instead, he asked if I bought old jazz records. His file, complete with Hot Discography *information on dates and personnel, was in that box. Items like New Orleans Rhythm Kings, Olivers, Gennetts of Morton, others on Columbia and Paramounts with sought-after names, all in E or better condition. I figured he'll want* *over $100 for them, and in those days, digging up $70 a month for rent was a chore. He admitted he was going to throw them in the trash on the morrow if I didn't want to buy, and I "stole" that collection for $75. Think of all the work I eliminated for the overworked trash man.*

During those years, the musicians, the kooks, and the out-of-town Record Finder *subscribers added to my day-to-day customers and kept things interesting. Some days were slow and I'd put a sign on the door that read, "I was here—where were you?" Then I'd go out junk shopping (you could find things in those days) or down the street to the model railroad shop.*

It was within those musty confines that I met Rex Stewart, Wingy Manone, several of the Rolling Stones, and hundreds of other "friends" I'd met in those 78 grooves. And it gave the more brazen customers a chance to get an autograph "for my sister." Then there was the day the owner of a nationwide Chicago meatpacking house called to see if I validated parking. His block-long Rolls Royce would have refused to enter that lot!

There were the interesting non-buyers, too. "Moses," with his gunny sack, robe, rope sandals, beard, long hair, and his tales of "the blue haze" at the North Pole during World War II. He knew of planes that flew into that haze, never to be heard from again. Or the tall black gal with her G.I. ankle-length raincoat (100 degrees outside), buck-fifty hand-rolled cigar, and nothing underneath but a dirty, pink half-slip. Or the blind man that tapped his way up my porch and, following the music into the shop, asked, "Is this the barber shop?" When I told him, no, it was a record shop, he replied, "Sure sounds like the barber shop" and tapped his way back to the street.

From the beginning, Brown decided that in order to stay in business, he needed to have something for everyone in the shop, not just jazz. So he bought single items from private collectors, scoured Salvation Armies and thrift shops, and bought thousands of records from radio stations.

Gary Hammond, who became one of Brown's best friends, was born in Salt Lake City in 1942 and moved to Los Angeles on New Year's Day, 1956. Hammond's mother was a concert pianist and his father was a jazz buff, so he became a music fan early when he was growing up. Hammond began collecting records by going to junk shops in Salt Lake City when he was only 10 or 11 years old. In the fall of 1955, Hammond's father was transferred to California, and the family eventually settled in Whittier. Upon graduating high school, Hammond entered USC as a freshman and began looking around for local places where he could buy old records. He had come across copies of Jazz Man 78s and knew the shop existed, but by that time, the shop had moved to 2689 Pico Blvd., within walking distance of the university.

Don was a steady, rock-solid kind of a guy. You would be around him for five minutes and then say to yourself, "This guy really knows what he's doing." The shop never changed during the years I was over there at 2689 Pico. There were tons and tons of records and a huge table in the middle of the store which had 25-cent records stacked on it. Then Don got tired of having them around and dropped the price to a dime and it was known as "The Dime Table" after that.

Don didn't chase his tail and run around town like Perry did, looking for records. Don waited until he had a good, solid lead and then he would go out and follow it up or even ask somebody else to do it for him. I ran down a lot of stuff for Don over the years.

When I was still at USC, I went down to Central Avenue and there was a store there that was going out of business. I took one look at this stuff and called Don and said, "Meet me. You're gonna want this." This store had choice, post-war blues 78s; a lot of really, rare things. About 3,500 to 4,000 records in all. So we hauled them back to the shop in a couple of trips. I had a '53 Buick back then and Don had this Dodge with overload springs that he'd installed for the purpose of hauling records. So we got all this stuff back to the shop and Don said, "Well, your commission is 50 records. Take whatever you want." So I did, and I've still got the 50. Some of the scarcest stuff in my blues collection came from that shop. But that's how Don operated. He was willing to work and not chase rainbows all the time.

The shop was so well-known and so many people came in because of Don's reputation and because of The Record Finder, *that he could always find things that he wanted for himself and still have plenty to stock the shop with.*

Stocking the shop was not the main objective for Don because he didn't want really rare stuff on the shelves since they tended to disappear. Don felt it was too much of a liability to have that stuff in there on a shelf when it might go for $100 to $125 on an auction. So he ran his own auction list for the really good stuff. He'd find an Oliver Gennett or an early Johnny Dodds and he'd set these aside and run them in his own auction in The Record Finder.

The building at 2689 West Pico Blvd. was, in Don Brown's words, "a classic."

I don't know when it was built, but I had one guy in there just looking around, reminiscing, and he was an old cat then. He had run a restaurant in that building and used to hunt rabbits where the Ambassador Hotel is and then serve them in his restaurant. I don't know when the Ambassador was built, but that goes back a long time. All the building was being held together by was the rust on the nails. If you put a coat of paint on it, the whole thing would have collapsed outwards. It reminded you of an old, neglected 1930s Woolworth's store, with the floors that waved and flowed. There was a trap door in the back that I kept a table over so nobody would fall into it. The floorboards were all rotted. There were apartments upstairs and other buildings along side of it, including a place that was a pool hall at one time and a music store where somebody gave private lessons.

Gary Hammond:

In the back of the shop was Don's work space. He had a lot of overstock in the back of the shop, a work table, and an old-fashioned mimeograph machine the he used to print The Record Finder *on. He cranked out every copy himself, collated them, stapled them, and mailed them. It was always a one-man operation.*

Like his predecessors, Don Brown decorated the Jazz Man with photos of musicians—many of them autographed—plus 78s with unusual or attractive labels which were thumb-tacked to the walls. What many customers remember, though, was the showpiece of the shop: an original poster from the 1929 film *St. Louis Blues* starring Bessie Smith in her only film appearance. Brown got the poster from a young collector named Marc Friend:

I don't know what year it was. Maybe '64 or '65. I used to go to Larry Edmunds' book store on Hollywood Blvd. At the time they had a catalog of their posters for sale. The St. Louis Blues *poster was listed in the catalog for $15 or something like that. I was pretty young and that was a lot of money, but I bought it. I held onto it for a couple of years and then decided to auction it off. The first place I thought of was Jazz Man Records. Don Brown had an auction list and he put it up there with a $25 minimum bid. I remember that it had been in Larry's catalog for a long time, at least a couple of years, but no one noticed it. So Don put it up there and nobody bid on it. After the auction, he said he'd give me $25 in store credit for the poster. The next thing I know, it's framed and on his wall. It's been a regret of mine ever since. But I consider it to be a pretty ugly poster.*

One of the major irritants Don Brown faced at 2689 was an eccentric who ran a business from another space in the building. Gary Hammond remembered him:

There was a crazy next-door neighbor by the name of Walter – I never knew what his last name was – but Walter was a nut case. He lived

Don Brown in front of 2689 Pico Blvd., April 1963 (Courtesy Darlene Brown).

next door to the shop on the second floor. His place came right out of a fever dream. The place was loaded with boxes and stacks of things. Walter was an upholsterer and his shop was next door to Don's. But he had another life, apparently, and every so often, he would go away and Don would pick up his mail for him. Well, there were a lot of big checks in that mail; dividend checks and things like that. We never found out exactly who Walter was. One time he actually broke through the walls of the shop when they cut his electricity off and tapped into Don's power outlet with an extension cord. The next day, I took a look at the damage. It wasn't the plaster that bothered me, it was that the timbers were all riddled with little bitty holes. And I said, "Don, you've

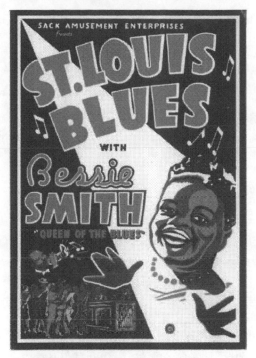

SACK AMUSEMENT ENTERPRISES

This 1929 poster was the most recognizable icon in the shop, where it resided for 20 years.

got a termite problem here." He said, "I think it's more than termites." Whatever was eating the place up was really doing a pretty thorough job.

Gary Hammond:

Graham Lang was a fixture in the shop, and was one of those guys who would run down 78s for Don. One time he made a terrible mistake. He tried to take Walter's picture and Walter went over the edge and chased Graham for about eight blocks down the street. Walter was a man to be afraid of. He was a little guy, but was built like a pocket Hercules. Once he carried a sofa that he had reupholstered all the way from the shop down to Santa Monica, about 12 miles. Graham was fast and hid out in a big box in the back of somebody's house and stayed there for a couple of hours. He didn't come back to the shop for a week or week-and-a-half.

Don Brown:

Walter reupholstered used furniture by taking material off, turning it inside out and tacking it back on. One of the stores in our building was a frame shop which, before I moved out, became a cleaning establishment. And Walter did all the wiring for the place. When the inspectors came, they ran out of the building screaming.

I remember one time, there was an apartment upstairs where a bunch of artists lived together. The rent was very cheap. Before they left, they must have had a great party because they pounded all the plaster off all the walls. So one day, I hear this thundering noise out on the back stairs that went up on angles – old rickety things that you were scared to walk on—here's this gigantic noise, and I go on out there, and here's Walter with almost a complete piece of slate off of a pool table that had a hunk taken out of it. And he, by himself, is struggling with this half-inch thick slate and got it upstairs. This was going to be his wallboard. And he's up there in a little cubbyhole pounding nails into this slate—just whamming away at it.

In the upper corners of the shop, all the pieces of plaster eventually started breaking loose. And my landlord, who was a typical slum landlord, came in and said, "Mr. Brown, what are you going to do with the plaster?" And I said, "Well, when it falls on the floor, I'll sweep it up." And he said, "Well, couldn't you get some glue and glue it back on?" I told him, "You gotta be kidding." But he was serious. One day, it all came down and the shelves underneath it were all filled with plaster dust. So I swept it all up. He came in a couple of days later and wanted to know what I did with the plaster. I thought he was going to make me go out to the trash, get it all back, and glue it back on, piece by piece. He said, "You could have put it in the potholes in the parking lot."

Gary Hammond:

In the old shop, there was an extremely high ceiling, so high that it could have been turned into a second story, but it wasn't. Walter's place had a dropped ceiling and a family from Honduras lived on the upper floor.

Over the years, Hammond got to know the Browns intimately. He saw in Don Brown a man with a brilliant mind, sharp wit, and equally honed business instincts. But, in Hammond's opinion, Brown curbed his ambitions to be a writer for good when he took over the Jazz Man.

Don had three passions. One was writing. I still have a folder at home with 40 or 50 things that he wrote over the years and threw away. I'd go through the trash can in back of the shop and pull them out and save them. Dar was grateful that I did save them. But he'd write wonderful things and then just pitch them. Once in a while, he'd put a piece into The Record Finder, *but he thought that he had failed himself to some extent by simply being a shopkeeper. But he kept his own illusions alive by continuing to write, and he wrote well. He was a very gifted writer.*

Baseball was number two. He was very, very, big on baseball. It didn't seem to matter what team it was. He just loved his baseball. Dar once told me that when he was a young man, he even had some thoughts on turning pro.

The third thing, of course, was records. The very first record that he owned was a Fats Waller recording on Victor. That's how he started his record collection. Fats remained a big ticket item with Don until the end of his life.

Unlike Marili Morden, who felt imprisoned by the shop, Don Brown felt that running his own place gave him the freedom to do things when he wanted to. If he wanted to take a vacation, he either paid someone to watch the shop for him or he simply closed the doors, took the money out of the cash register home with him, and put up a sign that said, "Back next Tuesday." If he found a hot tip, he'd shut the shop down for an hour, go check out the lead, and then come back later that day. Gary Hammond recalled Brown's changing personality.

Don was a mass of contradictions. He could be the sweetest guy in the world one day but if you rubbed him the wrong way once, you'd never get back on his good side again. Don had a Johnny Dodds Black Bottom Stompers record playing on his turntable; it was one he was planning on auctioning. Well, there was a guy in the shop who was really interested in getting that record. He played it several times and then asked Don what he wanted for it. "A hundred dollars." The guy hemmed and hawed and offered Don $65 and then $70 for the record. Finally, he said, "Look, I want that record and I'll pay you 75 bucks, and that's it." Don calmly said, "You know what I'm going to do before I sell you this record for $75?"

He had a hammer underneath the counter. He brought it out and whacked that thing until it flew into about 45 pieces. This guy walked out of the shop in tears. Don shouted after him, with expletives deleted: "Don't !$%&*!? come back!"

There was another guy who was trying to bargain the records on the quarter table down to a nickel apiece. Don was a very powerful man and he picked this guy up by the collar and literally threw him outside on the sidewalk. Don did not bargain. He priced records what he thought was a fair price and that was it.

But Don was also extraordinarily generous. One time, I got in over my head in an auction when I was in college. I won so many records I couldn't afford to buy them all. So I told Don about it and he bought all the records for me and said "Pay me back when you can." I did, gradually.

Don had very unusual tastes. He played piano and played well but didn't think much of his own playing. He loved Vladimir Horowitz and the piano music of Chopin and Beethoven. Another fellow he really liked a great deal was Jimmy Yancey.

Don didn't like anything at all that resembled rock 'n' roll, and he wasn't really fond of post-war blues either unless it was in a fairly traditional mode. He didn't care for amplified guitars. One time we got back to the shop after having lunch or something and somebody called and asked if he had any Beatles records. And Don said, "No, honey. In here, we step on 'em."

He tried to be patient with everybody because he was in business. It was only when someone really pushed him over the edge that Don would lose it. We had some regulars; one was a guy named Tony Thompson. Tony was a student at the university the same time I was there. He had a way of talking that made me grate my teeth together. He was a screwball. And he got to the point where Don would almost say, "Hey, Tony, get out of my sight." Tony had a habit of buying nothing but really cheap records. He'd buy off the dime table as much as he possibly could. One time, he was

Don Brown, early 1960s (Courtesy Darlene Brown).

shuffling records from place to place and finally, I walked in and found him on the top of the table. He'd just get up there and sit right on top of the table with records all around him.

Don was utterly devoted to Dar. Dar was the one thing in his life that was immutable as far as he was concerned. Around 1978 or '79, Dar came down with advanced colon cancer and had to have surgery. Every night, Don would talk to me and he never seemed to show much emotion but I could tell how worried he was about her.

Soon, record collectors, musicians, singers, and actors found out where the Jazz Man had moved and became semi-regulars, stopping in whenever they were in town to browse through Don's bins or check out the new reissue LPs that he was stocking. Some, like singer Mel Tormé, became friends. Gary Hammond recalled a few of the other personalities who frequented the shop.

The Rolling Stones used to come in from time to time. Don had the whole contingent in there once upon a time. They bought a lot of blues stuff. Don would unload two, three, four hundred dollars worth of stuff at a time to the Stones. Johnny St. Cyr lived in the neighborhood, so he was in all the time. He was quite a dapper fella. He always wore a three-piece suit and a tie. Even in the warmest weather, he was always dressed to the nines. Rosy McHargue came in quite often.

Don Brown:

I was the number one man in the neighborhood one day when two of the Rolling Stones came in. Charlie Watts and Ian Stewart. It was at the old shop when the Stones were big, big, big. Both of them wanted to buy old jazz records from the late '30s and early '40s: Albert Ammons and people like that. Ian was a boogie-woogie pianist and percussionist and wasn't really a part of the group; he was their road manager.

But the one thing Charlie Watts wanted to buy—that he didn't get to buy—was the Bessie Smith poster. When he saw that, he laid his wallet down on the counter after taking it out of his coat pocket. He kept it there because it wouldn't fold over because it had an inch-thick stack of hundred dollar bills in it. So he laid it on the counter and said, "You take out what you want out of that because I'm going to take that poster home with me." I didn't sell it to him, and when the shop closed for good, I took it home with me.

Gary Hammond:

I remember Woody Allen came in there a couple of times. Someone said once that Perry Como came into the shop. Sinatra was rumored to have come in, but I don't think that's true at all. A lot of the singers who were popular in the post-war years would come in and want to find some of their records. I was there when Jabbo Smith came in. He just shook his head and said that he couldn't believe people remembered him and his records. He said, "They were trying to make me into another Louis Armstrong."

Bob Hite and Henry Vestine, the co-founders of Canned Heat, used to have a skiffle band that played in the old shop. Bob was in his early 20s and he and Henry were right about the same age. Don was always self-deprecating about his musicianship, but he played guitar and one of the brass instruments besides piano. But his big thing was playing jug. On Saturday evenings, after the shop had closed, Bob, Henry, Don, and Bruce Bromberg got together and just had fun playing old blues, and that's where Canned Heat really got started. I remember them doing "Bullfrog Blues," with that wonderful guitar lick at the beginning by Henry Vestine. Vestine, even at that young age, was a budding alcoholic. Hite just became a druggie. I remember when their first LP came out, it was a doggone good record.

One day, I received a call from Bob Hite who informed me that Bukka White was playing at the Ash Grove, which was on Melrose Avenue in those days. He knew I had a portable reel-to-reel tape recorder and asked if I could bring it with me and pick up Bukka to take him to the shop for an impromptu session. Bukka and I arrived at about 11:00 on a Saturday morning. He was well supplied with a little liquid sustenance (i.e. 90 proof). We only had time to cut two pieces: "World Boogie" and his signature tune "Fixin' to Die." One of the mistakes I made was turning off the recorder when he had finished. As I recall, he talked to us for about a half hour afterwards. I still have that recording, which was made at the shop, and you can still hear Vestine and Bromberg in the background. One night after Vestine had had a little too much to drink, he said, "Let's start a band." And that's when Canned Heat was born.

On Wednesday, August 11, 1965, an event rocked the city of Los Angeles, which also had a permanent effect on the stability of the Jazz Man.

Less than ten miles southeast of the shop lay the residential district of Watts. At around 7 p.m. that evening, a white California Highway Patrol officer arrested a black motorist named Marquette Frye on suspicion of drunk driving. Racial tension had been building in the area, and the circumstances surrounding Frye's arrest as well as other members of his family triggered a citywide conflagration. By Friday, rioters had looted hundreds of business and set fires to others, prompting an 8 p.m. curfew as government officials tried to gain control of the community. While national guardsmen remained in the area to maintain order, the region surrounding central and south-central Los Angeles continued to be a tinder box. The next day, Gary Hammond and the other shop regulars showed up as usual for their weekly gathering of chatting and playing old records. They found, however, that there was still tension in the streets, and with gunfire going off and people shouting on Pico Blvd., the Jazz Man no longer was the safe haven it once was for record collectors. Gary Hammond:

On the one Saturday when all hell broke loose, Don closed the shop. It was about two or three in the afternoon and we were fearing for our lives. John Fraser and Keith Sawyer and I fled to Mar Vista and stayed with Don and Dar at their house. It was all on the news and I called my folks and said, "Don't worry. We're out of there and we're in Santa Monica right now."

Two weeks later, on August 28, when things had settled down somewhat, Joe Levi, an occasional customer of the shop, walked in with a special guest: the legendary Reb Spikes. The co-founder of the Spikes Brothers Music House and producer of the first recordings by Kid Ory in 1921 was now 77 years old, but still in good physical condition. Customers were still a little jittery about the racial unrest surrounding them, but there was a celebrity in the shop and the regulars greeted Spikes like a conquering hero. Don Gray was there that day:

Joe Levi was a very dapper black dude who was sort of a braggart. He loved jazz of all kinds. He liked the early stuff but also the post-war bop

A red-letter day at the Jazz Man: Don Brown (left) and Joe Levi (right) welcome Reb Spikes (center), August 28, 1965. The Watts riots had decimated Los Angeles for the previous two weeks, but life at the shop went on.

Former Jazz Man manager Harvey Newland (left) and shop regular Nat Ross (right), with Reb Spikes (center), August 28, 1965.
(Photos courtesy Darlene Brown).

by Dizzy Gillespie and Charlie Parker. We used to make fun of him. "What are you listening to that stuff for? That's for junkies and dope addicts." And he'd laugh and laugh and laugh. He got along real well with Nat Ross, despite the fact that they were total opposites. Nat was kind of a slob and you could hear his old smoking car coming a month away. Well, Joe had to have a Cadillac or an Oldsmobile. And he became a shop fixture. But after this, that braggart thing was over. There was no bullshit about him, I mean, here he comes with Reb Spikes, for crying out loud.

The Jazz Man's Saturday Crowd - August 28, 1965. Left to right: Nat Ross, Don Brown, Keith Sawyer, Joe Levi, Harvey Newland (partially hidden), Reb Spikes, Don Gray (Courtesy Darlene Brown).

Joe was kind of a Jelly Roll Morton type because he looked like a Creole. He was a lot of fun to be around, because he'd start bringing up names like Curtis Mosby and Reb Spikes. We were given fair warning that Joe was bringing Reb in so we were all there bright and early that Saturday morning. I brought in Reb's Columbia to autograph and he wrote on it, "Dear Don: Hope you keep this record 100 years. Reb Spikes." I looked it up afterwards and found out that the record was recorded on a Saturday. This happened during the riots. What we were doing out there I don't know. But I told Pete Whelan about Reb coming in and he was really impressed. He said, "Wow! You really met that dude!" and I said, "Yeah," and we got pictures of him and everything, standing out in front of the shop with Don. He spent about an hour in the shop that day.

But the Spikes visit was one of the last memorable moments at 2689. The effect the Watts riots had on the neighborhood took its toll and the neighborhood changed from a seedy area to a dangerous seedy area. As a result, foot traffic in the shop slowed to a crawl. Gary Hammond:

When he started out there, it was never really a problem walking down the street. Don and I would often go out to breakfast at a place across from the shop called Fay's. But as the mid-'60s turned into the late '60s, things started to get really tough in that part of Pico Blvd. Fay died and the restaurant closed. Then the convenience store across the street closed and Don began to see that this was a neighborhood that was in serious decline.

Then there were a couple of shootings on the street, so Don started doing some soul searching about what to do. A lot of his regular customers began to be afraid to come into that area. Then some really nasty incidents happened. A gal got raped in broad daylight right on Pico Blvd. and then a guy got shot to death, and I think Dar started getting very concerned about Don's safety and told him that he ought to think about moving the shop. So he started looking for a location that was closer to home. His eyesight was beginning to fail him and he was getting awfully tired of the drive from West Los Angeles.

He was not really comfortable about making a move because Don was a creature of habit. But 2689 wasn't a great location to begin with. And the building, which had been built around 1900, was quite old by then. There was always the fear of fire, especially with that lunatic Walter next door, who was more than capable of starting one by accident that would have taken out that entire strip of stores.

Three factors: the Watts riots, the condition of the shop, and the annoying antics of Walter convinced Brown that it was time to vacate 2689. The final straw happened when plaster began falling from the ceiling in chunks, which Brown took as a sign to load up and move somewhere else. It took nearly three years to come to the decision, but when he did, he found a suitable location, 11 miles west on Pico Blvd. in the more restful, casual community of Santa Monica. In the spring of 1968, only a month before the Martin Luther King, Jr. assassination sent the neighborhood again

Street view of West Pico Blvd., facing East. Nat Ross's 1929 Hudson is parked in front of the Jazz Man, c. mid-1960s (Courtesy John Fraser).

into a racial uproar, Don Brown faced the daunting task of hauling tens of thousands of 78s across town. The Jazz Man had moved over ten times since its inception on the Sunset Strip in 1939. It was at this next location, 3323 Pico Blvd., where it stayed for 15 years, the longest time it would spend at any one place.

Moving day...again. Spring 1968 (Courtesy Darlene Brown).

Chapter Twenty-One
An Atavist's Paradise

In the first issue of *The Record Finder* in 1968, Don Brown let his subscribers know that the Jazz Man's move to Santa Monica was imminent. In a brief note, Brown did not mention a specific address, but said, "It is a time of much confusion… and little accomplishment," advising his readers to "keep the faith" and "keep an eye open for a new address." He had initially hoped to move before the end of February, but it would be into March before he finally signed the lease on the new building, rolled up his sleeves, and started moving boxes of records. Although he had some help, Brown did most of the moving himself. On one of his trips, while carrying a heavy box of 78s, he stumbled over the threshold and fell headlong onto his face, fracturing his nose.

Don Gray:

He didn't get fully moved in until the middle of the summer. I remember coming in and seeing him with a broken nose and a bandage on his face. There were some guys who came to the old shop who had a truck and helped Don moved all the useless records that he had there.

Darlene Brown:

I was in Washington, D.C. at the time he moved. I had to go for my job. I used to work at System Development Corporation, which was a spin-off of the Rand Corporation. I had a top secret clearance there. My boss was

248

Don Brown takes time out from his moving 78s crosstown to pose for a picture in front of the Jazz Man's new home at 3323 Pico Blvd. in Santa Monica, spring 1968. Brown mistakenly assumed the shop got its start in 1938, which was actually one year prior to its actual beginnings on the Sunset Strip. (Courtesy Darlene Brown)

a chief scientist assigned to Washington, so I asked him, "What can I do to help?" and he said, "You can come and work for me." I talked to Don about it and he said that if I wanted to do it, I should do it. So I made a bargain with him. I was there for three months and came home when it was half over to visit Don and see how things were going with the move.

When he finally completed the move, he notified his customers through *The Record Finder,* and slowly, they made the transition to 3323 Pico Blvd. as well.

The one big complaint when I moved in here was "My God, you've lost all the atmosphere. You don't have atmosphere here anymore." And I said, "Yeah, I know it, because I was always sweeping it up down at the other place."

Gary Hammond:

Don didn't mind the move. He was happy that it brought him closer to his home in West L.A. But he was concerned about the impact that it would have on his business. When he moved to Santa Monica, he started paying a lot more rent than he did at 2689. After Don moved out there, the Mexican restaurant across the street started getting a lot of new business. He'd bring me along with John Fraser, Don Gray, and all the rest of those tortilla-loving guys who had been hanging around the shop for so many years. His neighbors loved him because these guys would come out on Saturdays and go invade this Mexican restaurant.

Saturday became the official "hang-out day" for the shop regulars. It began in the early '60s, when a few regular customers started spending the entire day at the shop, talking with Don, playing records, drinking beer in the back room, smoking cigars, and playfully insulting each other's tastes in records, clothing, favorite sports teams, and anything else that came to mind. Gary Hammond:

3323 was larger than 2689 so Don opened up the back room to people who wanted to browse. He had a lot of rhythm-and-blues back there. In the old shop, the back room was mainly for overstock and things that he was going to auction, so people really didn't have access to the back room there. 3323 was a lot nicer building, too. It was built sometime in the 1940s, while the old shop was literally falling apart.

The reason the Saturday Crowd got started was because of Don Gray and John Fraser. They both lived out in the Inland Empire and the only day they could come in was on Saturday. So I'd do the same thing and eventually, that became the day when everybody would get together. Don encouraged it because these guys would bring in their own records either to show off or to trade and Don figured that while they were there, they might buy some of his records also.

One by one, the Saturday Crowd grew, until there was a basic group of about two dozen regulars and semi-regulars. Others dropped in sporadically, like guest stars on a situation comedy, but the core group showed up faithfully, week after week. Then there were the oddballs, neighborhood derelicts who wandered into the shop accidentally, novice collectors who didn't know the difference between a 78 and an LP, and the occasional mysterious customer, whose unusual behavior or exotic musical taste baffled everyone. In his 23 years as owner of the Jazz Man, Don Brown claimed to have "seen 'em all" and was never shocked when somebody completely out of left field walked through the front door. Tom Ball, a collector who later became a professional blues singer and harmonica player, began frequenting the shop just after the move to Santa Monica:

I have loads of memories of the place, but mostly, I just think of it as an atavist's paradise, a quiet spot in the eye of the storm where one could go back in time and wade through tens of thousands of dust-covered relics. Oh, all the weird crap I culled from his famous dime table!

One of two dime tables in the front of the shop at 3323 Pico Blvd. Also seen are 78 stacks and LP displays (Courtesy Darlene Brown).

If you found something interesting or with an odd title, such as "Bring It on Home to Grandma" by the Mississippi Mud Mashers, Don would chomp his cigar, cough, and say, "What the hell, let's find out what it is" and allow you to give it a spin on his perpetually rotating turntable. In those days I was pretty broke and hardly ever bought anything, but Don was always helpful and put up with all my musical and discographical questions. In particular, I think he was kind of amused at those of us with a passion for blues. I often saw Bob Hite, Henry Vestine, Barry Hansen (aka Dr. Demento), and [independent record producer] *Bill Givens in the shop.*

Being a student at nearby Santa Monica City College, I usually stopped in during the week, so I wasn't part of the weekend Dixieland Mafia. I just recall seeing all the beer cans in the alley on the days after. Don was a very friendly guy, although on occasion he did not suffer fools easily. Little by little, as the years went by, his beard became more and more the color of nicotine, but his demeanor and laughter stayed young. And on the rare occasion when a City College coed wandered in, lost, and looking for the latest LP by the Archies, Don became smooth-tongued, courtly, and 25 all over again.

Back in the late '60s, Don had a weekly radio show called "Cobweb Corner," which was broadcast on KRHM. One night, I was listening to it and Don played the 78 "Who Put the Benzedrine in Mrs. Murphy's Ovaltine?" Me being 18 years old, and this being 1969, the height of the so-called "counterculture," I thought this record was just about the coolest thing possible, aside from blowing up a building, so the next day, I hitchhiked down to the Jazz Man to ask Don about it.

"Oh yeah," he said, chomping his cigar and grinning, "That's Harry 'The Hipster.' Slim Gaillard's on there, too. 1946."

"Do you have it in stock?" I asked. "Can I hear it again?"

Just then, the front door opened and a young Hare Krishna walked in, bald head, saffron robe and all. He said nothing, just stood by the door,

(Images courtesy Darlene Brown)

peering around, his eyes adjusting to the dim light. Don ignored him and fished around for the 78. "Here it is," he said finally, and put it on the turntable.

So we stood there, listening to Harry "The Hipster." When it was finished, I asked, "Is that for sale?" Don looked it over and held it up to the light. "It's only about VG," he said. "How 'bout a buck-and-a-quarter?" "Sold!" I said.

Suddenly the Hare Krishna guy piped up, "You like that record?"

I nodded and Don chomped his cigar and squinted non-committally.

"That's my daddy," said the Hare Krishna, opening the door to leave. "Harry 'The Hipster' Gibson is my daddy. He's a cab driver now." He closed the door and left.

Don and I looked at each other. "Think he's pullin' our leg?" I asked.

"Who knows?" Don said wearily.

One of the regulars who had been coming since the early '60s was Nathaniel Lester Ross. Like John Fraser, Nat Ross was a schoolteacher, a tall, burly black man with a sardonic sense of humor. In addition to records, Ross was a fan of vintage automobiles, and when the shop was at 2689, he would often show up, resplendent, driving a 1929 Hudson. As the years went by, Ross's automobiles got more and more dilapidated, and by the late '70s, he was driving clunkers, cars that were held together only by the rust on the rivets. His cars became his calling card, and the other regulars would often wonder: 1) What jalopy will Ross roll up in next week, and 2) How does he keep it running? Donald Lee Nelson:

Our favorite thing about Nat was that he was a car genius. When he would get a motor-driven instrument of any kind, it would immediately rust, become noisy, emit noxious odors, and frighten children, dogs, and all sorts of things for miles around. "But it runs" is what he would say with

Nat Ross and one of his famous indestructible automobiles. The trunk and driver's side door were tied shut with rope. Daylight could be seen through the floorboards in the front seat (Photos by Cary Ginell).

constant smiles.

Ross was an inveterate collector of jazz vocal groups such as the Mills Brothers, the Ink Spots, and the Boswell Sisters, and was also extremely knowledgeable about old movies. He wrote an impressive biography of legendary silent screen star Lon Chaney, and brought copies of the book to the shop to sell, while grumpily autographing them.

Ross formally immortalized the Saturday Crowd by issuing a slim, typewritten publication called *B-A-R-F* (an acronym whose meaning has vanished over the years), with a subtitle that he borrowed from Shakespeare's *Macbeth*: "A Monograph Full of Sound and Fury Signifying Nothing." The piece was prompted by a regular topic of discussion in the Jazz Man's back room: "If you lost all of your records but one and could decide which recording that one would be, which one would you choose?" Ross's tome, which was dedicated to Ira "Buster" Moten, the piano-playing nephew of Kansas City bandleader Bennie Moten, was dated June 2, 1975. The manuscript was only six pages long, and included an introduction that named the Saturday regulars and defined their respective tastes in music.

In his introductory paragraph, Ross wrote:

For the past dozen or so years, a group of individuals has gathered at Don Brown's Jazz Man Record Shop in Los Angeles-Santa Monica for the purpose of boasting about and demonstrating their own particular taste in music: a condition described by Doug Lawler as "anal cavity clearing."

The result of the informal survey was that the kind of music favored by a majority of the Saturday Crowd was black jazz. Minority votes went to such genres as hillbilly music (Eugene Earle and Donald Lee Nelson), country blues (Bob Hite's younger brother Richard), swing (Alan Roberts), Mexican (George Roblin), and others. The favored time period spanned from June 1926 to June 1933. After taking pot shots at virtually everyone on his list, Ross summed up his findings:

And as a final question one might ask: which of the twenty-two records discussed is the best and which selection demonstrates the epitome of taste. The answer, of course, is NONE, for as Doug Lawler so aptly put it in describing the Jazz Man habitués: "All of their taste is in their mouths."

"Playing the dozens," which in the sports world is now known as "trash talk," became a by-product of the Saturday Crowd, in which insulting everything about a person was the order of the day. To be a member-in-good-standing of this informal club, one had to be able to dish it out and take it with equal effectiveness. As the only African American in the group, Nat Ross was often the barb of mock-racist diatribes. This became a hallmark of the regular Saturday get-togethers, and innocent bystanders rummaging around in the back room were often privy to these seemingly threatening, but ultimately harmless verbal battles. Don Brown:

There was some guy in here once, and it was probably his first or second time here. And it was a Saturday. Well, whatever he was looking for turned out to be in the back room. And Nat and Gray are going at it in their typical mock "nigger/honky" style, and this guy turned around, came back out and said, "I'll see you Tuesday" and walked out. Tuesday he came back and he says, "You know, I was here on Saturday and I was going to go in the back room, but I heard those two guys and I thought there was going to be a race riot, so I left." A lot of people wouldn't come back on Tuesday after hearing all that. It would scare them away permanently. But if they were here three weeks in a row, they would realize that these guys loved each other. And they did.

The core members had their own unique quirks and personalities. John Fraser was the peacock of the Saturday Crowd. A junior college speech teacher, Fraser was dubbed "The Silver Fox" due to his neatly coiffed silver crewcut, stylish short-sleeved golf shirts, and brightly colored double-knit slacks. A fan of hot jazz and dance band music, Fraser always brought his own beer glass to the shop and was also known for his gargantuan appetite; no matter how much Mexican food or beer he consumed, it never changed his calm, bemused demeanor. Fraser's speech was peppered with "two-dollar words" and he always referred to himself in the third person, saying things like: "The Fox believes that Wingy Manone was a poor man's imitation of Louis Armstrong" and other such bon mots of musical wisdom.

John Fraser, "The Silver Fox." (Photo by Cary Ginell)

Don Gray (Photo by Cary Ginell)

Don Gray, who was nicknamed "Chubbsy," was the portly clown prince of the Saturday Crowd. One of the elder statesmen of the shop, he had been coming to the Jazz Man longer than anyone except Harvey Newland. Gray's quick wit and ability to mimic other members of the Crowd often had the back room roaring with laughter. He was the chief baiter of Nat Ross, but despite their constant name-calling, the two were good friends. Come mid-afternoon, either Gray or Fraser would break out cigars and the back room filled with the pungent odor of smoke amidst all the hilarity.

Donald Lee Nelson was a throwback to olden times. He fancied himself as one who came from the romantic old South: a true southern gentleman from antebellum days. Nelson was an avid collector of hillbilly music from Appalachia but also prided himself on his collection of rare Cajun 78s:

I had always liked that kind of music and when I was in my early 20s I started looking around for the original records. Eventually, I stumbled into the old shop over on Pico and Normandie. The place was Cockroach Heaven, but I started coming once a month and then twice a month, and then when he moved to Santa Monica, closer to where I live, it was every week. So I'd stay every week for an hour, then it got to be two hours, then it was four hours, and pretty soon it was all day, and then we started going out to dinner, and it really became quite a social organization.

Nelson, who worked as a buyer for the restaurant at the Ambassador hotel, always came to the shop in a three-piece wool suit, no matter what the weather. Despite his fastidious appearance, he engaged in ribald, often flowery insults with his fellow collectors, who often bristled whenever he brought in one of his G+ condition Cajun records by such artists as Joseph Falcon or Amedie Ardoin.

Donald Lee Nelson (Photo by Cary Ginell)

It was a privilege to come in to the Jazz Man every week. It was an honor. It was something a person got to do because he belonged. It was a completely unique club, and if you didn't fit in, you were frozen out. For me, it took a good six months of just being on the fringes of it, fitting in a little more and a little more each week. Everybody is nice to you and polite to you when you come in and that's when you really feel like you don't belong. But the more they alienate you, and degrade you, and pick at you, and insult you, the more you feel welcome. Don Gray and Doug Lawler were champions of that sort of thing, probably because they had very high I.Q.s and fast minds. And, they've got the guts to take it when they get it back. That's something you have to have here. If you can't take it, don't start it. Moral, racial, religious, psychological—you give an opinion on any of these things, you'll get nailed on it. There are virtually no sacred calves.

Nelson, who was an accomplished chef, could also be counted on to bring home-baked goodies. Once, he brought in an especially atomic-powered jalapeño bread, which caused the boys in the back room to lunge for their beer cans after taking a bite.

Doug Lawler, an aerospace engineer in his early 50s, collected jazz piano records of the late 1920s and early 1930s. Lawler stationed himself in the doorway that separated the front room from the back room. Wearing the same purple golf shirt every Saturday, Lawler was the shop's version of the mythological Cerberus, the guard dog of Hades, who passed muster on anyone who dared venture into the back room. Donald Lee Nelson:

Although Doug and I shared political views, musically, we were about as polarized as we could get. He's the North Pole, a typical Yankee, and I'm the South Pole. He came over and fixed my sound system once, so I invited him over for dinner and we became friends. Now, if my car is getting repaired, I might call Doug or Fraser for a lift, and they never grumble about what they're doing or gas or anything like that. It's "Sure. When do you want to go?" So even though it looks like we don't get along because of the vast differences in our tastes in music, we're really very close friends.

Doug Lawler (Photo by Cary Ginell)

Eugene Earle was a good-natured, rotund collector of vintage hillbilly recordings who became affectionately known as "Gentleman Gene." Earle, who worked for Hughes Aircraft, had a record collection that was unmatched, not only in the country but in the world, and he earned himself a respected "throne" in a wooden captain's chair in the back room. Earle ran regular mail auctions

"Gentleman" Gene Earle, jealously guarding his record box full of rare hillbilly 78s.
(Photo by Cary Ginell)

and it was an exciting day when a new edition came out and the hillbilly collectors pored greedily over the listings. Donald Lee Nelson:

Gene was always kind enough to share any auction list with us that he received, not just his. He was very generous in that fashion. So we'd give him our bids and he'd submit them for us. And this is where the trust comes in. I'd bid through him, he'd get the bill and pay for the records. Then he'd call me up and say "You owe me such-and-such amount," and I'd faint, and for the next few weeks I'd live on a diet of thin soup.

Gene was more sedate than the rest of the group. He didn't go for the violent insults. He gets a certain amount of violent insults simply because he's a hillbilly collector. Gene was a fiscal conservative, but if I were on the street corner selling pencils, Gene would stop and buy all the pencils I had. That's the kind of person he was.

Harvey Newland, the former manager of the shop, had gotten married in the 1960s after giving way to Don Brown and for years, did not show up on Saturdays. But in the 1970s, he returned, a tall, quiet presence who never spoke about his time as shop manager. Don Brown:

Harvey is a very quiet, almost mouse-like individual. He just sits around very quietly and absorbs anything that's being played, because he's like me; he's got very Catholic tastes and I don't really think that Harvey has ever heard a record from 1960 or older where he didn't have something good to say about it. He doesn't jump up and down and say, "Wow, what a great record this is!" He'll just sit there and nod his head, pick his imaginary guitar, or blow his imaginary trombone.

Newland rarely engaged in the raucous behavior in the back room. Usually, he was out front, listening to whatever 78 was on the turntable at the time. At times, the raucous talk in the back room threatened to alienate customers, but Brown could never bring himself to throw anyone out because, as in his own words, "Where would they go?" Over the years, the camaraderie amongst the collectors became close, and Brown became

Harvey Newland (Photo by Cary Ginell)

the unofficial father figure to the group. They would insult each other without mercy, but they were always respectful of Brown.

Stephen Bartron was one of the younger members of the fraternity. Bartron was known as the shop "changeling," who collected country blues one week, switched to jug bands, and then back again. He had a knack for finding rare 78s and trading them for whatever he was interested in at the moment. Many in the shop admired Bartron for always being in the right place at the right time when it came to record hunting, and when he showed up with a box of records, nattily dressed in a sport jacket, but never wearing a tie, everyone sat up and paid attention.

The Saturday Crowd knew each other's musical tastes and foibles, but were hard-pressed to know much else about their lives, yet they spent Saturday after Saturday together. Donald Lee Nelson:

If one of the regulars didn't show, we'd call. Nobody knew if something hadn't happened to that person and they were in a bad spot and needed our help. We couldn't stand to think that the poor wretch might be laying on the floor, clutching a mint Gennett in his hand—"A" side up.

On Saturday, each person brings in his own little black or gray or white or purple or metal or monogrammed box and plays his own records. And anybody who didn't like that particular record utters obscenities, runs out of the room, and retires to the

Stephen Bartron (Photo by Cary Ginell)

back to get Fritos and a Coors Light, not necessarily in that order, while the rest of us sneer in the direction of the back room, making obscene comments and making great effort to show how much we appreciate whatever is being played that drove them back there, no matter how God-awful it is. Doug is against it all, and that's why I love him.

Don Brown had fathered a unique social network. He was fully aware of the role that he played as "den father," arbiter of arguments, and keeper of the flame. His ever-present beard and cigars became his trademarks, and as the years rolled by, musicians, collectors, and other visitors to the shop not only depended on Brown to find what they wanted for them, but viewed him as the one and only Jazz Man.

Brown was there every Saturday, rain or shine, opening up promptly at 10 a.m. The hillbilly collectors arrived first, followed by Gray, Fraser, Ross, and the rest, each laden with beer, chips, or other munchies, and a box of 78s to share on Brown's turntable. The front room was reserved for record playing and discussion of the relative merits of whatever was playing at the moment. In the back room, there was joke-telling, trivia contests, commentary on the events of the day, and talk of everything except records. Donald Lee Nelson:

Don Brown had probably the only cash drawer in the city of Los Angeles that was completely open. We all made change for people, we all ran up sales for customers when he was busy; Don could go out for the whole day and nothing would happen. There was a certain honor that prevailed.

Don was a nice, nice man. He's the guy who let us use the shop as a playroom or as a clubhouse. Every once in a while he had to verbally bop somebody over the head for getting a mite out-of-hand but he was the root of the tree, and we were

Don Brown, 1983. (Photo by Cary Ginell)

*3323, shortly after Brown moved the shop to Santa Monica.
(Courtesy Darlene Brown)*

all of the branches and twigs. If it was anybody else but Don who was running the shop, we would all be tossed out on our ears.

When a collector from out-of-town came to Los Angeles, invariably, he would be directed to the Jazz Man on Saturdays, where he would be greeted and welcomed by the Crowd, followed by a sumptuous dinner at the Mexican restaurant across the street after the shop closed that evening. One such collector who Don Brown didn't welcome with open arms was Robert Altshuler. A leading collector of vintage jazz 78s and a former executive with Columbia Records, Altshuler, who was un-affectionately referred to as "Altie" or "The Big Kahuna," made irregular visits to the West Coast, but when he did, he would show up at the Jazz Man to find buyers for pricey items he always seemed to have on hand, many of which he absconded with from Columbia's vaults. Brown thought Altshuler's visits were more self-serving than social, and hated the disruptions caused when he came out. Don Gray:

One time, Don was already having a bad day when he heard that Altie was going to be coming in. This must have been '72 or '73, somewhere around in there. When he walked into the shop, we saw that he had suitcases in both hands and we all said, "Oh, shit, we're outta here." Doug Lawler said, "I don't think it's going to be much fun." That was the day that Lew Upton did what he shouldn't have done. He told Altie, "Hey, you want to make Brown happy? Bring him some free records, man, he's an Ellington collector." So Altie brought Don a couple of Cameos or something—not great stuff, but pretty good stuff. Don looked at them and threw them on the counter and I heard one of them break. All the time Altie was dealing in the back room, Don was out in front, getting madder and madder by the minute. He started playing an LP and turned the volume up so high you couldn't hear anything else. Well, that's when I looked at Doug, winked and went out the back door. I thought that fireworks were going to start going off. Well, curiosity got the best of me, so in a half an hour I came back. I never did do much dealing with Altie. I did get a few things from him in the mail, but as far as buying things from him in the shop, I left that to George Robin and John Fraser because nobody else I know ever bought anything from him because his prices were just too high.

Donald Lee Nelson:

I always got a kick out of the greed and the buttering up some people did in order to get a record they wanted. I am sure that no junior member of the diplomatic service curries favor or licks boots more than some of the people did to get a record.

Celebrities continued to find the Jazz Man as well. Mel Tormé made the transition from 2689 and could often be seen during the week thumbing through the latest LP reissues of vintage jazz in the stacks Don had set up in the front room. Other visitors included pianist Mary Lou Williams, trumpeter Jabbo Smith, and on one occasion, even the great Louis Armstrong, who autographed a publicity photo that hung proudly on the wall in back of the counter until the shop closed. Gary Hammond:

Don and I did a radio program together on what was purported to be Louis Armstrong's 70th birthday in 1970. It wasn't prepared; it was sloppy, but apparently, everybody liked it, because Barney Bigard called in to the studio while we were on the air and then later came into the shop. Rex Stewart was kind of a regular there, too, and when I was teaching a course on jazz at USC, I had Don in to do a lecture with me and he brought Rex in. So we had a pretty good contingent. Some of them I did not meet. Monette Moore was one, but I never saw her in the shop. She gave Don the copy of the handwritten lyrics she wrote for "Burgundy Street Blues" that she recorded with George Lewis.

Occasionally, there were some incidents, usually involving regulars who consumed too much alcohol. One of these was Bill Givens, the founder of an early LP reissue label called Origin Jazz Library. Born in Kentucky in 1930, Givens received a degree in English from New York University. In 1961, he and a friend from boarding school named Pete Whelan decided to start their own record label for the purpose of reissuing rare country blues on LP. Their first release, an LP of vintage recordings by Delta blues singer Charlie Patton, became a highly influential record, and was followed by a succession of other records with similar artists. Origin Jazz Library turned people on to a music that was all but dead. Budding rock guitarists like Keith Richards, Eric Clapton, and Jimmy Page bought OJL's blues reissues and helped carry country blues into a new generation of influence. Whelan bowed out of the record company in 1967, but Givens took over the label by himself. He moved from Washington, D.C. to the West Coast and found his way to the Jazz Man, where he fit in perfectly with the eccentric Saturday Crowd. Givens became the shop sage, always ready to pontificate on any subject, turning the mundane into something of mad ironic wit.

Givens was boisterous and rough on the outside, but a generous man at heart. His major failing was his consumption of alcohol, which would often get him in trouble, even with the accepting Saturday Crowd. Don Gray remembered one occasion when Givens had too much to drink, which resulted in the only physical altercation witnessed in the back room of the shop:

Canned Heat's Bob Hite (left) vs. Jazz Man regular Bill Givens (right).
(Photo at right by Cary Ginell)

The only fight I ever saw in the shop was between Givens and Bob Hite of Canned Heat. That was a knock-down-drag-out, with bodies rolling all over the place. It was all Givens' fault. This was the early '70s and Bob had on his Alan Ladd jacket; a buckskin thing with a big hat, and he had a long beard and long hair and was going through the records in the back room. Givens was there drinking wine, and he started making catty comments about Canned Heat and about how fat Bob was. Finally, he said something that crossed the line and I saw that there was going to be a problem. And I mean a bad one. I think somebody said to him, "Bill, shut the fuck up," but by then he was out of control. When he got like that, you couldn't tell him anything. Sure as hell, they tangled right there in the back room, and I mean rolling on the floor and knocking over boxes. I'm sure there were broken records that resulted from this. Don got to the point where I thought he was going to call the cops, but he managed to separate them.

After that, Givens showed up less frequently, but when he did, there was always the possibility of another explosive confrontation. Fortunately, the Hite rumble in the back room never repeated itself.

In addition to veteran collectors like Givens, Gray, and Fraser, the shop also attracted younger ones like Jonathan Pearl, who first encountered the shop when he was 17 years old:

In 1974, I had a friend who collected 78s, but he always got his at Salvation Army and Goodwill stores for ten cents apiece. At that time, second-hand stores were starting to die out, but he wouldn't spend what Don was charging for a 78 so I had to come in by myself. The first time I came in to the shop, Don had one of the strangest customers he's ever had to this day. It was a guy who looked like an emaciated Buffalo Bill who wore Western regalia, was very thin and old, and had hair that came down to his shoulders. I remember he was playing 78s and was telling Don that the ghost of Louis Armstrong lived in his closet and played trumpet with him every night. But he feared that people were stealing the music on his tape recorder. I got about halfway into the store and listened to this guy talk for about five minutes and said to myself, "This is too weird for me," and I left.

The second time I came in, a guy was in the shop and said to me, "Oh! You look like one of the Marx Brothers." I didn't last very long that time either. It wasn't until late 1975 that I had the nerve to start coming in regularly.

For several years, the regulars of the Saturday Crowd were tolerant of Pearl's presence but ignored him, as they did with most outsiders. It wasn't until they started insulting him the way they insulted each other that he finally felt that he belonged. Don Brown had nothing but nice things to say about Pearl:

If somebody asks a question, you know he'll have an answer. And 99% of the time, he's right. He's one of the most knowledgeable young cats I've run into. If he doesn't know, he'll be at the UCLA library Monday morning to find the answer.

Over the course of the shop's stay at 3323 Pico Blvd., minor incidents occurred that were normal for an independent retail store in Los Angeles, including windows broken by vandals, burglary attempts, power outages, and the effects from periodic California earthquakes, which threatened to bring down the heavy 78 cabinets on the heads of browsers. In 1983, Don Brown remembered:

Even today, when I walk in the door, the first thing I do is look in the back room to see if it's light or dark. If it's dark, the back door is still closed. No matter what you're doing at home, you can be gassed out of your mind or whatever, you still wonder if someone is trying to break in through the front window or the back door, either accidentally or on purpose.

One of the reasons I stayed 23 years is because once you dig yourself into a 15-foot hole, the more you try to dig your way out, the deeper your hole gets. But seriously, it was all the crazy people I met. As any collector knows, anybody that collects anything is basically crazy. They have an anal complex, as one of John Fraser's friends told him; they have to suck in everything. A lot of them know just as much as you do; some of them know less but think they know more, like the guy who heard me playing a record by Tommy Dorsey and said, "Yeah, I have a record his father made: Thomas A. Dorsey."

Running the Jazz Man was always a struggle for Don Brown. In 1977, he decided to discontinue *The Record Finder*, which had finally become too much trouble for what it was bringing in. He kept hosting his Sunday night radio program, *Cobweb Corner*, which aired first on KRHM and then on KCRW. Although he was the owner of one of the world's most comprehensive collections of records by Duke Ellington, Brown liked many different kinds of music. When he went home at night, he would often listen to classical piano music. (His favorite composer was Frederic Chopin.) Brown played piano, but only at home. Many shop regulars were never aware of Brown's musical talent. Brown was fond of saying, "When you work for a candy company, you don't go home after work and eat candy." Brown once listed his top "Desert Island Discs," which showed his

The Jazz Man Record Shop aged Don Brown prematurely. The above photo was taken in 1970 when Brown was 47. Below, Brown at 59 in the shop's back room in 1982.
(Top photo courtesy Gary Hammond. Lower photo by Cary Ginell)

sophisticated breadth and knowledge of popular and classical music:

    "Washboard Wiggle" – Tiny Parham & his Musicians

    "Diabelli Variations" – Ludwig Van Beethoven

    "Lonely Villa" – The Casino Dance Orchestra

    "Mountain City Blues" – Clarence Williams

    "Starvation Blues" – Jesse Stone

    "Bucket's Got a Hole in It" – Tom Gates

    "How Long Blues" – Jimmy Yancey

    "Alone in San Francisco" – Thelonious Monk

    "Flock of Blues" – Sioux City Six

Although Saturdays were always busy, Brown spent many solitary hours on weekdays, sitting in the shop waiting for customers to come in. In the early '60s, he would come to work in a coat and tie. As the years wore on, he became more casual in his attire, until, toward the end, he was favoring Bermuda shorts and Hawaiian shirts during the hot summer months. The daily grind of opening and closing the shop, hunting down records to sell, keeping up with his distributors and mail order customers, and dealing with the day-to-day stress of running a business by himself took a physical toll on Brown. He aged noticeably in the 1970s, and by the early '80s, although he was not yet 60, he looked considerably older. Darlene Brown:

Toward the end, when he was getting tired and the rent was increasing, he would worry and say to me, "What am I going to do with all these records?"

Rumblings about the Jazz Man shutting down began in late January 1983. In early May, the owner of the restaurant next door, an Irish pub called Fran O'Brien's, wanted to expand into Don Brown's space. O'Brien made an offer to Brown's landlord, who accepted it, and gave Brown 60 days to clear out. The news reached the Saturday Crowd six weeks before the official last day of business on July 10. The final few weeks were bittersweet. The Saturday Crowd came in as usual, but it was hard for anyone to believe that the shop was actually going to close for good. The dime table was still there, the back room refrigerator was still empty, the crushed beer cans still had not been brought to the recycler, and the records on the dusty shelves were still standing at attention in their brown and green sleeves. It was almost a celebratory atmosphere. There was laughter and much loud music was played on the turntable in the front room, with well-wishers coming to pay their respects to Brown.

Brown had long since decided not to attempt another move. He was, however, faced with the decision of what to do with the records he had accumulated in the shop. To nearly every customer who came in, Don would half-jokingly ask, "Wanna buy 60,000 records?" Graveyard humor pervaded the back room for the next few weeks. Brown made a miniature effigy of Fran O'Brien out of Styrofoam and proceeded to treat it like a voodoo doll, poking it with the end of his lit cigar. He also created a sign that read "The End Is Near—July 10th Goodbye," which was posted on the front counter. In the last few weeks, Brown declared a 50% off sale on all records in the shop.

A local television station, KIIJ Channel 9, broadcast a brief feature on the Jazz Man's demise. An unctuous street reporter named Hank Plant treated the closing as just another human interest story, but the television cameras in the shop caused a minor stir. Members of the Saturday Crowd put on their best faces when queried about the shop's forthcoming demise.

Plant: *"This is kind of a sad, sad affair."*
John Fraser: *"Unfortunately, you are accurate on that."*
Plant: *"What does this shop mean to you?"*
Fraser: *"Oh, it means a lot in terms of recreation, fun, things like that, camaraderie with the others."*

Stephen Bartron, a relatively recent habitué of the shop, was more forthcoming in his more meaningful answer to the same question:

It was a great place to learn, you know? More than any university

Don Brown, at the Jazz Man "wake" barbecue held in his back yard for the Saturday Crowd, friends, and family, May 1983. The doomsday sign he is holding was displayed in the shop during its final days. (Photo by Cary Ginell)

could ever teach you. What little I know, I learned here. I'll miss the place.

Don Gray, who had been frequenting the shop longer than just about anyone, delivered the understatement of the day.

Plant: "What are you going to do with your Saturdays now?"

Don Gray: "That does present a problem."

When Plant finally got around to interviewing Don Brown, Don pointed out the role the shop played in the community:

Plant: "I have a feeling I'm watching the end of an era here, not just for the shop, but for what it represents."

Brown: "I think so, because there are so many young kids that are coming up and there are so many people that call on the phone and they have questions. A lady today wanted to know the proper spelling of Earl Klugh's name. And they've got no place to turn. You call a commercial chain store, and they'll say, 'Who?'"

Plant ended the piece by misquoting former U.S. Secretary of the Navy Gideon Welles, who had made the somber pronouncement after the death of Abraham Lincoln, "Now he belongs to the ages."

And so the Jazz Man goes the way of Ellington and Armstrong, Monk and Jelly Roll. They all belong to the ashes, but their music belongs to us. Nothing has ever equaled jazz as a truly American art form, and the Saturday Crowd here at the Jazz Man knows that a significant part of all of this is going to die July 10th. In Santa Monica, this is Hank Plant, Channel 9 News.

Don Brown shut the doors of the Jazz Man for the last time on a Saturday, July 2, 1983. The shop was crowded that day, as record buyers snapped up whatever they could at bargain basement prices. The following Tuesday, many of the shop regulars came to help clear the place out. Some (me included) took home shelving as souvenirs. Others helped load records onto a truck. The following Saturday, the Crowd was invited over to the Browns' house for a potluck feast. Burgers and chicken were barbecued, and music, laughter, and stories continued through the afternoon and into the evening. The next day, the Jazz Man ceased to exist. But the venerable shop would have one more breath of life before expiring for good.

JAZZ MAN RECORD SHOP
"SPECIALISTS SINCE 1938"

DON BROWN
OWNER

3323 PICO BOULEVARD
SANTA MONICA, CALIF. 90405
PHONE 828-6939

The Saturday Crowd Gallery

Don Gray, Michael Kieffer, Eugene Earle

John Tippet and Harvey Newland

(Photos by Cary Ginell, except for top right, courtesy Darlene Brown)

Don Brown, Bob Vinisky, Don Gray, December 11, 1971. Note the poster of St. Louis Blues, which hung on the wall throughout Don Brown's tenure at 3323 Pico Blvd.

The Saturday Crowd poses for one last portrait in May 1983, six weeks before the shop closed down. Left to right: Don Gray, John Fraser, Norm Fist, Don Brown, Cary Ginell, Nat Ross, Doug Lawler, Donald Lee Nelson, Harvey Newland, Stephen Bartron, Jonathan Pearl, Eugene Earle.

Chapter Twenty-Two

End Groove

Six weeks after Don Brown closed down the Jazz Man Record Shop, it rose from its own ashes, Phoenix-like, in the city of Burbank, 25 miles from Santa Monica. The shop and its contents were rescued by Jonathan Pearl, now 26, and a bonafide member of the Saturday Crowd. Pearl, who was unemployed, couldn't stand to see the shop close after more than 40 years, so his mother, who was apparently well off financially, agreed to bankroll the purchase of the Jazz Man for $6,000, which was to be paid in monthly installments of $500.

The shop's new home was in an outdoor shopping mall called the Burbank Golden Mall. Designed and constructed in 1967, the Golden Mall was an experiment in urban design created by blocking off traffic on North San Fernando Road six city blocks long and two blocks wide. The futuristic design included hexagonally-shaped planters and fountains with restaurants, restrooms, and storefronts, which were only accessible to pedestrians. The complex was designed for "pleasurable shopping and browsing in a relaxed and attractive atmosphere." Ground was broken for the mall on May 6, 1967 and residents looked forward to its opening with the eager anticipation one felt for a new ride at Disneyland.

By the time the Jazz Man moved in, however, the mall had fallen upon hard times. Initially charmed by the novelty of a traffic-free shopping area, customers began to complain about having to walk from distant parking lots to get to the mall, when they were used to parking directly in front of stores on San Fernando Road. Within a few years, stores began to close. During the 1970s, the mall's high profile department stores: Thrifty Drug, Sav-On, Newberry, Woolworth's, and J.C. Penney's all began to disappear. Affluent banks and jewelry stores also vacated, to be replaced by shabby mom-and-pop book and thrift shops. The fountains were neglected and dried up, and a job assistance office opened up. By the early 1980s, derelicts and homeless men could be seen loitering in the mall. In 1983, when Jonathan Pearl moved the Jazz Man to Burbank, the Golden Mall was anything but golden. But the rent was cheap—at $250 per month, it was half of what Don Brown had been paying in Santa Monica.

Ribbon-cutting day at the Jazz Man's new (and final) home in Burbank's Golden Mall, August 20, 1983. The Saturday Crowd pauses for an alumni snapshot. Left to right: Doug Lawler, John Fraser, Cary Ginell, Eugene Earle, Stephen Bartron, Jonathan Pearl, Tim Fitak, Alan Roberts, Nat Ross, Lewis Upton, Harvey Newland, Don Gray.

On August 20, 1983, the new Jazz Man opened up with a private ribbon-cutting ceremony for the Saturday Crowd. Although the mall had fallen upon hard times, it was still far from the rundown neighborhood where the shop had been located during the Watts riots. A used book store next door housed a wealth of interesting memorabilia, from magazines to movie posters. There was also a deli and an ice cream parlor nearby, so the Saturday Crowd was encouraged, thankful that at least the shop still existed somewhere.

Pearl hired Saturday Crowd regular Stephen Bartron to help manage the shop. He reasoned that someone had to be the proprietor while the other scoured the neighborhoods for records to sell, and there was no one better suited for this than Bartron. They spent the first month unpacking crates of records and stocking the shelves. The new shop was larger and brighter than the previous building on Pico Blvd., but it had a spacious back room and resembled a stripped-down version of the Santa Monica shop. Pearl installed a counter in the front room, with a turntable in the same location as before. The high ceilings dwarfed the six-foot-high record shelves, and no

Jonathan Pearl (center) goes through boxes at the Jazz Man. At left, Doug Lawler.
(Photo by Cary Ginell)

matter how much Pearl put in the store, it always looked cluttered but empty at the same time. The official grand opening of the new shop took place on Saturday, September 10, and everyone had high hopes for a successful business. But after a month of meager sales and slow traffic, Bartron bowed out, leaving the entire operation to Pearl. Stephen Bartron:

He and I were supposed to be partners. There was a lawyer who was going to draw up a partnership agreement, but that never happened. When I left the shop, John gave me around $1,000, but that was it. The shop was making no money, so I had to leave and go find a job. The street was closed down, and there was not much traffic. It turned out to be a poor location for any store. Many days we had no sales at all. We were young and had no idea how to run a record shop.

The Saturday Crowd remained loyal and showed up every week as usual. Even Don Brown made some appearances as the shop's elder statesman. But the drive to Burbank was farther for most people and many of the regulars looked like fishes out of water in the clean, barren store. Old-time collectors Bob Vinisky and Lewis Upton, who used to frequent the old shop at 2689 Pico, showed up to play and share some records, but they didn't remain long. The only celebrity musician who showed up was ragtime pianist John "Knocky" Parker, who I brought in one Saturday. But the mood was different in Burbank, and nobody paid much attention to him. There were no decent restaurants nearby, so there was no socializing in the evening after the shop closed. Everyone simply got in their cars and made their way home. One Saturday in December, only Harvey Newland and Barton showed up. The journey to Burbank had proven to be too much for most of the Saturday Crowd.

By early 1984, even Pearl was getting discouraged and on Saturday, February 18, he wrote an open letter to his customers:

JAZZ MAN
RECORD SHOP
432 N. Golden Mall, Burbank, California 91502   (213) 843-3730

MAGI AND RAY:
THANKS MUCH.
J. P.

February 18, 1984

Dear Friends,

    The Jazz Man is closing its doors once again. As many of
you already know, the City of Burbank is planning to condemn
the building in which the shop is housed to make way for a
dandy new shopping center. I have decided it is better for
me to throw in the towel at this point than to duke it out
with the pugs from City Hall. Moving to another location is
out of the question. This store is too much of a Humpty Dumpty
for it to be put back together again from thirty thousand
pieces every six months or so, subject to the whims and caprices
of landlords and politicians.

    All of the 78s have already been sold to a dealer from
Kansas City, and the new LPs have flown the coop as well.
A few used LPs remain and will be available until February 24.

    Thank you all very much for all the kindness and support
you have shown me over the last few months.

                                       Sincerely,

                                      Jonathan Pearl

                                      Jonathan Pearl

P.S. Former Jazz Man owner Don Brown is still handling jazz LPs
via mail order at this address: DON BROWN #72 2801-B OCEAN PARK BLVD
                                      SANTA MONICA, CA 90405

Jonathan Pearl closes the Jazz Man for good. (Courtesy The L.A. Institute of Jazz).

In an interview with the *Los Angeles Daily News*, Pearl tried putting a positive spin on what was plainly a hopeless situation:

We were attracting people from Burbank and Glendale who had not known about it when it was in Santa Monica. I think, in time, it would have been comparable if it had been allowed to stay. I would have had to move in the fall anyway. It was starting to be profitable, but if I moved to another location, it would be too much of a transition in too short a time. I didn't want to go through the long aggravating thing that Don Brown went through. I just wanted to get out now.

This time, it was for keeps. The Jazz Man's 44-year life ended the same way it began, quietly and without fanfare. It is believed that at the time of its closing, the Jazz Man was the oldest operating used record store in the country. But times were changing and the record industry was on the threshold of a major transition. The 78 rpm record died in the late 1950s, and at the time Jonathan Pearl was struggling to keep the shop alive in Burbank, the 78's successor, the 33 1/3 long-playing record, was experiencing its own death knell. A new format had been recently introduced, a silvery four-and-a-half-inch diameter item called the compact disc, which would soon revolutionize the recording industry. The Internet was still a decade away, but the demise of the Jazz Man signalled the beginning of the end for the traditional mom-and-pop record store. In a few short years, another major Los Angeles 78 haven, Ray Avery's Rare Records in Glendale, would also shut down, and in time, even major chain stores such as the Wherehouse and Tower Records also gave way to the futuristic world of downloading, iPods, and MP3s.

Since it first opened on the Sunset Strip in 1939, the Jazz Man Record Shop survived at least a dozen moves, a World War, local riots, and even an eccentric upholsterer. It is unlikely that anything like the Jazz Man will ever exist again. The reason for this is that it wasn't the music that kept the shop alive; it was the people; the entrepreneurs who ran the shop and the customers who sought it out. When John Fraser was asked what the Jazz Man meant to him, he didn't talk about the music or the countless 78s he had heard or bought there, he talked about the camaraderie, the fellowship with other collectors, and the bond he and other collectors formed with the owners of the shop and with each other. The interpersonal relationships that developed at the Jazz Man included not only the establishing of lifelong friendships, but marriages involving three of its owners. For Donald Lee Nelson, coming to the Jazz Man was much more than a habit.

For most of us, record collecting was an avocation. When a person gets into record collecting as deeply as most of us are, it is no longer a hobby. A hobby is something that you can put away. It becomes an avocation when it encompasses a goodly portion of your life, your interests, and even routes your thinking. Records are the things that brought us all together, but it was the enjoying of each other's company that was what the Saturday Crowd was all about.

The Jazz Man was a tradition. The word tradition is easily bandied about these days and has almost lost its meaning. But it was a place where a widely diversified group of people have been coming for many, many years and it's just a shame to see something like that end. The people found that record collecting was more than just listening to the sounds; they got into the very history of it, the feeling of it, and actually getting into the confines of the musicians themselves who were performing 30, 40, 50 years ago.

The closing of the Jazz Man in 1984 was a harbinger of things to come. Since that time, another quarter century has passed, and one by one, other collectors shops, retail stores, giant conglomerate chains, and traditional mom-and-pop shops have all bitten the dust. Most record collectors spent precious hours in these stores. As Stephen Bartron said, they proved more educational than any book, university, or even the Internet. Neighborhood record stores were places where we listened and learned, met other collectors, and discovered the wondrous sounds of our musical past.

With each store's closing, a piece of us dies with it. The fellowship collectors share is exceeded only by the bond we have for those black, scratchy dust catchers. To paraphrase former New York Yankees pitcher Jim Bouton in *Ball Four,* we spend our lives gripping our 78s, 45s, and 33s, but in the end, it's the other way around.

L.A. WEEKLY JULY 1-7, 1983

A Jazz Rarity Goes Under

Horrible news for jazz fans. Don Brown's Jazzman Record Shop in Santa Monica, which is listed in the Smithsonian Collection of Classic Jazz as one of only seven sources of rare jazz in the country, is shutting its doors on July 10 after 45 years in business. Brown recently received notice to vacate because of expansion of a restaurant next door, and rather than move the oft-dislocated shop once again and have to pay higher rent elsewhere, Brown, who is in his mid-60s and tired, has decided to do only mail order business in the future, making it impossible for jazz aficianados to be able to browse through his 60,000 78 rpm records, none of them recorded after 1955. (The only LPs stocked are reissues of early recordings or modern recordings of traditional jazz tunes.)

The shop dates back to 1938 and at one time produced its own Jazzman label (first recording Jelly-Roll Morton) in order to provide cuts of many artists the record companies ignored. When Brown took it over in 1960, it had deteriorated to the degree that its stock consisted of 21 LPs and one truly rare record, a Clarence Williams that had been left in the sink. Brown rebuilt the collection over the years, primarily by painstakingly tracking down widows and family members of jazz artists and getting them to dig out their usually boxed or buried records.

Brown is selling out his entire rare stock at 50 percent or more off, with the intention of only handling reissues through the mail. Sitting under a sign saying "The end is near," he remarked about his loyal clientele: "Most are unhappy. I've gotten a lot of wet coat-collars from people crying on my shoulder. Most have learned all they know about jazz from hanging around the store." For those who want to buy while it's possible, the store is at 3323 Pico Blvd., Santa Monica. For those who want to hear Brown's personal jazz collection, he has a radio show on KCRW Sunday nights from 10 p.m. to midnight.

—David Ackerly

Jonathan Pearl: Fall, 1983 (photo by Cary Ginell)

Afterword

Without a Song

When the Jazz Man closed its doors for the last time, the various owners of the shop were still living. But within a few short years, four of the six major players in the shop's 44 years of existence were gone.

Dave Stuart worked for Lester Koenig at Good Time Jazz until 1960. By that time, he had switched careers again, having established a successful Los Angeles art gallery in 1957, specializing in primitive and pre-Columbia art. He died of a heart ailment on March 15, 1984, only a few weeks after the demise of the record shop he founded in 1939. Stuart was 73. A two-paragraph obituary in the *Los Angeles Times* failed to mention any of his music-related activities, including the founding of the Jazz Man and the initial, revolutionary recordings by Lu Watters that he produced in 1941.

Dave Stuart (photo at left courtesy Charles Campbell)

286

Marili Levin, Santa Monica, 1959.
(Courtesy Art Levin)

Marili Morden married her third husband, musician Art Levin, in 1956. Levin was a tuba player who met Marili when she was still running the Jazz Man in the early 1950s. After she sold the shop, he didn't see her for about a year. Selling the Jazz Man liberated Marili and she enjoyed a variety of hobbies, including traveling, photography, and writing short stories, many of which she submitted to *The New Yorker* magazine. Although Levin recalled that she was a good writer, none of her work was ever published. At one time, she owned 10 acres of land in Twentynine Palms, a small desert community in San Bernardino County.

After leaving the shop, Marili worked as a bookkeeper, and then got a job as a color coordinator for a construction company. In March 1965, Art Levin became the senior keeper at the Los Angeles Zoo and Marili, who was very fond of animals, was soon hired to run the children's zoo. Marili and Levin's marriage lasted 12 years. They were divorced in 1968. Levin regretted divorcing Marili for the rest of his life.

The biggest mistake in my life was leaving her. I knew immediately that I shouldn't have done it. She was a really nice person, but she was always into her own thoughts. That's kind of what attracted me to her, but there was always a barrier between us because of this."

Marili lived out her remaining years in North Hollywood. She died of cancer on August 12, 1988 at the age of 68.

Nesuhi Ertegun

Nesuhi Ertegun joined his brother Ahmet as a partner in Atlantic Records in 1955. He was put in charge of Atlantic's roster of jazz artists and soon shifted the label's focus from singles to LPs. Through his leadership, Atlantic signed the Modern Jazz Quartet, Charles Mingus, John Coltrane, Herbie Mann, Bobby Darin, Roberta Flack, and many other artists to the label.

When Atlantic was purchased by Warner Communications in 1967, Ertegun stayed with the company and founded WEA International and East-West Records. He was the first president of the National Academy of Recording Arts and Sciences and chairman of the International Federation of Phonographic Industries, which sought to prevent piracy of records, tapes, and sheet music.

Ertegun's wide range of interests continued after he left the Jazz Man. He founded the New York Cosmos soccer team of the North American Soccer League and also amassed a large collection of Surrealist art. Nesuhi Ertegun died on July 15, 1989, following cancer surgery. He was 71. In 1991, he was posthumously inducted into the Rock and Roll Hall of Fame. In 1995, he was awarded the Grammy Trustees Award for his lifetime achievements in the music industry. His legacy was cemented when, in 2004, Jazz at Lincoln Center established the Nesuhi Ertegun Jazz Hall of Fame. A bust of Ertegun can be seen in Lincoln Center's Rose Hall.

After selling the Jazz Man Record Shop to Jonathan Pearl, Don Brown continued to run his mail order business, selling LP reissues of vintage jazz recordings. Refusing to break up, the Saturday Crowd met monthly at the home of Donald Lee Nelson in Westwood. Brown was an honored guest at those get-togethers, which included record playing and the usual joshing and dozens playing that had taken place in the back room of the Jazz Man for so many years. On May 29, 1985, Brown hosted his regular *Cobweb Corner* radio program on KCRW. The next day, he collapsed and died of a sudden heart attack at his home. He was 62. Gary Hammond recalled:

The Saturday Crowd meets at the Westwood home of Donald Lee Nelson, March 1985. Don Brown died two months later. Left to right: Stephen Bartron, Peter Tanner, Harvey Newland, Donald Lee Nelson, Doug Lawler, John Fraser, Don Brown. (Courtesy John Fraser)

Dar called me the day that Don passed, so I went over there the following morning to help her make the arrangements. One of the things she wanted was a New Orleans-style brass band at the funeral. So I called up a colleague of mine from the Red Cross who played trombone. His name was Wally Craig. Wally, of course, knew everybody in town, mainly guys who were with the South Frisco Jazz Band and the Hot Frogs. So Wally put together a brass band. We had an old-fashioned viewing, then the services, and the burial was out at Woodlawn Cemetery. The band sent Don out in good order. The pallbearers were myself, John Fraser, one of the people from KCRW, and Don's brother-in-law, Ted.

Darlene Brown lived until February 13, 2010 when she passed away after a stroke. She was 88. Dar's service, like that of her husband, featured a New Orleans-style jazz band, which played songs like "Pennies from Heaven" and Duke Ellington's "Creole Love Call."

The whereabouts of Albert Van Court and Jonathan Pearl remain unknown, but as of this writing, both are presumed to be still living.

* * * * * * * * * *

In October 1975, I was a freshman at California State University Northridge, majoring in Radio-Television-Film. In my first film production class, I was given the assignment of making a movie about any subject I chose. The assignment said that no more than fifty dollars could be spent. I immediately thought of the Jazz Man and decided to make an old-fashioned silent comedy short with a musical soundtrack. The plot I devised concerned a rabid collector of Al Jolson records who invades the Jazz Man searching for an elusive copy of "Toot Toot Tootsie, Goodbye" with which to complete his collection. I titled my film *Without a Song*, with Jolson's 1940s Decca rendition of the tune played over the opening credits.

When I presented the idea to Don Brown, he agreed to let me use the shop as my "set." I asked two friends of mine, David Hongisfeld and a fellow record collector named Steve Bergere, to star in the film, but I needed somebody to play the record shop owner. Don volunteered. His only caveat was that I shoot the film in one day, preferably on a weekday when traffic in the shop was slow.

The weather was dreary and drizzling rain when I showed up at the shop the next Thursday with my Super-8 silent movie camera, several rolls of film, a few spot lights on stands, and a couple of props. Since this was a silent film, there was no script, but I showed a crude storyboard to my three actors and basically directed their actions while shooting. In the story, Don shows the Jolson collector (played by Bergere) to the back room where all the high-priced Jolson 78s are kept on shelves that take up an entire wall. (In actuality, the wall housed Brown's stock of country and hillbilly 78s.) When he can't find the record, Bergere gets increasingly frustrated and starts breaking and throwing 78s in disgust. Don, who has fallen asleep in a chair in the front room, is oblivious to what is going on in the back, but awakes to find Bergere dejectedly sitting amongst the rubble he has created and throws him out of the shop. While putting on his jacket to leave, Bergere notices the elusive Jolson record, sitting on top of a stack of 78s on the dime table. He tosses Don a dime from across the room and exits, leaving Don to give the camera a priceless Oliver Hardy camera look of utter despair and a heavy sigh as he stares at the coin.

I had no idea whether Don Brown was reliving similar real life encounters he had experienced while running the shop, but in retrospect, I'm sure there was some déjà vu as we shot the film. Brown turned out to be a great actor; he rarely needed more than one take to give me the facial expressions I needed.

At one point, I has to change film in my camera, and with no dark room available, I had to do it by feel, changing reels with the camera under a blanket. While I was struggling with this, the front door to the shop opened and Mel Tormé walked in. I had known that Tormé was a frequent customer and would occasionally stop by to see what new LPs were in stock. After greeting Don, Tormé sauntered over to the LP stacks and started thumbing through the latest arrivals. Don introduced me and I said hello while still on the floor, groping with the recalcitrant camera. I didn't know what else to say, so I grumbled "Show business is rough" in Tormé's direction. Without looking up, he muttered, "Tell me about it, kid." Before I could finish what I was doing, Tormé had found something he wanted, paid Brown, and walked out. I didn't realize until later the opportunity I had just squandered. Imagine getting Mel Tormé to appear in my college film! I would have been the idol of everyone in my class. Don thought the whole thing was very funny and we finished shooting the film late that afternoon. I edited the pieces together and synched the whole thing with Lu Watters records. I got an "A."

The whole experience may have been a memorable one for me, but it was just another day in the life of the Jazz Man Record Shop. Each day, something entirely different would happen. Whether it was Dave Stuart arguing about the merits of New Orleans jazz with swing fans, Marili Morden quietly smoking while adolescent collectors gazed longingly in her direction, or the impeccably dressed Nesuhi Ertegun going through Jelly Roll Morton outtakes, the day-to-day existence of the Jazz Man and its owners was something that could only happen in Hollywood. No screenwriter could come up with characters like Walter the upholsterer or the members of the Saturday Crowd.

It has been more than a quarter of a century since the Jazz Man closed, and since that time, thousands of other independent record stores, each unique in its own quirky fashion, have also shut down. In the impersonal world that the music industry has become, it is unlikely that stores of this nature will ever return. When Don Brown held up his sign that said "The End Is Near," little did he know how prophetic it would be, and that the death of the Jazz Man Record Shop would also signify the beginning of the end of a remarkable social community: the neighborhood record store.

The author at the front counter of the Jazz Man's Burbank location, 432 N. Golden Mall, Fall 1983.

Sources

In its 44-year life span, the Jazz Man was run by six wildly different owners in at least twelve different addresses. Tracking the shop's various locations required careful scrutiny of surviving correspondence, jazz periodicals, newspapers, copies of the Jazz Man record labels, and Los Angeles city directories. Piecing together the elusive history of the Jazz Man is not unlike working on a giant jigsaw puzzle while blindfolded, but bit by bit, it fell into place. I'd like to acknowledge the following individuals, whose assistance helped me trace the history of the shop, the lives of its various owners, and those who frequented it: George Avakian, Paul Bacon, Tom Ball, Stephen Bartron, Michael Biel, Manfred Borman, Tim Brooks, the late Darlene Brown, the late Don Brown, Charles Campbell, Mark Cantor, Robert Celaschi, Irwin Chusid, Jim Cooprider, Stan Cornyn, Gene Deitch, Frank Driggs, Selma Ertegun, Paul Ewing, Holly Fraser, John Fraser, Marc Friend, Richard Ginell, Vince Giordano, Don Gray, Travis Haase, Richard Hadlock, Gary Hammond, Terri Hinte, Harry Huryk, Orrin Keepnews, John Koenig, Steven Lasker, the late Doug Lawler, Jim Leigh, David Lennick, Art Levin, Dan Levinson, Bill McClung, Donald Lee Nelson, Patty O'Connor, Hank O'Neil, James Parten, Doug Pomeroy, Malcolm Rockwell, Chris Strachwitz, Jeff Sultanof, and Ken Swerilas.

In addition, I am indebted to the following institutions for allowing me access to their historical collections: Ken Poston and Eric Fankhauser of the L.A. Jazz Institute; the Los Angeles Public Library; Aurora Perez,

Andrea Castillo, and Jerry McBride of the Archive of Recorded Sound at Stanford University; Bill Belmont and Ralph Kaffel of the Concord Music Group; Bill Carter of the San Francisco Traditional Jazz Foundation; Emily Ferrigno of the Irving S. Gilmore Music Library at Yale University, and Eric Seiferth of the Williams Research Center of the Historic New Orleans Collection. My apologies to anyone I may have omitted.

Books:
Alicoate, Jack (editor). *The 1942 Radio Annual.* New York: The Radio Daily, 1942.
Bastien, Alfred. *Lettering Alphabets for Draughtsmen, Advertisement Designers, Architects, & Artists.* West Drayton, Middlesex: Bastien Brothers, 1942.
Berg, Chuck & Tom Erskine. *The Encyclopedia of Orson Welles.* New York: Checkmark Books, 2003.
Brothers, Thomas. *Louis Armstrong: In His Own Words.* New York: Oxford University Press, 1999.
Buchanan, John. *Emperor Norton's Hunch: The Story of Lu Watters' Yerba Buena Jazz Band.* Middle Dural, New South Wales: Hambledon Productions, 1996.
Carter, William. *Preservation Hall.* London: Bayou Press, Ltd., 1991.
Cornyn, Stan. *Exploding: The Highs, Hits, Hype, Heroes, and Hustlers of the Warner Music Group.* New York: HarperCollins, 2002.
Crystal, Billy. *700 Sundays.* New York: Warner Books, 2005.
Dance, Helen Oakley. *Stormy Monday: The T-Bone Walker Story.* Baton Rouge: Louisiana State University Press, 1987.
Delaunay, Charles. *Hot Discography.* Paris, New York: Charles Delaunay, 1936, 1938.
Delauney, Charles, ed. Walter E. Schaap and George Avakian. *New Hot Discography.* New York: Criterion, 1948.
Gennari, John. *Blowin' Hot and Cool.* Chicago: University of Chicago Press, 2006.
Goggin, Jim. *Turk Murphy: Just for the Record.* San Leandro: San Francisco Traditional Jazz Society, 1983.
_____ & Peter Clute. *The Great Jazz Revival.* Sacramento: Donna Ewald, 1994.

Gottlieb, William P. *The Golden Age of Jazz.* New York: Simon and Schuster, 1979.

Higham, Charles. *Orson Welles: The Rise and Fall of an American Genius.* New York: St. Martin's Press, 1985.

Hillman, Christopher. *Bunk Johnson.* Turnbridge Wells, Kent: Universe Books, 1988.

Jasen, David A. *Recorded Ragtime: 1897–1958.* Hamden: Archon Books, 1973.

_____ & Trebor Jay Tichenor. *Rags and Ragtime: A Musical History.* New York: Dover Publications, 1978.

Jones, John Bush. *The Songs That Fought the War: Popular Music and the Home Front, 1939–1945.* Waltham: Brandeis Publishing, 2006.

Kernfeld, Barry Dean. *The Blackwell Guide to Recorded Jazz.* Cambridge: Blackwell Publishers, 1995.

Leigh, James. *Heaven on the Side: A Jazz Life.* James Leigh (privately published), 2000.

Levin, Floyd. *Classic Jazz: A Personal View of the Music and the Musicians.* Berkeley and Los Angeles: University of California Press, 2000.

Meckna, Michael. *Satchmo: The Louis Armstrong Encyclopedia.* Westport: Greenwood Press, 2004

Olmsted, Tony. *Folkways Records: Moses Asch and His Encyclopedia of Sound.* New York: Routledge, 2003.

Pastras, Phil. *Dead Man Blues: Jelly Roll Morton Way Out West.* Berkeley/ Los Angeles: University of California Press, 2001.

Raeburn, Bruce Boyd. *New Orleans Style and the Writing of American Jazz History.* Ann Arbor: University of Michigan Press, 2009.

Reich, Howard & William Gaines. *Jelly's Blues: The Life, Music, and Redemption of Jelly Roll Morton.* Cambridge: Da Capo Press, 2003.

Ramsey, Frederic Jr. *A Guide to Longplay Jazz Records.* New York: Long Player Publications, 1954.

_____ & Charles Edward Smith. *Jazzmen.* New York: Harcourt, Brace & Company, 1939.

Rose, Al & Edmond Souchon. *New Orleans Jazz: A Family Album.* Baton Rouge: Louisiana State University Press, 1967.

Russell, William. *Oh, Mister Jelly: A Jelly Roll Morton Scrapbook.*

Copenhagen: Jazz Media, 1999.

Rust, Brian. *Brian Rust's Guide to Discography*. Westport: Greenwood Press, 1980.

_____. *Jazz and Ragtime Records (1897–1942)*. Denver: Mainspring Press, 2002.

Smith, Charles Edward, with Frederic Ramsey, Jr., Charles Payne Rogers, and William Russell. *The Jazz Record Book*. New York: Smith & Durrell, 1942.

Smith, Kathleen E.R. *God Bless America: Tin Pan Alley Goes to War*. Lexington: The University Press of Kentucky, 2003.

Souther, J. Mark. *New Orleans on Parade: Tourism and the Transformation of the Crescent City*. Baton Rouge: Louisiana State University Press, 2006.

Stoddard, Tom. *Jazz On the Barbary Coast*. San Francisco/Berkeley: San Francisco Traditional Jazz Foundation and the California Historical Society, 1982.

Sutton, Allen. *Cakewalks, Rags and Novelties: The International Ragtime Discography (1894–1930)*. Denver: Mainspring Press, 2003.

_____ & Kurt Nauck. *American Record Labels and Companies: An Encyclopedia (1891–1943)*. Denver: Mainspring Press, 2000.

Teachout, Terry. *Pops: A Life of Louis Armstrong*. New York: Houghton Mifflin Harcourt, 2009.

Welles, Orson & Peter Bogdanovich. *This Is Orson Welles*. New York: HarperCollins Publishers, 1992.

Wright, Laurie. *Mister Jelly Lord*. London: Storyville Publications, 1980.

Yanow, Scott. *Jazz on Film: The Complete Story of the Musicians & Music Onscreen*. San Francisco: Backbeat Books, 2004.

Periodicals:

Billboard Music Year Book (1944)
Record Retailing Yearbook (1945, 1946)
Also, selected issues of *Clef, Down Beat, Jazz, Jazz Information, The Jazz Record, The Jazz Session, Joslin's Jazz Journal, LiterRarely, Metronome, The Record Changer, The Record Finder*, and *The Second Line*.

Articles

"60-Year-Old 'Bunk' Johnson, Louis' Tutor, Sits in the Band" by Louis

Armstrong (*Down Beat*, August 15, 1941).

"All Jazzman Masters Sold to Good Time." (*Billboard*, April 26, 1952).

"Area Emporium for Nostalgic 78 Records Closes" by Richard S. Ginell. (*Los Angeles Daily News,* February 25, 1984).

"August Grapes to the Jazzman Record Shop." (*Jazz*, August 1942).

" 'But This Music Is Mine Already!': White Woman as Jazz Collector in the Film *New Orleans* (1947)" by Sherrie Tucker. In Rustin, Nichole T. & Sherrie Tucker, Editors. *Big Ears: Listening for Gender in Jazz Studies.* Durham, N.C.: Duke University Press, 2008.

"Collecting Hot, 1927-1947" by Marili Ertegun. (*The Record Changer*, October 1947).

"CRD Distribs Indie Wax in S. California." (*Billboard*, February 3, 1951).

"Crusader for Jazz" (article on Nesuhi Ertegun) by Floyd Levin. (*The Second Line,* Nov.-Dec. 1952)

"Hot Society" (*Time*, May 17, 1937).

"The Jazz Man: A Legend Passes" (*Joslin's Jazz Journal*, November 1983).

"Jazz Man Records Links People with Bygone Glories" by Eliot Tiegel (*Billboard*, July 26. 1975).

"The Jazz Man Settles in Burbank" by Neil Wertheimer (*Los Angeles Daily News,* 1983).

"A Jazz Rarity Goes Under" by David Ackerly (*L.A. Weekly,* July 1983).

"Keep on Diggin' Lu Watters, Man" letter by Frances Downey (*Down Beat,* May 1, 1942).

"The Kid Comes Back" (*Time,* February 5, 1945).

"Kid Ory" by Dave Stuart (*Jazz Information,* November 22, 1940).

"Kid Ory Comes Back to Bizz." (*Down Beat*, September 1, 1942).

"Listen to What Ory Says" by Rudi Blesh (*The Jazz Record*, October 1945).

"The Lu Watters Band" by Nesuhi Ertegun (*The Record Changer,* April 1946).

"Louis Film Director Slaps at Duke." (*Metronome*, November 1941).

"Lu Watters' Yerba Buena Band" by Eugene Williams (*Jazz Information,* November 1941).

"McPartland May Get a Part in Orson Welles' Movie on Jazz" by Eddie Beaumonte. (*Down Beat*, August 15, 1941).

"Memories Linger, Melodies Fade" by Robert W. Stewart (*Los Angeles Times,* July 17, 1983).

"More Bootleg Blues" by William Grauer, Jr. (*The Record Changer*, June 1951).

"A Must for Jazz Buffs" by Charles M. Weisenberg (*Santa Monica Evening Outlook,* October 16, 1981).

"New Orleans Jazz" by Marili Ertegun (*Clef,* August 1946).

"New Orleans On the Air" by Nesuhi Ertegun (*The Jazz Record*, May, 1944).

"New Show Airs Only Jazz from Pre-swing Era." (*Down Beat*, March 15, 1943).

"On Being a Record Collector in Dixon, Illinois" by Don Brown (*Joslin's Jazz Journal,* August 1982).

"On the Record" by Charles Payne Rogers (record reviews). (*Jazz*, March 1943).

"Orson Welles Jazz Movie Will Star Louis Armstrong" by Charlie Emge. (*Down Beat*, August 15, 1941).

"Papa Mutt Carey" by Gene Williams and Marili Stuart. (*Jazz*, March 1943).

"Popular Music and the Post-War World" by Charles Edward Smith (*Record Retailing Yearbook, 1945*).

"Profiles: Don Brown" column by John Peer Nugent (*Santa Monica Evening Outlook,* January 24, 1979).

"Rare Record Store Rises from the Ashes in L.A." by Sam Sutherland (*Billboard,* October 15, 1983).

"The Real Sultan of Swing: Ahmet Ertegun" by Michael Gross. (*The Sunday Correspondent Magazine,* October 1990) (www.mgross. com).

"'Robbed of Three Million Dollars,' says Jelly Roll" (*Down Beat,* October 1, 1940).

"Recording Studios of the Pacific Northwest" by Peter Blecha. HistoryLink.org essay 8946, July 26, 2009.

"S.F. Band Leader Shot by Father of U.C. Coed, 19. (*San Francisco Examiner,* October 7, 1941).

"Specialty Stores Failing, But 2 Flourish in L.A." (*Billboard,* July 4, 1981).

"The Spikes Brothers: A Los Angeles Saga" by Floyd Levin (*Jazz Journal,*

Vol. 4, No. 12, December 1951).

"Stuart to Exit Contemporary." (*Billboard,* May 30, 1960).

"Talent Array Set By New Jazz Man Diskery on Coast." (*Billboard*, March 6, 1954).

"Watters' Band Brings Dixie Jazz to Frisco," by Frank O'Mea. (*Down Beat*, March 1, 1941).

"Wax Job: Hot Music Gets a Cool Start at Twelfth and Central" by Charles M. Weisenberg (*Westways,* [*Los Angeles Times* supplement] June 1979).

"Welles Jazz Film May Be Shelved." (*Down Beat*, May 1, 1942).

"West Coast Jazz" by Paige Van Vorst (*JazzBeat,* December 21, 2006).

"What Did Ory Say?" (*Clef*, March 1946).

"Whatever Became of Those Great Old Hot Jazz Record Shops?" by Paige Van Vorst (*The Mississippi Rag,* September 1981).

"White Woman as Jazz Collector in the Film *New Orleans* (1947) (*Institute for Studies in American Music,* Vol. XXXV, No. 1, Fall 2005).

"Who the Hell's Dave Stuart?" (*Down Beat,* September 1, 1940).

"Who's Stuart?" (*Down Beat,* August 1, 1940).

"Wife Takes Over as 'Jazz Man' Joins Up" (*Down Beat,* September 15, 1942).

"Yerba Buena Ork Plays Without Lu Watters" by Dave Houser. (*Down Beat,* August 1, 1942).

"Yerba Buena Jazz Band Sounds Good on Wax" by Hal Holly. (*Down Beat,* February 15, 1942).

Correspondence

Personal letters from Dave Stuart and Marili Stuart to William Russell (1940–1971), housed in the Historic New Orleans Collection of the Williams Research Center in New Orleans, Louisiana.

LPs and Compact Discs:

"Billy Crystal Presents The Milt Gabler Story" (Verve B0003911-00), notes by Billy Crystal and Ashley Kahn

"Bunk Johnson & his Superior Jazz Band," (Good Time Jazz M-12048), notes by David Stuart.

"The Commodore Story" (GRP, CMD-2-400, 1997), notes by Dan

Morgenstern.

"The Complete Recordings of Lu Watters & his Yerba Buena Jazz Band" (Good Time Jazz, 4 GTJCD-4409-2), notes by Philip Elwood and John Koenig.

"The Compositions of Jelly Roll Morton" (Timeless), notes by Charles Campbell.

"The Contemporary Records Story (Contemporary CCD-4441-2), notes by Richard S. Ginell (profile on Lester Koenig).

"George Lewis: Volume 1" (Jazz Man LJ-331), notes by Wayne C. Lockwood.

_____: "Doctor Jazz" (Good Time Jazz GTJCD-12062-2), notes by Scott Isler.

"The Good Time Jazz Story" (Good Time Jazz 4GTJCD-4416-2), notes by Floyd Levin and Ralph Kaffel.

"Hommage à Nesuhi: Atlantic Jazz, a 60th Anniversary Collection," (Rhino/Atlantic, unnumbered box set, 2008).

"From Spirituals to Swing" (1938 & 1939 Carnegie Hall Concerts) (Vanguard, 1999), notes by Steve Buckingham, John Hammond, and Charles Edward Smith.

"Kid Ory's Creole Jazz Band: 1944/45." (Good Time Jazz GTJCD-12022-2), 1957, 1991, notes by Nesuhi Ertegun.

"Kid Ory, Portrait of the Greatest Slideman Ever Born" (The Complete 1944 Orson Welles Airshots) (Upbeat Jazz URCD-187, 2003), notes by Mike Pointon.

"Rosy McHargue's Ragtimers: The Complete Recordings (1952-1956)" (Jump JCD-12-2), notes by Dan Levinson and Floyd Levin.

Miscellaneous

"B-A-R-F" (A Monograph Full of Sound and Fury, Signifying Nothing) by Nathaniel Lester Ross, unpublished monograph, June 2, 1975.

"A Guide to Collectors' Items: Phonograph Records: Recognizing Them, Grading Them, Selling Them" by Don Brown (privately published pamphlet, 1977).

Original 78, 33, and 45 rpm issues on the Jazz Man and Crescent record labels (see discography).

𝕵𝖆𝖟𝖟 𝕸𝖆𝖓

Discography
By Cary Ginell

This discography consists of original Jazz Man issues (except for unissued titles) and foreign 78 rpm releases. All releases are 10" 78 rpm singles or 10" 33 1/3 rpm LPs, except for Jazz Man 501, which is a 12" 78, and EJ-451, which is an extended play 45 rpm.

All Jazz Man releases from 1-15 were issued with white labels with red print (1942-1946) and then on green labels with silver print (after 1947).

Title and songwriter information are indicated as listed on the original record releases.

LU WATTERS' YERBA BUENA JAZZ BAND
Picto Sound Studios, 130 Bush St., San Francisco, Calif.
December 19–20, 1941
Lu Watters, cornet; Bob Scobey, trumpet; Ellis Horne, clarinet; Turk Murphy, trombone; Walter "Wally" Rose, piano; Clarence "Clancy" Hayes, Russ Bennett *, banjos; Dick Lammi, tuba; Bill Dart, drums. (MLB-111 features Rose, Bennett, Hayes, & Dart only). Session produced by Dave Stuart and Lester Koenig.

MLB-106-3	Muskrat Ramble* (Ed Ory)	Jazz Man 3, Melodisc 1125 (GB)
MLB-107-2	At a Georgia Camp Meeting* (K. Mills)	Jazz Man 4
MLB-108-2	Original Jelly Roll Blues* (Jelly Roll Morton)	Jazz Man 4
MLB-109-3	Maple Leaf Rag* (Scott Joplin)	Jazz Man 1, JM 1 (GB)
MLB-110-2	Irish Black Bottom (Percy Venables)	Jazz Man 2, JM 2 (GB)
MLB-111	Black & White Rag (George Botsford)	Jazz Man 1, JM 1 (GB)
MLB-112-2	Smokey Mokes* (Abe Holzman)	Jazz Man 3, Melodisc 1125 (GB)

MLB-113-2   Memphis Blues (W.C. Handy)   Jazz Man 2, JM 2 (GB)

• JM 1 and JM 2 were reissued in Great Britain in the early 1950s by Tom Cundall. Labels were silver print-on-yellow.
• JM 1, 2, 3, & 4 were originally issued in a 4-pocket album.
• Dave Stuart was dissatisfied with the master for MLB-111 and remade the song at Watters' second session on March 22, 1942. Subsequent issues of Jazz Man 1 included the later take of "Black & White Rag."

KFRC Studios, 1000 Van Ness Avenue, San Francisco, Calif.
March 22, 1942
Wally Rose, piano; Russ Bennett*, Clarence Hayes, banjos; Bill Dart, drums

MLB-117	Hot House Rag* (Paul Pratt)	Jazz Man 17
MLB-118	Temptation Rag* (Harry Lodge)	Jazz Man 7
MLB-119-3	Black & White Rag (George Botsford)	Jazz Man 1

KFRC Studios, 1000 Van Ness Avenue, San Francisco, Calif.
March 29, 1942
Lu Watters, Bob Scobey, trumpets; Ellis Horne, clarinet; Turk Murphy, trombone; Walter "Wally" Rose, piano; Clarence "Clancy" Hayes, Russ Bennett*, banjos; Squire Girsback, tuba; Bill Dart, drums. (MLB-131 features Rose, Hayes, Bennett & Dart only)

MLB-120	Come Back Sweet Papa (Russell & Barbarin)	Jazz Man 6
MLB-121	Terrible Blues (Williams)	Jazz Man 15
MLB-122-A	Fidgety Feet (LaRocca & L. Shields)	Jazz Man 7
MLB-122-B	Fidgety Feet (LaRocca & L. Shields)	unissued
MLB-123-A	London Blues[1] (Jelly Roll Morton)	Jazz Man 14
MLB-123-B	London Blues (Jelly Roll Morton)	unissued
MLB-124-A	Sunset Cafe Stomp* (Venable)	Jazz Man 14
MLB-124-B	Sunset Café Stomp* (Venable)	unissued
MLB-125-A	Daddy Do* (Fred Longshaw)	Jazz Man 13
MLB-125-B	Daddy Do* (Fred Longshaw)	unissued
MLB-126	Milenberg Joys* (Jelly Roll Morton)	Jazz Man 13
MLB-127	Riverside Blues (Jones & Dorsey)	Jazz Man 5
MLB-128	Cake Walking Babies (C. Williams)	Jazz Man 5
MLB-129-A	High Society* (Williams & Steele)	Jazz Man 15
MLB-129-B	High Society* (Williams & Steele)	unissued
MLB-130	Tiger Rag (LaRocca)	Jazz Man 6
MLB-131-A	Muskrat Ramble (Ed Ory)	unissued

1 Originally published as "London Café Blues."

• Some copies of MLB 131A have MLB 131-2 embedded in the wax, indicating that it was an alternate take. In addition, Jepsen notes that while the majority of pressings of Jazz Man 3 used this master, "some copies use master MLB 106 from the 1941 session."

(Jepsen, Vol. 8: 223)

• White label copies of Jazz Man 13, 14, & 15 have 1221 N. Vine St. address at bottom of label.
• Green label copies list 6420 Santa Monica Blvd.
• All of the unissued Lu Watters titles were released on "Lu Watters' Yerba Buena Jazz Band: The Complete Good Time Jazz Recordings" (Good Time Jazz box set 4GTJCD-4409-2)

KFRC Studios, 1000 Van Ness Avenue, San Francisco, Calif.
April 24, 1942
Lu Watters, Bob Scobey, trumpets; Turk Murphy, trombone; Ellis Horne, clarinet; Wally Rose, piano; Clancy Hayes, banjo/vocal *; Russ Bennett, banjo; Squire Girsback, tuba; Bill Dart, drums.

Fidgety Feet	unissued
South	unissued
Piano Rag	unissued
Terrible Rag	unissued
St. James Infirmary	unissued
That's A Plenty	unissued
Careless Love *	unissued
Auntie Skinner's Chicken Dinners *	unissued

• Three titles from the above session were to be released on Jazz Man 78s, using the master numbers MLB 132, 133, and 134. After the Bunk Johnson session of June 1942, Jazz Man canceled the idea of issuing these Watters titles and reassigned the masters to the Johnson titles, beginning with MLB132.

BUNK JOHNSON'S ORIGINAL SUPERIOR BAND
Grunewald's Music Store, 327 Daronne Street, 3rd floor, New Orleans, Louisiana
June 11, 1942
Bunk Johnson, trumpet; George Lewis, clarinet; Jim Robinson, trombone; Lawrence Marraro, banjo; Austin Young, bass; Walter Decou, piano; Ernest Rogers, drums.

MLB-132-1	Yes, Lord, I'm Crippled (Traditional)	Jazz Man Ltd. Edition 2B, Jazz Man 17
MLB-133	Down By the River (Traditional)	Jazz Man 8
MLB-134	Storyville Blues (Traditional)	Jazz Man 10
MLB-135-1	Weary Blues (Matthews)	Jazz Man 9
MLB-136	Bunk's Blues (Bunk Johnson)	Jazz Man 10
MLB-137-1	Moose March (Traditional)	Jazz Man 9
MLB-138-2	Pallet on the Floor (Traditional)	Jazz Man 16
MLB-139-2	Ballin' the Jack (Smith & Europe)	Jazz Man 16
MLB-140	Panama (W.H. Tyers)	Jazz Man 8

• Some later issues of Jazz Man 9 (green label) were pressed on red vinyl.
• Original white label pressings have "Co-sponsored by Jazz Information" printed beneath the artist's name.
• MLB 133 was recorded as "I Ain't Gonna Study War No More."
• MLB 133 has no take number in wax on JM 17, although it is the same performance.
• MLB 134 was recorded as "Those Draftin' Blues."
• MLB 136 was recorded as "Old Time Blues."

WILLIE BUNK JOHNSON
Grunewald's Music Store, 327 Baronne Street, 3rd floor, New Orleans, Louisiana - June 12, 1942
Bunk Johnson, speech; questions posed by Eugene Williams.

MLB-141	Interview – part 1	Jazz Man Ltd. Edition 1A
MLB-142-1	Interview – part 2	Jazz Man Ltd. Edition 2A
MLB-143-1	Interview – part 3	Jazz Man Ltd. Edition 1B

• Fifty hand-numbered copies of the two Jazz Man Limited Edition 78s were pressed, with possibly a second pressing. Most were autographed by Bunk Johnson and are exceedingly rare. Artist credit on the three interview sides is to "Willie Bunk Johnson." Labels for these issues were blue print on white background. It is not known whether or not these two discs were sold as part of an album set.

JELLY ROLL MORTON
Washington, D.C. - December 1938
Jelly Roll Morton, piano, vocal*

MLB-144	Honky Tonk Music #2 (Jelly Roll Morton)	unissued
MLB-145	Finger Buster (Jelly Roll Morton)	Jazz Man 12, Blue Star (Fr) 185, Vogue GV-2256
MLB-146	Creepy Feeling (Jelly Roll Morton)	Jazz Man 12 Blue Star (Fr) 185, Vogue GV-2256
MLB-147	Winin' Boy Blues* (Jelly Roll Morton)	Jazz Man 11 Blue Star (Fr) 170 Vogue GV-2255
MLB-149	Honky Tonk Music (Jelly Roll Morton)	Jazz Man 11 Blue Star (Fr) 170 Vogue GV-2255

• An unissued test of MLB-144 exists, with artist credit to "Ferd Morton." Single sided tests were pressed by Allied Phonograph & Record Manufacturing Co., Hollywood, California.
• MLB-148 is a dub of "Cake Walking Babies from Home" by Clarence Williams, from

master 73083A, issued on OK 40321.
• English pressings of JM 11 exist on vinyl with yellow label and silver print.
• Original white label pressings have "Co-sponsored by Nesuhi Ertegun" beneath the artist's name.

KID ORY'S CREOLE JAZZ BAND
Hollywood, Calif. – August 3, 1944
Mutt Carey, trumpet; Kid Ory, trombone, vocal*; Omer Simeon, clarinet; Buster Wilson, piano; Bud Scott, guitar; Ed Garland, bass; Alton Redd, drums.

CPM-10-32-1-A	Get Out of Here (and Go On Home) (Kid Ory-Bud Scott)	Crescent 2, Jazz Man 22, JM 22 (GB)
CPM-10-33-1-A	South (Moten-Hayes)	Crescent 1, Jazz Man 21
CPM-10-34-2-A	Blues for Jimmy (Kid Ory)	Crescent 2, Jazz Man 22, JM 22 (GB)
CPM-10-35-2-A	Creole Song* ('C'est L'autre Cancan) (Kid Ory)	Crescent 1, Jazz Man 21

• Title of CPM-10-32-1A on Jazz Man 22 is "Get Out of Here" (no subtitle).
• Title of CPM-10-34-2-A on Jazz Man 22 is spelled "Blues for Jimmie."
• JM 22 reissued in Great Britain by Tom Cundall. Label was silver print-on-yellow. Title on the British reissue of JM 22 is "Blues for Jimmie." There is no subtitle for "Get Out of Here" on the British reissue.

JOHNNY WITTWER TRIO
KOL Radio Studio, 1220 3rd Avenue (basement), Seattle, Washington September 26, 1944
Johnny Wittwer, piano; Joe Darensbourg, clarinet, vocal *; Keith Purvis, drums.

3889	Joe's Blues * (Darensbourg)	Jazz Man LP LJ-332
3890	Wolverine Blues (Jelly Roll Morton)	Jazz Man LP LJ-332
3891	Come Back, Sweet Papa (Russell-Barbarin)	Jazz Man LP LJ-332
3892	Tiger Rag (La Rocca)	Jazz Man LP LJ-332

• The above sides were originally released on Exner 1 & 2.
• Jazz Man 10" LP LJ-332 was released April 12, 1954.

KID ORY'S CREOLE JAZZ BAND
C.P. MacGregor Studios, 729 S. Western Ave., Hollywood, Calif.
February 12, 1945
Thomas "Papa Mutt" Carey, cornet; Kid Ory, trombone; Edward Garland, bass; Albert "Buster" Wilson, piano; Alton Redd, drums; Arthur "Bud" Scott, guitar; Joe Darensbourg,

clarinet, vocal *

EX5	Dippermouth Blues (Joe Oliver)	Jazz Man LP LJ-332
EX6	Savoy Blues (Edward Ory)	Jazz Man LP LJ-332
EX7	High Society (Clarence Williams)	Jazz Man LP LJ-332
EX8	Ballin' the Jack * (Chris Smith)	Jazz Man LP LJ-332

- The above sides were originally released as Exner 3 & 4.
- Jazz Man 10" LP LJ-332 was released April 12, 1954
- Disc label shows record number to be LP2.

Hollywood, Calif. – August 5, 1945
Mutt Carey, trumpet; Kid Ory, trombone, vocal*; Omer Simeon, clarinet; Buster Wilson, piano; Bud Scott, guitar; Ed Garland, bass; Minor Hall, drums.

CRE-1006	Panama (W.H. Tyers)	Crescent 7, Jazz Man 27
CRE-1007	Unknown title	
CRE-1008	Unknown title	
CRE-1009	Careless Love (W.C. Handy)	Crescent 5, Jazz Man 25
CRE-1010	Do What Ory Say* (C. Williams)	Crescent 5, Jazz Man 25
CRE-1011	Under the Bamboo Tree (Cole & Johnson)	Crescent 7, Jazz Man 27

Hollywood, Calif. – September 8, 1945
Mutt Carey, trumpet; Kid Ory, trombone; Darnell Howard, clarinet; Buster Wilson, piano; Bud Scott, guitar; Ed Garland, bass; Minor Hall, drums.

CRE-1013	1919 (Traditional)	Crescent 4, Jazz Man 24
CRE-1015	Maryland (Traditional)	Crescent 3, Jazz Man 23
CRE-1018	Down Home Rag (Wilber Sweatman)	Crescent 4, Jazz Man 24
CRE-1019	Oh Didn't He Ramble (W.C. Handy)	Crescent 3, Jazz Man 23

- CRE-1014/1016/1017 unknown titles
- Writer credit on JM 23 for "Oh Didn't He Ramble" is to Will Handy

Hollywood, Calif. – November 3, 1945
Mutt Carey, trumpet; Kid Ory, trombone; Darnell Howard, clarinet; Buster Wilson, piano; Bud Scott, guitar; Ed Garland, bass; Minor Hall, drums.

CRE-1022	Original Dixieland One-Step (La Rocca)	Crescent 6, Jazz Man 26
CRE-1023-4	Maple Leaf Rag (Scott Joplin)	Crescent 8, Jazz Man 28
CRE-1024-2	Weary Blues (Matthews)	Crescent 8, Jazz Man 28
CRE-1025-2	Ory's Creole Trombone (Kid Ory)	Crescent 6, Jazz Man 26

- Note: All Jazz Man releases of recordings originally issued on Crescent were issued between 1946 and 1947.

JOHNNY WITTWER
Probably San Francisco, Calif. - December 1945
Johnny Wittwer, piano

MLB-150	Ragtime Nightingale (Joseph Lamb)	Jazz Man 20
MLB-151	Aunt Hagar's Blues (W.C. Handy)	Jazz Man 18
MLB-152	Ace in the Hole (Traditional)	Jazz Man 19
MLB-153	Two Kinds of People (Traditional)	Jazz Man 19
MLB-154	Ragged but Right (Traditional)	Jazz Man 18
MLB-155	Bill Bailey (James Cannon)	Jazz Man 20

PETE DAILY'S RHYTHM KINGS
Hollywood, Calif. – December 24, 1947
Pete Daily, cornet; Warren Smith, trombone; Rosy McHargue, clarinet; Skippy Anderson, piano; George Defebaugh, drums.

CPM-1026-B	Sobbin Blues (Kassel-Burton)	Jazz Man 29
CPM-1027-B	Jazz Man Strut (Rosy McHargue)	Jazz Man 29
CPM-1028-C	Yelping Hound Blues (Lada-Nunez)	Jazz Man 30
CPM-1029-C	Clarinet Marmalade (Shields-Ragas)	Jazz Man 30

TURK MURPHY'S BAY CITY STOMPERS
San Francisco, Calif. – December 31, 1947
Bob Scobey, trumpet; Turk Murphy, trombone, vocal; Bob Helm, clarinet; Burt Bales, piano; Harry Mordecai, banjo.

CPM-1030	Shake That Thing (Charlie Jackson)	Jazz Man 31
CPM-1031	Kansas City Man Blues (Williams & Johnson)	Jazz Man 31
unknown	Willie the Weeper	unissued
unknown	unknown title	unissued
CPM-1036	Yellow Dog Blues (W.C. Handy)	Jazz Man 32
CPM-1037	Brother Lowdown (Turk Murphy)	Jazz Man 32

DARNELL HOWARD'S FRISCO FOOTWARMERS
San Francisco, Calif. — April 29, 1950
Bob Scobey, trumpet; Jack Buck, trombone; Darnell Howard, clarinet; Burt Bales, piano; Clancy Hayes, guitar; Squire Girsback, bass; Gordon Edwards, drums; Nesuhi Ertegun, vocal *

CPM-1038	Pretty Baby (Tony Jackson)	Jazz Man 34
CPM-1039	Some of These Days (Shelton Brooks)	Jazz Man 33
CPM-1040	Dippermouth Blues * (Oliver-Armstrong)	Jazz Man 33
CPM-1041	St. Louis Blues (W.C. Handy)	Jazz Man 34

• On "Dippermouth Blues," Nesuhi Ertegun shouts the obligatory "Oh, play that thing!"
• This was the last Jazz Man session before the sale of its masters to Good Time Jazz, on January 15, 1952 for $5,500.00.

PUD BROWN'S DELTA KINGS
Capitol Records Studios, 5515 Melrose Ave., Hollywood, Calif.
October 10, 1951
Pud Brown, tenor saxophone; Charlie Teagarden, trumpet; Jack Teagarden, trombone, vocal *; Jess Stacy, piano; Ray Bauduc, drums.

DR-1001	Lovin' to Be Done * (Brown-Teagarden-O'Connor)	Jazz Man LP LJ-334
DR-1002	Jersey Bounce (Wright Player-Bradshaw-Johnson)	Jazz Man LP LJ-334
DR-1003-D1	Pretty Baby (Van Alstyne-Kahn)	Jazz Man LP LJ-334
DR-1004-D1	Charmaine (Rapee-Pollack)	Jazz Man LP LJ-334

• The above sides were originally released as West Craft 1 and 2. Jazz Man LP LJ-334 ("Dixieland Contrasts") was issued c. November 1954, with the group listed as "The Delta Kings."

ROSY MCHARGUE'S RAGTIMERS
Radio Recorders, 7000 Santa Monica Blvd., Hollywood, Calif.
April 8, 1952
Bob Higgins, cornet; Moe Schneider, trombone; Rosy McHargue, clarinet, C-melody saxophone; Earle Sturgis, piano; Ray Leatherwood, bass; George Defebaugh, drums; Rink Leslie, lead vocal *. Group vocal by "The Gentlemen of the Ensemble" (Higgins, Schneider, Leatherwood, McHargue, Defebaugh).**

J-???-X	Night Wind (McHargue)	Jazz Man LP LJ-334
J-???-Y	Mysterious Rag ** (Irving Berlin-Ted Snyder)	Jazz Man LP LJ-334
J-???-Z	Don't Send Me Posies */** (Fred Rose-Billy McCabe-Clarence Jennings)	Jazz Man LP LJ-334
J-127-1	They Gotta Quit Kicking My Dawg Around ** (Cy Perkins-Webb M. Oungst)	Jazz Man LP LJ-334

• The above sides were originally released on Jump LP 12-2, except for "They Gotta Quit Kickin' My Dawg Aroun'," which was issued on a 78 rpm single, Jump 34B. They were reissued c. November 1954 on the "A" side of the Jazz Man LP "Dixieland Contrasts," backed with Pud Brown's Delta Kings. The Jazz Man LP label omits Berlin's name in the credit for "Mysterious Rag." Songwriter credit for "Don't Send Me Posies" is listed as "McCabe-Perkins." The original 10" LP showed the group name spelled "Rosy McHargue's Rag Timers."

GEORGE LEWIS' RAGTIME BAND
Capitol Records Studios, 5515 Melrose Ave., Hollywood, Calif.
October 26, 1953
Avery "Kid" Howard, trumpet, vocal%; Jim Robinson, trombone; George Lewis, clarinet;
Alton Purnell #, piano, vocal; Lawrence Marrero, banjo; Alcide "Slow Drag" Pavageau,
bass; Joe Watkins, drums, vocal*; Monette Moore **, vocal.

unknown	Panama (William Tyers)	unissued
CB-675-2	Doctor Jazz* (Oliver-Morton)	Jazz Man 101, LP LJ-331
CB-676-3	Down by the Riverside * (Traditional)	Jazz Man 101, LP LJ-331
CB-695-D1	A Closer Walk With Thee *% (Traditional)	Jazz Man 501, LP LJ-331
CB-696-D1	Lou-Easy-An-I-A # (Joe Darensbourg)	Jazz Man 501
CB-717-1	Ice Cream *% (Johnson-Moll-King)	Jazz Man LP LJ-331
CB-718-2	Saints Go Marching In (Traditional)	Jazz Man LP LJ-331
unknown	Burgundy Street ** (Lewis-Marrero-Moore)	Jazz Man LP LJ-331

- CB-695-D1 issued as "Closer Walk With Thee" on LJ-331.
- Jazz Man 501 released November 18, 1953.
- LJ-331 released Dec. 25, 1953.
- Alton Purnell's name is misspelled as "Parnel" on Jazz Man 501.
- "Panama" was issued on CD by Good Time Jazz in 1999.
- "Burgundy Street" features clarinet, bass, drums, and vocal only.

OCTAVE CROSBY'S ORIGINAL DIXIELAND BAND
Capitol Records Studios, 5515 Melrose Ave., Hollywood, Calif.
January 1 or 25, 1954
Octave Crosby, piano, vocal **; Alvin Alcorn, trumpet; Albert Burbank, clarinet, vocal *;
Irving "Cajun" Verret, trombone; Jim Davis, bass; Chester Jones, drums.

DB-110-D1	Gettysburg March (Traditional)	Jazz Man 102
DB-111-D1	None of My Jelly Roll ** (Clarence Williams-Spencer Williams)	Jazz Man 102
DB-112-D1	Paddock Blues (Traditional)	Jazz Man 103
DB-113-D1	Ting a Ling * (Britt-Little)	Jazz Man 103

PETE DAILY & HIS CHICAGOANS
Capitol Records Studios, 5515 Melrose Ave., Hollywood, Calif.
February 1, 1954
Pete Daily, cornet; Warren Smith, trombone; Jerry Fuller, clarinet; Skippy Anderson,
piano; Bernie Miller, bass tuba; Lenny Esterdahl, banjo; Hugh Allison, drums.

DB-117-D1	Quaker Town (There's a Quaker Down Down in Quaker Town) (Solman-Berg)	Jazz Man 104,

		EJ-451, LP LJ-333
DB-118-D1	Closer Walk with Thee (Traditional)	Jazz Man 104,
		EJ-451, LP LJ-333
DB-119-D1	New Tin Roof Blues (Make Love to Me) (Copeland-Norvas-Pollack-Brunis-et.al.)	Jazz Man 105,
		EJ-451, LP LJ-333
DB-120-D1	Swanee River (Stephen Foster, arr. Warren Smith)	Jazz Man 105,
		EJ-451, LP LJ-333

• Title of DB-119 on Jazz Man 105 is "Make Love to Me." Matrix prefixes on labels of Jazz Man 104 & 105 read "CB" instead of "DB," as it is inscribed in the wax.
• EJ-451 is a 45 rpm EP.
• Jazz Man 105 was reportedly issued on a 45 rpm single. No evidence of copies has turned up.
• LP LJ-333 was issued in May 1954.
• Also issued on UK EP Tempo EXA 60.

JOHNNY LUCAS & HIS BLUEBLOWERS
Capitol Records Studios, 5515 Melrose Ave., Hollywood, Calif.
February 1954
Johnny Lucas, trumpet, vocal *; Matty Matlock, clarinet, flute **; Mike Hobi, trombone; Jess Stacy, piano; Lenny Esterdahl, guitar; Bob Stone, bass; Monte Mountjoy, drums.

DB-145-D1	Lazy River (Arodin-Carmichael, arr. Esterdahl)	Jazz Man 106, LP LJ-333,
DB-146-D1	Loveless Love * (Handy-Lucas, arr. Hobi)	Jazz Man 106, LP LJ-333
?	High Society ** (C. Williams, A.J. Piron)	Jazz Man 107, LP LJ-333
?	Hindustan (Weeks-Wallace)	Jazz Man 107, LP LJ-333

• Jazz Man 106 & 107 were issued in April 1954.
• LP LJ-333 was issued in May 1954.

MARVIN ASH
Capitol Records Studios, 5515 Melrose Ave., Hollywood, Calif.
September 14, 1954
Marvin Ash, piano solo.

Music Box Rag (C. Luckyth Roberts)	Jazz Man LP LJ-335
Shakespearean Rag (David Stamper)	Jazz Man LP LJ-335
Ragtime Romeo (Williem B. Friedlander)	Jazz Man LP LJ-335
Old Folks Rag (Wilbur C. Sweatman)	Jazz Man LP LJ-335
Searchlight Rag (Scott Joplin)	Jazz Man LP LJ-335
Those Ragtime Melodies (Hodgkins)	Jazz Man LP LJ-335

Old Man Jazz (Gene Quaw)   Jazz Man LP LJ-335
A Ragtime Skeedadler's Ball (George
    Rosey)   Jazz Man LP LJ-335

JOE VENUTI & TONY ROMANO
Gold Star Studios, 6252 Santa Monica Blvd., Hollywood, Calif.
October 1954
Joe Venuti, violin; Tony Romano, guitar, vocal *, unknown mandolin & second vocal
(Venuti's optometrist). **

You Know You Belong to Somebody Else
    (West-Siras-Monaco)   Jazz Man LP LJ-336
Free and Easy (Venuti-Romano)   Jazz Man LP LJ-336
Almost Like Being in Love (Lerner-Loewe) Jazz Man LP LJ-336
Autumn Leaves * (Mercer-Kosma-Prevert) Jazz Man LP LJ-336
I Want to Be Happy (Caesar-Youmans)   Jazz Man LP LJ-336
Summertime (Gershwin-Heyward)   Jazz Man LP LJ-336
Joy Ride (Four String Original) (Venuti-
    Romano)   Jazz Man LP LJ-336
Angelina */** (Venuti-Romano)   Jazz Man LP LJ-336

- Jazz Man 10" LP LJ-336 was released c.November 1954.
- Romano is noted as playing Eddie Lang's guitar, a Gibson L-5 model.

Two foreign releases of Jazz Man masters. On left, British Melodisc, on the right, French Blue Star.
(From the author's collection)

Known Jazz Man Addresses

DATE	LOCATION	OWNER
c. December 1939	8960 Sunset Blvd., Hollywood	Dave Stuart
February 1940	1221 N. Vine St., Hollywood	Dave Stuart
c. July 1940	1053 N. Vine St., Hollywood	Dave Stuart
Late 1940	1731 N. Vine St., Hollywood	Dave Stuart
July 1941	6331 Santa Monica Blvd., Hollywood	Dave & Marili Stuart
December 1944	1221 N. Vine St., Hollywood	Marili Morden
November 1945	6420 Santa Monica Blvd., Hollywood	Marili Morden/ Nesuhi Ertegun
Spring 1954	1538 Cassil Place, Hollywood	Albert Van Court
July-August 1954	532 Alandele Ave., Los Angeles	Albert Van Court
November 1954	7511 Santa Monica Blvd., W. Hollywood	Albert Van Court
c. December 1954	2689 W. Pico Blvd., Los Angeles	Albert Van Court / Don Brown
Summer 1968	3323 Pico Blvd., Santa Monica	Don Brown
July – Sept. 1983	CLOSED	
September 1983	432 N. Golden Mall, Burbank	Jonathan Pearl
February 1984	CLOSED	

DATE	OWNERS
c. December 1939 – July 1942	Dave Stuart
July 1942 – February 1946	Marili Stuart/Morden
February 1946 – January 1952	Marili & Nesuhi Ertegun
January 1952 – Summer 1953	Marili Morden
Summer 1953 – January 1960	Albert Van Court, Jr., owner (managed by Jerome Weiss, L. Harvey Newland, Perry Pugh, Don Brown)
January 1960 – July 1983	Don Brown
July 1983 – February 1984	Jonathan Pearl

Index

"WHAT??? You sold your last Bolden disc to Cary Ginell???"

The author is deeply grateful to Gene Deitch for drawing this "Cat" cartoon specifically for this book.

About the Author

Cary Ginell is a four-time winner of the ARSC Award for Excellence for music journalism and discographical research. His book *Good Vibes*, written with jazz vibraphonist Terry Gibbs, won the ASCAP Deems Taylor Award. He lives in Thousand Oaks, California with his wife Gail, sons Brian and Adam, and about 30,000 records, many of which were purchased at the Jazz Man Record Shop.

The author, holding the "3323" address shingle from the Jazz Man's Santa Monica location (1968-1983). (Photo by Gail Ginell)

The
Jazz Man
Records Anthology

A special CD is being offered to purchasers of *Hot Jazz for Sale: Hollywood's Jazz Man Record Shop,* produced by Origin Jazz Library under license from Concord Jazz Records. The CD includes highlights from the 13-year catalog of recordings made by Jazz Man from 1941 to 1954 and includes an unreleased recording of "Fixin' to Die" by blues legend Bukka White, which was recorded at the Jazz Man Record Shop in September 1963. (The story of this session is documented on page 241 of this book.) To order the CD, visit www.originjazz.com. The CD comes complete with a self-adhering plastic sleeve that you can affix to the bottom of this page. Contents are listed on the opposite page. For recording details, see the discography, which starts on page 301.

Affix Jazz Man
CD here

CD Contents

1. Muskrat Ramble   Lu Watters' Yerba Buena Jazz Band
2. Memphis Blues   Lu Watters' Yerba Buena Jazz Band
3. Black and White Rag   Wally Rose
4. Sunset Cafe Stomp   Lu Watters' Yerba Buena Jazz Band
5. Moose March   Bunk Johnson's Original Superior Band
6. Interview - part 1   Willie Bunk Johnson
7. Finger Buster   Jelly Roll Morton
8. Blues for Jimmy   Kid Ory's Creole Jazz Band
9. Get Out of Here (and Go on Home)   Kid Ory's Creole Jazz Band
10. Joe's Blues   Johnny Wittwer Trio
11. Do What Ory Say   Kid Ory's Creole Jazz Band
12. Ragtime Nightingale   Johnny Wittwer
13. Clarinet Marmalade   Pete Daily's Rhythm Kings
14. Brother Lowdown   Turk Murphy's Bay City Stompers
15. Dippermouth Blues   Darnell Howard's Frisco Footwarmers
16. Lovin' to Be Done   Pud Brown's Delta Kings
17. Don't Send Me Posies   Rosy McHargue's Ragtimers
18. Ice Cream   George Lewis' Ragtime Band
19. Burgundy Street   George Lewis' Ragtime Band, featuring Monette Moore
20. Ting a Ling   Octave Crosby's Original Dixieland Band
21. Quaker Town   Pete Daily and His Chicagoans
22. Loveless Love   Johnny Lucas and His Blueblowers
23. Searchlight Rag   Marvin Ash
24. You Know You Belong to Somebody Else   Joe Venuti and Tony Romano
25. Fixin' to Die   Bukka White

CD produced by Cary Ginell and Bill Belmont.
Label design by Holly Fraser.

Made in the USA
Lexington, KY
12 May 2012